D1613804

CONVERSATIONAL LEARNING

CONVERSATIONAL LEARNING

An Experiential Approach to Knowledge Creation

Ann C. Baker
Patricia J. Jensen
David A. Kolb

Q

QUORUM BOOKS
Westport, Connecticut • London

Library of Congress Cataloging-in-Publication Data

Baker, Ann C.
Conversational learning : an experiential approach to knowledge creation / Ann C. Baker, Patricia J. Jensen, David A. Kolb.
p. cm.
Includes bibliographical references and index.
ISBN 1-56720-498-8 (alk. paper)
1. Conversation. 2. Experiential learning. I. Jensen, Patricia J. II. Kolb, David A., 1939- III. Title.
LC15.B35 2002
302.3'46—dc21 2001058934

British Library Cataloguing in Publication Data is available.

Library of Congress Catalog Card Number: 2001058934
ISBN: 1-56720-498-8

First published in 2002

Quorum Books, 88 Post Road West, Westport, CT 06881
An imprint of Greenwood Publishing Group, Inc.
www.quorumbooks.com

Printed in the United States of America

The paper used in this book complies with the Permanent Paper Standard issued by the National Information Standards Organization (Z39.48-1984).

10 9 8 7 6 5 4 3 2 1

To Lee, Sarah, Sandra, Jon, and all the conversation partners who contributed to the meaning of this work

Contents

Preface

This book grew out of a research program on conversational learning that began at the Department of Organizational Behavior in the Weatherhead School of Management at Case Western Reserve University in 1992. Our intention in writing this book has been to understand conversational learning in ways that have practical applications for scholars, teachers, facilitators, consultants, and managers in their own fields of practice and, more generally, for all those who are seeking to explore and understand a better way to communicate and learn from one another through conversation.

As proponents of experiential learning, we are increasingly aware that much of learning that occurs through experience emerges out of the interaction among people, especially through their conversation with each other. Thus, one intention here is to further elaborate existing theory of experiential learning to illustrate the social and interactive dimensions of conversation.

Each of us brings a unique perspective to this book. Ann C. Baker is on the faculty of George Mason University, Program on Social Organizational Learning and Women's Studies in the School of Public Policy. She brings to her academic setting as well as to her consulting practices her passion and lifelong commitment for creating receptive conversational spaces where all individuals are given voice to explore their assumptions, share their experiences, articulate their ideas, express their feelings, and stay in conversation in collaborative ways that foster communities of learning.

Patricia J. Jensen's interest in learning through conversations became focused as a doctoral student at Case Western Reserve University in the early 1990s. This interest was born out of ten years of teaching women at Alverno College, an ability-based liberal arts college, and her experience in studying adult learning and development theory, especially as it has been informed by recent scholarship on the centrality of relationships to women's development. As a teacher she has taught varied models of task-focused group interaction, and uses small and large conversational groups in classes to assist both undergraduate and graduate students to explore, apply, and test out their understanding of varied concepts and their own experiences. As a faculty member she interacts regularly with varied groups of colleagues in a highly collaborative academic environment.

David Kolb's interest in conversational learning grew out of his work with experiential learning. In using experiential learning in his teaching over the years, he has noticed that experiences alone, be they classroom simulations, exercises, internships, or field projects, produce some learning, but that when learners participate in conversations about the experiences, learning is greatly enhanced. Indeed, he has come to believe that placing conversations in a central role can do much to reform and transform education.

Later in our research we were joined by three colleagues who made substantial contributions to this book. We would like to thank Esther D. Wyss-Flamm, who extended the theory and practice of conversational learning into the realm of multicultural teams where her prior experience as scholar and practitioner was shaped. D. Christopher Kayes's research on how individual experience is transformed into group knowledge greatly enhanced and deepened our understanding of theoretical and practical implications of conversational learning at the group as well as the organizational levels. Alice Y. Kolb's qualitative analysis of conversational interactions by doctoral seminar members at Case Western Reserve University over a twelve-year period helped clarify and bridge our understanding of theory and practice of conversational learning. The life experiences and diverse perspectives we brought into this collaboration have in many ways shaped and enriched our thinking as we learned together in countless conversations about conversation.

Chapter 1, Learning and Conversation, offers a broad overview of what it means to learn in conversation. It introduces the reader to different forms of conversation that take place in diverse contexts and settings.

Chapter 2, Conversation as Communion: Spiritual, Feminist, Moral, and Natural Perspectives, invites the reader to understand conversation in communion with others as well as with all living beings that are part of our natural world. Scholars, practitioners, and readers who are interested in exploring a holistic understanding of life through conversation will find this chapter nourishing and insightful.

Chapter 3, Looking Back: Precursors to Conversational Learning in Group Dynamics, traces several key aspects of conversational learning back to classic group dynamics literature and informs us how this historical evolution has influenced the theory and practice of conversational learning. Scholars and Organizational Development (OD) practitioners will find this chapter helpful to enhance their understanding of how different streams of philosophy and practice have shaped conversational learning.

Chapter 4, Conversation as Experiential Learning, offers a theoretical framework from which to understand conversational learning. Essentially, this chapter offers five dialectical processes for conversational learning that together frame the space within which such learning takes place. These dialectical processes are referred to in several subsequent chapters.

Chapter 5, The Evolution of a Conversational Learning Space, bridges the theory of conversational learning to its practice through a case study of the evolution of conversational learning from the traditional discourse model of education to a conversational approach to education. Chapters 4 and 5 are especially recommended to scholars and teachers who are interested in adopting conversational learning as an alternative approach to classroom teaching.

Chapter 6, Receptive Spaces for Conversational Learning, addresses how a receptive space that fosters learning through conversations can be created and sustained. Those who will benefit from this chapter are scholars, practitioners, teachers, and others who are concerned about creating receptive conversational spaces for people, groups, organizations and communities.

Chapter 7, Streams of Meaning-Making in Conversation, reports an empirical study of how individuals make sense of their experiences and learn through conversations, thus revealing an individual's unique and distinct pattern of meaning-making processes that occur in conversation. Scholars and teachers will find this chapter very helpful to understand their students' as well as their own pattern of conversation, thus becoming more aware of how conversation impacts students' and their own learning.

Chapter 8, Conversational Learning in Multicultural Teams, takes the theory and practice of conversational learning into the multicultural realm through an extensive qualitative study of culturally diverse team interactions that emphasizes the importance of psychological safety in conversation. This chapter is particularly relevant to practitioners whose work involves interaction with highly multicultural environments. Scholars and teachers should find this chapter equally engaging and relevant, given the highly ethnic and culturally diverse student body that characterizes today's university campuses across the country.

Chapter 9, Extending the Conversation into Cyberspace, brings conversational learning into cyberspace by taking advantage of Internet technology. This chapter offers teachers and practitioners very useful guidelines to introduce conversation as a powerful tool to enhance learning through the convenience of the Internet.

Chapter 10, Extending the Conversation into Professional Conferences, explores conversation as an alternative way to create a more meaningful and richer learning experience for conference attendees. Practitioners, administrators, and conference organizers from both the academic and corporate worlds will benefit from the more interactive and relational approach to conference organizing suggested in this chapter.

Chapter 11, Conversational Learning in Organization and Human Resource Development, offers a provocative perspective by proposing ways in which the conversational approach can become a powerful tool to transform individual experience into group knowledge, hence increasing organizational effectiveness and overall well-being in a sustained fashion. Human resources managers, OD consultants, as well as scholars of organizational and human resource development will find this chapter particularly relevant to their work.

Finally, Chapter 12, The Practice of Conversational Learning in Higher Education, is a lively conversation among Ann C. Baker, Patricia J. Jensen, and D. Christopher Kayes on their current practice of conversational learning in higher education. This chapter is particularly relevant to teachers and trainers who are interested in adopting conversational learning in their various training and educational settings.

We begin the book by emphasizing the theoretical foundations of conversational learning and close with concrete examples of applications of these ideas. Overall, the work is intended as a stimulus for thought, consideration, and conversation rather than as a treatise to be adopted or rejected. The essential nature of conversational learning encompasses a continuous unfolding of collaborative learning, a widening circle of thought and practice. Thus, our intention throughout is to be provocative rather than definitive.

1

Learning and Conversation

Ann C. Baker, Patricia J. Jensen, and David A. Kolb

> Children do not converse. They say things. They ask, they tell, and they talk, but they know nothing of one of the great joys in life, conversation. Then, along about twelve, give or take a year on either side, two young people sitting on their bicycles near a front porch on a summer evening begin to talk about others that they know, and conversation is discovered. Some confuse conversation with talking, of course, and go on for the rest of their lives, never stopping, boring others with meaningless chatter and complaints. But real conversation includes asking questions, and asking the right ones before it's too late.
>
> Charles Schulz (1999)

Conversation is at once the most ordinary and most profound of human activities. It is ubiquitous, ever present, and all around us. In its many forms—face to face, telephone, among written texts, or in cyberspace—conversation is a process of interpreting and understanding human experience. This conversational sense-making can be described as a process of experiential learning, the roots of which go back to the works of Dewey (1938, 1964), Lewin (1951), Piaget (1965), James (1977), Vygotsky (1978), and Freire (1992), all of whom articulated the inseparable nature of learning and experience. Experiential learning is thus defined here as "the process whereby knowledge is created through transformation of experience" (Kolb, 1984, p. 41). The human species is distinguished by its capacity to learn, to make meaning from experience. This unique ability to learn from experience is what makes us human.

How humans learn from experience can be divided into two basic questions: How does what is outside get in? and How does what is inside get out? Piaget (1951), for example, identified imitation as an outside-in process of learning and play as an inside-out process of learning. Learning from experience thus involves balancing surrender and mastery, taking in experiences and others' views of them and expressing one's own conclusions in thought and action. It is a solitary act that occurs in relationship with others. Through learning together the human community is created and re-created. Yet ultimately the choice of when and what to learn is a private one. To paraphrase Annie Dillard, be careful what you learn, because that determines what you know.

The idea of difference is inherent in the concept of learning. To have learned something means being somehow different than before. Events experienced as strange and different are the source of learning. Learning is the process of making the strange familiar.

Paradoxically, learning is also the process of making the familiar strange. Unlearning old ideas is necessary to learn new ones. The artificial-intelligence expert Roger Schank (1991) says that learning only occurs when we encounter the unusual and the different. He says that the human mind uses scripts to understand the world and that "people come to rely upon situations where they know the scripts. Often they are afraid to venture into new areas because they do not know the scripts and are afraid of looking foolish. The ability to learn depends on the ability to abandon scripts that are failing and to acquire new scripts. This becomes more and more difficult as one gets older" (p. 92).

In a classic article entitled "The Need to Know and the Fear of Knowing," Abraham Maslow (1962) described how individuals work to preserve and defend their point of view, their values, and their definitions of good. Still, they are curious, intrigued, and excited by the new and different. For Maslow, the key variable is psychological safety, a concept that has been empirically explored and elaborated by Amy Edmondson (1999, 1996). When individuals are psychologically safe and secure, they are more likely to be asking questions, to be taking risks, and to be open to differences. Stress, threat, and being treated disrespectfully produce a defensive clinging to the familiar and the known.

Contemporary theories of adult learning also give the "fear of knowing" component a prominent role. Jack Mezirow (1991), basing his learning model on the critical theory of Jurgen Habermas (1972, 1984, 1991), considers how unexamined assumptions produce errors in learning. Mezirow says, "Because symbolic models, meaning perspectives, metaphors, and meaning schemes are all or almost all products of unreflective personal or cultural assimilation, the possibility of distortion of assumptions and premises makes reflection and critical discourse essential for validation of expressed ideas" (p. 118). Likewise, Chris Argyris (1994) advocates the confrontation of differences between espoused theories (an organization's "talk") and theories in use (an organization's "walk") as a means of learning and uncovering incongruence. Conversational learning that embraces differences as a source of new understanding and questions previous assumptions and prejudices can be called deep learning.

DEEP LEARNING IN CONVERSATION

The idea of deep learning is in some ways analogous to Arne Naess's (1973) distinction between shallow and deep ecology. Shallow ecology is the self-interested protection of the environment to maintain our way of life, while deep ecology refers to a fundamental transformation in perspective from human centeredness to a larger sense of global identification and connectedness to humanity.

Deep learning is not only transformative but also possibly transcendent. Paulo Freire (1992) contrasts the shallow learning that results from the banking concept of education with the transcendent deep learning that results from problem-posing education. The banking concept refers to a mode of education where learners passively absorb information imparted by the teacher with no opportunity to critically reflect and transform their own experiences into meaningful knowledge. On the other hand, says Freire, "Problem posing education is revolutionary futurity. Hence it is prophetic.... Hence it affirms men as beings who transcend themselves.... Hence it identifies with the movement which engages men as beings aware of their incompletion" (p. 72).

When Freire proposes problem-posing education based on dialogue as a means for promoting deep learning, he is not alone. Many other scholars also see conversation and dialogue as a powerful transformative process. For example, Mortimer Adler's (1982) *Paideia Proposal* suggests a model for educational reform where teachers play three roles: the teacher lecturing about declarative knowledge, the coach developing critical skills, and the facilitator of a Socratic dialogue that produces *maieusis*, the birthing of new ideas. Some other relevant perspectives on learning include Rorty's (1980) edification through conversation, Habermas's (1984) emancipation through ideal speech situations, Vygotsky's (1978) development through the proximal zone of development, Taylor's (1991) aligning horizons of significance through dialogue, Gadamer's (1994) fusion of horizons, Freire's (1992) liberation through dialogue among equals, and feminist scholars who write about development through relationality.

In his theory of organizational knowledge creation, Nonaka (1994) says, "Although ideas are formed in the minds of individuals, interaction between individuals typically plays a critical role in developing these ideas" (p. 15). His premise is that it is the "continual dialogue between explicit and tacit knowledge which drives the creation of new ideas and concepts" (p. 15). This distinction between explicit and tacit knowledge (Brown & Duguid, 1991, 2000; Lave & Wenger, 1991; Polanyi, 1966; Wikstrom & Norman, 1994) is fundamental to conversational learning. While explicit knowledge (i.e., the "knowing about" and "knowing that") is more content- and information-based knowledge, it is not accessible for practical use without its tacit dimensions. Tacit knowledge—the uncodified "knowing how"—develops along its own unique path within each person through observation, trial and error, and practice.

The interplay of tacit and explicit dimensions of knowledge manifest themselves in conversational learning as individuals come together in a joint meaning-making process. Conversation can serve as an essential foundation for mutual trust and sharing of experiences among members of an organization. When organizational spaces such as communities of practice and self-organizing teams emerge, conversation can catalyze visions, innovations for new development, and learning. Nonaka (1994) describes the kind of learning that can be generated in these receptive spaces as a "challenging task [that] involves repeated, time-consuming dialogue among members. . . . A key way to build mutual trust is to share one's original experience—the fundamental source of tacit knowledge. Direct understanding of other individuals relies on shared experience that enables team members to 'indwell' into others and to grasp their world from 'inside'" (p. 24). This kind of repeated sharing of experiences out of relationships of mutual trust is at the heart of conversational learning.

According to Francis Fukuyama's (1995) groundbreaking work, *Trust: The Social Virtues and the Creation of Prosperity*, on the interdependency of social capital and economic prosperity, global prosperity hinges on "the ability of people to work together for common purposes in groups and organizations" (p. 10). Huy's (1999) new multilevel theoretical model of radical change suggests that individual and organizational receptivity to change is increased with the experiencing and reconciliation of emotion through conversations. Conversational learning can be a fundamental component at the micro, interpersonal level of Fukuyama's macro concept of social capital and of being able to accept and adjust to the radical change that Huy is describing at a more abstract level. Implicit within the works of Fukuyama and Huy is the capacity for having ongoing collaborative conversations where learning and changing perceptions is possible.

According to Alan Webber (1993), formerly a managing editor and editorial director of the *Harvard Business Review* and a founding editor of *Fast Company*, "The most important work in the new economy is creating conversations. . . . But all depends on the quality of the conversations. . . . Conversations—not rank, title, or the trappings of power—determine who is literally and figuratively 'in the loop' and who is not" (p. 28). The current knowledge-intensive environment is dependent upon the ease, frequency, and quality of interactions among people in organizations.

To be deprived of good conversation can be devastating. While Nobel laureates and large proportions of other successful people come from families that talked around the dinner table, many children today have no one to talk with and often no dinner table. One can turn to one's peers who are equally deprived, or participate in a media conversation that at least sometimes gives voice to a part of the world, or withdraw into a world of imaginary conversations that can become self-fulfilling prophecies. The deprivation then serves to drain the lifeblood away from the individual and collectively drain away the heart of the culture.

This deprivation takes many forms. It may be a by-product of unintentional neglect to create a "dinner table" in the family or the school or the workplace or the community. It may be a decidedly intentional result of avoiding interaction. Either way, deprivation of conversation is a wound that leaves lasting scars, or worse.

There are many forms of conversation, each with its own particular dynamics. Some of these are described in the following sections.

PRIVATE AND PUBLIC CONVERSATIONS

A private conversation, as we are using it in this context, is one where the participants have more control over who is included and who is excluded. In these private spaces with family, friends, or colleagues, there are opportunities to explore sensitive, intimate, confusing, and important topics about oneself, others, and the world. Often it is more risky to talk about many of these issues in public. In public conversations, what is said becomes open, in varying degrees, to everyone. Just one "outsider" can turn a private conversation into a public one.

One of the many stories told about Herb Shepard, the founder in 1960 of the Organizational Behavior Department at Case Western Reserve University, illustrates the difference between public and private conversation. Herb, serving as a consultant to a senior management team at Wright Patterson Air Force Base, was sitting in on a meeting of the team. The commanding officer (CO) was leading the group through the agenda, and at one point turned to Herb and said, "What do you suggest?" "I think we should take a break," he replied. The team spontaneously broke into groups of two or three people and began talking among themselves. After reconvening and continuing the agenda, the CO again turned to Herb for advice and Herb again suggested a break. When this sequence was repeated for a third time, the CO in frustration asked, "Why do you suggest a break every time I ask what we should do?" Herb replied, "Because that's the only time anything is happening."

Herb's insight was that conversation in the public forum of the CO's meeting was guarded and formal. Free exchange about the real issues was constrained by many factors in the situation: the presence of a strong, directive power figure, competing interests among subgroups, even Herb's presence as an "outsider." When individuals were free during the breaks to gather in subgroups of their own choice, they felt freer to speak their minds.

The expanse of public conversation extends from those where one outsider is present to the collective public conversation of a community or a culture or society. How to bring some of the most valued qualities of good private conversations—speaking more honestly and openly to build relationships—into the public arena is an especially timely concern. Most observers today view the state of public conversation with alarm. Public conversation comes to us in many forms, from face to face to newspapers to television to congressional debate to television to talk radio to musical lyrics. The airways and print media seem to bombard us with images of violence, fear, partisanship, hatred, selfishness, endless investigations, the short term, and parochial views. Perhaps as important as the actual words or specific messages conveyed is the spirit that gets called forth in each person when surrounded by these images.

Yet public conversation could call forth a quite different spirit. Robert Reich, secretary of labor in the Clinton administration, speaking on the importance of public conversation in national decisions, said, "Policy-making should be more than, and different from, the discovery of what people want. It should entail the creation of contexts in which people can critically evaluate and revise what they believe" (Heinrichs, 1995, p. 42). What a different spirit would be called forth if public conversation allowed for genuine consideration of alternatives and revisions of perceptions through new learning. The ways people talk to each other privately and publicly contribute to creating the reality of their worlds. As such, conversations can serve as a bridge that unites differences and promotes mutual understanding among individuals, families, and communities at large.

CONVERSATIONS AMONG DIVERSE GROUPS

Intergroup conversations can be among the most difficult conversations, and in today's pluralistic world may be among the most important. In contrast to the kinds of conversation that Reich describes, much of the current conversation among diverse groups is combative (Tannen, 1998). It seems that the only thing that can stop ethnic wars, for example, is conversation among the parties. It is only when the Jews and the Palestinians persistently stay in difficult and ongoing conversations, both in private and official spaces, that real hope for peace in the Middle East emerges. Similarly, it is only when people from different neighborhoods and in more official policy-making arenas across the United States or among nations enter and sustain conversations with each other that they begin to hear the commonality of their concerns and learn from their differing experiences and expectations. Whether in the Middle East, the United States, Eastern Europe, or Latin America, when people share their hopes, values, and despair caused by the loss of community in a effort to understand how their differing experiences contributed to their current stands on issues, possibilities for reconciliation can emerge.

As an example of how conversations with and among diverse groups of people can generate new forms of sense-making, one of the authors of this book, Ann Baker, served as a consultant in a communitywide project designed to bring diverse stakeholders in a moderate-size metropolitan area to focus on the needs of children. People from highly diverse backgrounds in this community in the southeastern part of the United States were asked to come together for the project. As part of their early work together, attention was given to creating receptive conversational spaces, and they were asked to share stories from their past experiences, both together as a group and in individual interviews with the consultant. Insight from those stories into what was happening in their world came with a laserlike sharpness.

In a warm and humble home, one African-American woman spoke about growing up in that same neighborhood, where the woman across the street would tell her mother if she misbehaved while the same woman was also always there to help her whenever needed if her mother was not home. She went on to describe how different her neighborhood is now for her grandchildren, where people do not look after each other. A white woman in a similarly warm yet large and exquisitely designed and appointed home told the same story, though she had grown up in another part of town in an upscale neighborhood.

An African-American man who described a period of his childhood spoke of another version of the story. On Monday evenings he and a group of his childhood friends would go to the home of a man in their neighborhood to recite short texts they had memorized. As a reward and incentive to return and to continue to prepare their "speeches," they were given delicious home-baked cookies and lots of attention. He remembered these experiences as contributing substantially to the development of his own sense of self-esteem. He described growing up in an integrated community in the South where black and white people had helped shape the man he became, a man widely known as a devoted family man and highly respected family court judge. Yet he was bemoaning how segregated most neighborhoods are now and how adults seldom spend time with young people who are not family members.

In each of these three stories, individuals were describing their individual sagas of lost community. Yet until they worked together in this community project, they were unaware of how similar their experiences were. Before the community project began, for the most part, they had never been in conversations with each other across racial and class boundaries. They had been more aware of the differences—in terms of economic and racial inequities—among their neighborhoods rather than their shared values, experiences, and concerns.

As neighborhoods and groups within much of the United States have become more mobile and bifurcated, the sense of children growing up in extended families and communities has almost disappeared. People too seldom have symbolic "dinner tables" around which to talk in their own neighborhoods or ethnic groups, much less across neighborhoods or ethnic groups. The cultural idols of autonomy and "busyness," combined with fear, have too often mushroomed into seemingly impenetrable barriers that are increasingly insurmountable. When groups of people are not in conversation with each other, they are not living "in community" with each other. When groups are not in conversation with each other, their misunderstandings and folklore about each other go unexplored and the barriers can grow even thicker and more impermeable.

CONVERSATIONS AMONG TEXTS

Another facet of conversations are those that occur among texts. These are forms of talk among readers and writers, instances of conversations that continue historically over time as texts react and interact with one another. In addition to the sharing of texts with others that serve as fodder for further conversations, one of the advantages that hard-copy texts and electronically generated texts (i.e., e-mail, online conversations, etc.) offer is that they are available for repeated revisiting and reflection.

MacIntyre (1984) beautifully articulates the process of each person engaging in the "conversations among the texts" from their own vantage point: "Texts are always moments in conversations and are to be interpreted from the standpoint of the participants in those conversations, each of whom is apt to bring to his or her participation a different history and with it a different point of entry into that conversation and sometimes . . . a different understanding of what is involved in having such a conversation. And from those facts stem both conflict and misunderstanding" (p. 196).

TECHNOLOGICAL CONVERSATIONS

In today's technological world, face-to-face conversation is being replaced or at least expanded by technologically mediated conversations. One of the ways that conversation by telephone, e-mail, or even written letters is unique is that the exchange among participants is constrained to the spoken or written word and lacks visual cues. Yet a widely accepted premise of communication theory is that most communication is nonverbal. Perhaps there is a sense of loss that many people feel when technology intervenes in conversation. Yet there are also those who feel liberated and comforted by the structure dictated by technology. E-mail and voice mail give time to reflect and a sense of visual, nonverbal anonymity. Cyberspace is not confined to the physical constraints of having to be in the same space at the same time, allowing for asynchronistic, more spontaneous, and yet reflective and thoughtful conversations.

IMAGINARY CONVERSATIONS

The conversations that take place in our heads and dreams especially illustrate the ubiquitous nature of conversation. In *Dialogic Imagination*, the Russian philosopher M. M. Bakhtin (1981) suggests that thoughts are internalized conversations. Thus, people make meaning of their experiences and create and tell themselves stories immersed in their own internal conversations, some audible, some silent, and some imaginary.

CONVERSATION AND DIALOGUE

Contemporary research on learning and meaning making in conversation is expanding in many fields: philosophy, information systems, management, organizational behavior, psychology, and sociology. One major line of this work is organized around the concept of dialogue, while another tradition is focused on the concept of conversation. While there is much agreement between those two traditions and many researchers use the terms interchangeably, there are, in fact, important differences.

While some dictionaries define conversation and dialogue as synonyms or define both words as "talk," a deeper etymology reveals very different roots for the two words. The origin of the word "conversation," according to the Oxford English Dictionary (Simpson & Weiner, 1989) gives the earliest recorded usages in the 1340s as "living or having one's being *in* a place or *among* persons . . . living together, commerce, intercourse, society, intimacy . . . sexual intercourse . . . to be united in heaven in conversation," all usages that embrace collaborative, contextual interactions (vol. 3, p. 868). The current word seems to originate from Latin through the Old French words meaning "frequent abode, intercourse." Nearly all of the definitions emphasize the communal, sensual, and emotional aspects of conversation.

The English word "dialogue" can be traced through French to Latin and ultimately to the Greek *dialectos* (Simpson & Weiner, 1989), and is defined as "conversation, to talk, to speak alternately," as well as various kinds of "discussion" that are found throughout its two definitions (vol. 4, pp. 601–602). Unlike conversation, the etymology of dialogue includes frequent references to words like "debate" and "discussion." The original definitions of the word debate include "strife . . . dissension, quarrelling . . . fight, conflict . . . dispute, controversy . . . to beat down, bring down, lower, reduce, lessen, diminish . . . take away," while discussion means "drive away, dispel . . . to shake off, to set free . . . remove . . . to examine or investigate, to try (as a judge) . . . to sift the considerations for and against . . . to consume" (vol. 4, p. 309). Thus, the root of "dialogue" is more related to "opposing voices in search of truth," a definition that emphasizes conflict and a more rhetorical approach than "conversation."

Traditionally, the word dialogue generally is preferred by critical theorists, classicists, and other theorists who are epistemologically oriented, those who see "talk" primarily as an intellectual process of refining knowledge. Edgar Schein (1993), one of the early leaders of the sensitivity-training approach to group dynamics, makes this point by contrasting dialogue with communication in sensitivity-training settings:

> Most communication and human relations workshops emphasize active listening. . . . Dialogue is focused more on the thinking process and how our perceptions and cognitions are preformed by our past experiences. . . . In the typical sensitivity training workshops we explore relationships through opening up and sharing, through giving and receiving feedback, and through examining all of the *emotional* problems of communication. In dialogue, however, we explore all the complexities of *thinking and language*. We discover how arbitrary our basic categories of thought and perception are, and, thereby, be-

come conscious of imperfections or bias in our basic *cognitive* processes. (p. 43; emphasis added)

The term "conversation," in contrast, is used by more ontologically oriented writers (Gadamer, 1994; Rorty, 1980, 1989; Palmer, 1998), who focus more on human understanding and human experience than on abstract knowledge about ideas. According to White (1993), "Gadamer's hermeneutics illuminate an approach to understanding where interpersonal communication or *conversation* reveals . . . or embodies the *world* between people. His point is that interpersonal understanding does not consist of the transmission of preexistent meanings from one person to another but is a creative or *productive* understanding that occurs in conversation" (p. 84). To paraphrase Gadamer, conversations of inquiry and explorations can create learning opportunities that are larger than could be accomplished by any single participant.

This approach is especially appropriate in the context of learning, because it implies a somewhat softer approach to method. Gadamer's (1994) *Truth and Method*, for example, emphasizes the limitations of using a method to search for a truth. On the other hand, the introduction to the *Organizational Dynamics* special issue on dialogue, in which Schein's (1993) earlier quote appears, refers to dialogue as a "communications technology."

Hard method can lead to the objectification of others, where a facilitator's or leader's actions and words are privileged over other participants in the conversation. Instead, the conversational learning approach developed in this book is seen as a process of reaching interpersonal understanding where all participants' contributions are equally valued. The intention here is not to prescribe a method or technique for conversation. This conversational approach is much more attuned to the traditions of group dynamics and conversation as communion, traditions that will be explored in the next two chapters.

REFERENCES

Adler, M. J. (1982). *Paideia proposal: An educational manifesto*. New York: Macmillan.

Argyris, C. (1994, July–August). Good communication that blocks learning. *Harvard Business Review*, 77–85.

Bakhtin, M. M. (1981). *Dialogic imagination: Four essays*. Austin: University of Texas Press.

Brown, J. S., & Duguid, P. (1991). Organizational learning and communities-of-practice: Toward a unified view of working, learning and innovation. *Organization Science*, 2 (1), 40–57.

Brown, J. S., & Duguid, P. (2000). *The social life of organization*. Boston: Harvard Business School Press.

Dewey, J. (1938). *Experience and education*. New York: Macmillan.
Dewey, J. (1964). *John Dewey on education*. New York: Modern Library.
Edmondson, A. (1996). Learning from mistakes is easier said than done: Group and organizational influences on the detection and correction of human error. *Journal of Applied Behavioral Science, 32*, 5–28.
Edmondson, A. (1999). Psychological safety and learning behavior in work teams. *Administrative Science Quarterly, 44*, 350–383.
Freire, P. (1992). *Pedagogy of the oppressed*. New York: Continuum.
Fukuyama, F. (1995). *Trust: The social virtues and the creation of prosperity*. New York: Free Press.
Gadamer, H. G. (1994). *Truth and method* (2d rev. ed.). New York: Crossroad.
Habermas, J. (1972). *Knowledge and human interests*. Boston: Beacon Press.
Habermas, J. (1984). *The theory of communicative action*. Boston: Beacon Press.
Habermas, J. (1991). *Moral consciousness and communicative action*. Cambridge: MIT Press.
Heinrichs, J. (1995, July–August). How Harvard destroyed rhetoric. *Harvard Magazine*, 37–42.
Huy, Q. N. (1999). Emotional capability, emotional intelligence, and radical change. *Academy of Management Review, 24*, 325–345.
James, W. (1977). Percept and concept: The import of concepts. In J. McDermott (ed.), *The writings of William James* (pp. 217–247). Chicago: University of Chicago Press.
Kolb, D. A. (1984). *Experiential learning: Experience as the source of learning and development*. Englewood Cliffs, NJ: Prentice-Hall.
Lave, J., & Wenger, E. (1991). *Situated learning*. Cambridge: Cambridge University Press.
Lewin, K. (1951). *Field theory in social science*. New York: Harper Torchbooks.
MacIntyre, A. C. (1984). *After virtue*. Notre Dame, IN: University of Notre Dame Press.
Maslow, A. H. (1962). The need to know and the fear of knowing. In *Toward a psychology of being* (pp. 57–64). Princeton, NJ: D. Van Nostrand.
Mezirow, J. (1991). *Transformative dimensions of adult learning*. San Francisco: Jossey-Bass.
Naess, A. (1973). The shallow and the deep, long-range ecology movement: A summary. *Inquiry, 16*. (A summary of the introductory lecture at the Third World Future Research Conference, Bucharest, September 3–10).
Nonaka, I. (1994). A dynamic theory of organizational knowledge creation. *Organization Science, 5* (1), 14–37.
Palmer, P. (1998). *The courage to teach: Exploring the inner landscape of a teacher's life*. San Francisco: Jossey-Bass.
Piaget, J. (1951). *Play, dreams and imitation in childhood*. New York: W. W. Norton.
Piaget, J. (1965). *The moral judgment of the child*. New York: Free Press.
Polanyi, M. (1966). *The tacit dimension*. Garden City, NY: Doubleday.
Rorty, R. (1980). *Philosophy and the mirror of nature*. Oxford: Basil Blackwell.
Rorty, R. (1989). *Contingency, irony, and solidarity*. Cambridge: Cambridge University Press.
Schank, R. C. (1991). *The connoisseur's guide to the mind*. New York: Summit Books.

Schein, E. (1993). On dialogue, culture, and organizational learning. *Organization Dynamics, 22* (2), 40–51.

Schulz, C. (1999). *Peanuts: A golden celebration*. New York: HarperCollins.

Simpson, J. A., & Weiner, E.S.C. (Eds.). (1989). *Oxford English Dictionary* (2d ed., vols. 1–20). Oxford: Clarendon Press.

Tannen, D. (1998). *The argument culture: Moving from debate to dialogue*. New York: Random House.

Taylor, C. (1991). *The ethics of authenticity*. Cambridge: Harvard University Press.

Vygotsky, L. S. (1978). *Mind in society: The development of higher psychological processes*. Cambridge: Harvard University Press.

Webber, A. M. (1993, January–February). What's so new about the new economy? *Harvard Business Review*, 24–42.

White, J. (1993). *The role of individual characteristics and structure of social knowledge on ethical reasoning using an experiential learning framework*. Unpublished Ph.D. diss., Case Western Reserve University, Cleveland, OH.

Wikstrom, S., & Norman, R. (1994). *Knowledge and value: A new perspective on corporate transformation*. New York: Routledge.

2

Conversation as Communion: Spiritual, Feminist, Moral, and Natural Perspectives

Patricia J. Jensen and David A. Kolb

> We always retain the ability to alter or suspend any particular instance of participation. Yet we can never suspend the flux of participation itself.
>
> David Abram (1996)

> Because within every meeting other meetings occur. They take place in the mirror of consciousness. To exist is to reflect and consider. One meets oneself, one sees a trajectory, a certain possible path into what is yet unknown, recalling histories, detecting patterns, weaving the fabric of existence out of every moment. And for each of us, as for every community, village, tribe, nation, the story we tell ourselves is crucial to who we are, who we are becoming.
>
> Susan Griffin (1995)

To be in communion with others, with our natural world, with the source of being of all living things, is to deeply experience being at one with the other, in and beyond time and space. It is an experience that we know as a feeling of being fully alive. Being in communion, we sense something of the mystical, the mysterious, an intermingling of souls and spirits. We feel together, in the intimacy of conversation with others, in sensing that we share in the abundance of life we encounter in deserts, forests, mountains, and prairies. In our experience of the numinous, we feel grounded, connected, in communion.

When we attempt to name and communicate these experiences, we are perhaps best served by our poets, mystics, and naturalists, as they put into words the particular nuances of experiences that we know and with which we resonate. Philosophers, psychologists, theologians, and scientists give their attention to the universal that helps us conceptualize the human experience of connection. At heart we are relational beings and come to more fully know others and ourselves in communion with that which is both deeply within and profoundly beyond us.

Communion, from the Latin, *communio,* means "mutual participation." The word conveys a sense of strong and deep relationships, all the way from particles joining together as they create varied complex life forms, to individuals being emotionally present to one another as we participate in each other's experiences and feelings together, to the ways we sense our primal connections with nature, for relationship is the essence of existence. Whatever our individual perspectives, fundamental ways of relating between men and women, between human beings and our natural world, and between human beings and our common source of life, these ways of relating are integral to shaping our daily lives, our public policy deliberations, and perhaps ultimately the destiny of our earth. One of the primary ways we connect with others is in conversation. The contexts for conversation range from the intimate to the electronic, from the casual to the critical, and from the local to the global. The purpose of this chapter is to explore the varied ways spiritual, feminist, moral, and natural perspectives offer distinctive views on conversation as communion. This admittedly brief and selective sampling of these perspectives will highlight and suggest aspects of broad contexts relevant to an understanding of conversation as communion.

HOSPITABLE SPACE: A SPIRITUAL CONVERSATION

The great religious traditions of the world, with their respective spiritualities and religious practices and rituals, offer varied ways of being in communion with ultimate reality, the source of being, and one another. Writing within the Christian tradition, Henri Nouwen (1975) and Parker Palmer (1983, 1990, 1998), describe hospitality to the stranger and the strange as being at the heart of a spiritual life. Nouwen characterized life in the last decades of the twentieth century as living in a world full of strangers who are estranged not only from their own historical and environmental contexts, but from "their deepest self and their God" (p. 46). Such estrangement finds us yearning and searching for places of hospitality where we can be welcomed and welcoming, creating a community of integrity and wholeness. Drawing upon several biblical stories of individuals welcoming strangers into their homes, Nouwen interpreted them as examples of "when hostility is converted into hospitality then fearful strangers can become guests revealing to their hosts the promise they are carrying with them" (p. 47). He described hospitality as

> the creation of a free space where the stranger can enter and become a friend instead of an enemy. Hospitality is not to change people, but to offer them space where change can take place. It is not to bring men and women over to our side but to offer freedom not disturbed by dividing lines. It is not to lead our neighbor into a corner where there are not alternatives left, but to open a wide spectrum of options of choice and commitment. It is not an educated intimidation with good books, good stories and good works, but the liberation of fearful hearts so that words can find roots and bear ample fruit. . . . The paradox of hospitality is that it wants to create emptiness, not a fearful emptiness, but a friendly emptiness where strangers can enter and discover themselves as created free; free to sing their own songs, speak their own languages, dance their own dances; free also to leave and follow their own vocations. Hospitality is not a subtle invitation to adopt the life style of the host, but the gift of a chance for the guest to find his own. (p. 51)

To convert hostility into hospitality, we need to create "friendly empty space where we can reach out to our fellow human beings and invite them into a new relationship" (p. 54).

Nouwen (1975) goes on to explain that creating friendly open space is challenging, because our desire for power and immediate results, rivalry and competition, impatience and frustration, and fear make forceful demands and tend to fill every empty corner of our lives. It is out of our own fear of emptiness that we run from solitude so we can avoid the "uncertainties and hostilities" of life. As a result we fill our emptiness with criticism, advice, and opinions, and we hold those as most valuable (p. 53). Nouwen describes the ways that hospitality can serve as a model for creative interchange between people within the context of education. For example, "students and teachers can enter into a fearless communication with each other and allow their respective life experiences to be their primary and most valuable source of growth and maturation" (p. 60). This space "asks for a mutual trust in which those who teach and those who want to learn can become present to each other, not as opponents, but as those who share in the same struggle and search for the same truth" (p. 60). It is in such free and fearless spaces that mental and emotional development can occur.

Within this view of hospitality, a good host is one "who believes that his guest is carrying a promise he wants to reveal to anyone who shows genuine interest" (Nouwen, 1975, p. 61). Emphasizing the importance of receptivity, Nouwen holds that unless we can see our gifts as being accepted and acceptable, we will be hesitant to openly share them. Thus the idea of genuine receptivity becomes an important part of the communal conversation process. Friendly, empty space is characterized by a receptivity that means inviting the stranger into our world on his or her terms, not on ours. However, receptivity is only one side of hospitality; the other is confrontation. Nouwen reminds us that receptivity to others does not mean that we simply become neutral and vacant in relationship to another. Rather, receptivity "asks for confrontation because space can only be a welcoming space when there are clear boundaries, and boundaries are limits between which we define our own position. Flexible limits, but limits nonetheless" (p. 69).

Compassionate confrontation gives to others an "unambiguous presence" where we honestly share our own perspectives and values in such a way as to challenge others to explore their own stances and to be invited into a critical exploration of them (Nouwen, 1975, pp. 69–70). Stating that receptivity and confrontation need to be kept in careful balance, Nouwen describes how receptivity without confrontation potentially leads to bland neutrality that serves no one, while confrontation without receptivity can lead to an oppressive aggression that hurts everyone.

Drawing upon Henri Nouwen's concept of hospitality, Parker Palmer (1983) writes, "To teach is to create a space in which obedience to truth is practiced" (p. 69). Three essential dimensions characterize this space: openness, boundaries, and hospitality. Openness is removing "the impediments to learning that we find around and within us, to set aside the barriers behind which we hide so that truth can seek us out" (p. 71). Palmer states that the fear of "not knowing" often leads us "to pack the learning space with projections and pretensions" (p. 71). To open space for learning, we must be aware of our fear of not knowing and see this as a step toward truth. Describing an open learning space as defined by its boundaries, Palmer states that the openness of this space can be experienced as a threat. He characterizes this space in talking about silence. It is in silence that we are potentially faced with our own barrenness. Afraid of being empty, we find masterful ways to fill up the spaces, which ultimately prevents us from encountering true and genuine connection with each other:

> If you doubt this, try creating a long silence in your classroom. . . . Feel the anxieties that arise . . . anxieties so powerful that fifteen seconds of silence is about as much as the typical group can tolerate. . . . Before we encounter truth, we must first wrestle with the demons of untruth that arise in the silence, demons that come from our own need to manipulate and master truth rather

> than let truth transform us. . . . For that temptation often arises just at the point where the true knowing begins, the point where we are forced to face our illusions. . . . Good teachers know that discomfort and pain are often signs that truth is struggling to be born among us. Such teachers will not allow their students, or themselves to flee. . . . They will hold the boundaries firm, and hold us all within them, so that truth can do its work. (pp. 72–73)

If such truth is to "do its work" we need to create space that is hospitable and not filled with fear. Such hospitality requires us to make the space an inviting yet bounded one, where conversation can be "conducted with passion and discipline." Palmer (1990) explains that such a process will lead us to the kind of truth that is embedded in community and therefore is "not in the conclusions so much as in the process of conversation itself. . . . If you want to be in truth, you must be in the conversation" (p. 12). Therefore, for Palmer, teaching and learning happen within the context of a community of truth. Such a community is one where "many stories can be told and heard in concert" (p. 13), and learners not only come to know the ways in which the world works but also come to know their inner selves. In such a context, both the story of the individual and the story of the discipline can be held in concert with each other, thus creating opportunities for illumination and creativity.

When the space does not allow for a range of voices to be heard, some may leave the conversation, silencing their own wisdom and keeping private their own gifts. Palmer (1990) reminds us that what is called for is to "establish settings where silenced voices can be heard into speech by people committed to serious listening . . . to make the classroom a hospitable space" (p. 15). Without such serious listening to each other, silence and fear hold sway over the conversation. In such conditions, fear of conflict is likely to result. Fears about conflict are often born of experiences where difference is not tolerated or the power of one perspective squashes openness to ambiguity or a communal sense of truth. Palmer speaks to the spirit of courage that such truth telling requires when he says, "Truth requires many views and voices, much speaking and listening, a high tolerance for ambiguity in the midst of a tenacious community" (p. 15). Through this process we can arrive at "consensual truth" by "exposing one's ignorance, challenging another's facts or interpretations, claiming one's own truth publicly and making it vulnerable to the scrutiny of others" (p. 15). Palmer sees this process as critical to learning, since "consensual truth is the only truth we have" (p. 15).

Nouwen and Palmer both describe hospitality as residing in the creation of friendly, open spaces where we can reach out to our fellow human beings and invite them into new relationships. The research and writing of several feminists during the past thirty years offer perspectives on what these new relationships can be.

FEMINIST PERSPECTIVES ON COMMUNION

According to Ken Wilber (1995) in *Sex, Ecology, Spirituality*, liberal feminism and radical feminism hold two fundamentally distinctive positions regarding men and women. He characterized liberal feminists' position as "men and women are fundamentally equivalent in capacities," and radical feminists' position as "men and women represent two quite different value spheres, the former being hyperautonomous, individualistic, a bit power-crazed, but generally *agency-oriented*, the latter being more relational, nurturing, and *communion-oriented*" (p. 160).

In *The Duality of Human Existence: An Essay on Psychology and Religion*, David Bakan (1966) uses the terms "agency" and "communion" to characterize "two fundamental modalities in the existence of living forms." He uses agency to describe the existence of an organism as an individual and communion to describe the individual's participation in some larger organism of which the individual is a part:

> Agency manifests itself in self-protection, self-assertion and self-expansion; communion manifests itself in the sense of being at one with other organisms. Agency manifests itself in the formation of separations; communion in the lack of separations. Agency manifests itself in isolation, alienation, and aloneness; communion in contact, openness, and union. Agency manifests itself in the urge to master; communion in noncontractual cooperation. Agency manifests itself in the repression of thought, feeling and impulse; communion in the lack and removal of repression. One of the fundamental points which I will attempt to make is that the very split of agency from communion, which is a separation, arises from the agency feature itself; and that it represses the communion from which it has separated itself. (p. 15)

Writing on the development of women's sense of self, Jean Baker Miller (1986), draws upon Bakan's (1966) concepts of agency and communion but offers a different interpretation. She suggests that the concept of "agency-in-community" describes the experience of actively using one's resources while not aggressing on others. She refers to this process as "doing" in such a way as to engage the self in relationship with others in developmentally and increasingly complex ways (p. 21). In this way, issues of self and communion are intrinsically woven together as women define themselves not so much as separate others, but as beings who are able to develop and nurture relationships around them (p. 83).

Unlike the perspectives of theorists from Erik Erikson (1982) to Daniel Levinson (1978) that describe human development as a process of separating from others to become autonomous and independent, Miller (1986) notes the importance of relationship over pure agency in her ideas about the developmental process. Moving from a focus on male experience of identity formation, Miller and others (Gilligan, 1982; Surrey, 1991; Belenky, Clinchy, Goldberger, & Tarule, 1986) have forged a type of evolution in the understanding of development, an evolution that goes beyond the view of the mature self as being separate and other to propose the importance of a "self-in-relationship," thus emphasizing "agency-in-community."

What is different about this perspective is that it embodies the possibility for identity to develop within the context of the web of relationships within which the self resides. Identity need not be sacrificed for the sake of relationship. Neither does relationship have to be sacrificed for the identity to form and mature. Rather, it is the relational identity that is the more whole, and the self only matures when developing in relationship to other selves (Surrey, 1991). Thus comes the importance of a "communion" that takes all selves seriously. Mutuality and resonance, relational mutuality, mutual intersubjectivity, mutual empathy, and mutual recognition are all terms that these writers use to help clarify the communion that takes place when the balance of self in relation to other is taken seriously.

Ruthellen Josselson (1992) describes this mutuality as "emotionally being with another, joining in" (p. 148). She sees in such mutuality a resonance between the self and other and cites this mutuality as a "pure form of communion with another person" (p. 150). While such resonance may be difficult to describe in objective terms, we humans have a proclivity to orient our own experiences to others around us. We do this in all kinds of ways: physically, intellectually, and emotionally, either through direct experience of the ways we encounter others or through the stories others tell of their own joining.

Still others describe the weaving of agency and communion as a paradoxical process that involves the need to both assert the self and recognize the other at the same time. Jessica Benjamin (1988) speaks of this intersubjective perspective as one where individuals grow through relationships to other subjects and develop capacities that can only emerge in the interaction between self and others. She describes assertion and recognition as constituting poles of a delicate balance that is integral to the process of "differentiation," an individual's development as a self who is aware of its distinctness from others. In Benjamin's paradox, recognition from others helps the self to make meaning of its own actions, feelings, and intentions. However, this recognition can only come from another individual whom we recognize as a person in his or her own right. In Benjamin's view, the need for recognition is the concept that unifies intersubjective theories of the self:

A person comes to feel that "I am the doer who does, I am the author of my acts," by being with another person who recognizes her acts, her feelings, her intentions, her existence, her independence. Recognition is the essential response, the constant companion of assertion. The subject declares, "I am, I do," and then waits for the response, "You are, you have done." Recognition is, thus, reflexive; it includes not only the other's confirming response, but also how we find ourselves in that response. (p. 21)

Judith Jordan (1991) describes mutual relationships and mutual intersubjectivity as being "mutual exchanges" where each participant is being equally affected by the other. In this process of mutual intersubjectivity people are genuinely attuned to each other and open and vulnerable to the experiences of both the self and the other. The process of relationship is a responsive and responding one, where each person actively engages with the other and maintains openness to the experiences of the other. In relationships characterized as mutual, individuals experience themselves as subjects through assertion and recognition and through active initiative and receptivity. Conversation in such a self-in-communion process is expansive and keenly aware of the other, while at the same time being respectful of the self and one's own experience and place in the world.

Janet Surrey (1991) describes the fundamental processes of mutual relationship as "mutual engagement (attention and interest), mutual empathy and mutual empowerment" (p. 167). Mutual engagement, empathy, and empowerment take place when the relational context provides both safety and encouragement to take the risks of tensions and conflicts. The process that Surrey describes is one of enlarged vision and energy, stimulated through interaction within a context of emotional connection. Surrey describes this process within group conversation as having a kind of "zest" that empowers each person to contribute to a greater awareness and effectiveness. At the same time that each individual voice is valued and each person finds his or her own clarity of experience, the contribution to the group energy and experience brings forth a larger vision and imagination than any one individual contributes. Such engagement does not diminish the single voice, but rather brings out the clear, resonating tones of personal understanding in light of the group experience. In this view of relational empowerment, conversation is a primary way of making and sustaining important emotional connections.

When engaged in conversation that is truly intersubjective and where "agency-in-community" is deeply respected, there is not room for "power over" claims or one agent overpowering another. In fact, power dynamics and power games interfere with the experiences of mutual understanding. Jordan (1991) points out that "a motivation for personal power and ascendancy directly contradicts the notion of mutuality" (p. 93). When trying to claim one's own perspective as the most powerful or most truthful, any one person will miss the value of experiencing the presence of another voice, another opinion, or an action that could have ultimately been helpful. Mutuality and domination cannot coexist. Communal conversation leaves no room for manipulation, as the heart of the idea is that each voice, each experience, leads to greater understanding for both the speaker and the listener. Therefore, if one is engaged in conversation for the sake of trying to maintain agency alone, the conversation will be an isolated one and will not benefit from the mutuality of the communal intersubjective process.

Likewise, if those who are engaged in the conversation each give up his or her voice, thinking that everyone else has the better idea or that one's own experiences have no value, then the energy of intersubjectivity is flattened. Without the voices of the individuals to create the dynamic of communal experience, communion becomes a process of cooption. When a participant does not take his or her experience seriously, it is difficult to contribute to a relational process in a way that is healthy and lively. Thus there is a need for the encouragement of individual voices who may not have spoken before to speak their experience and to be heard by both others and self.

Wilber (1995) sets the concept of a self-in-relationship in a broad historical perspective:

> There is literally *a million years* of rich tradition of the wise woman who feels the currents of embodiment in nature and communion, and celebrates it with healing rituals and knowing ways of connecting wisdom, a wisdom that does not worship merely the agentic sun and its glaring brightness, but finds in the depths and the organic dark the ways of being linked in relationship, that puts care above power and nuturance above self-righteousness, that reweaves the fragments with concern, and midwives the communions and the unsung connections that sustain us each and all. And finds, above all, that being a self is always being a self-in-relationship. (p. 183)

Author Susan Griffin (1995) places the communal experience within the body, pointing out that the mind and body have been described within the genre of agency. She points out that even when we try to talk about the mind and body as a dynamic kind of communion, we tend to portray the body as a kind of puppet with which the mind can enact its reasoning. She offers the reminder that "physical experience preceded the language that uses the body as metaphor," clarifying that the body has a knowledge that "like the gestures of a mime, bespeaks a world significant unto itself . . . [to] bring on to wonder at the texture and complexity of existence" (p. 190). Furthermore, Griffin artfully poses that our bodies feel the presence of others and the influences of time and place. She carries the concept of self-in-relation almost to a cellular level. Her poetic description of this process reads as follows:

> Just beyond your own body you can feel the presence of another body, amorphous but massive as it surrounds you. A body made up of trees and sidewalks and idea, of oceans and the sound of your neighbor's voice, of the taste of strawberries and the memory of the first strawberries you ate, of what your grandmother said to you when you were six years old and what you read in the newspapers this morning. This body presses into you, becomes you. (p. 81)

This decisive awareness of the body and all that is in communion with the body-self tells the story of interconnectedness that is rooted within time and space and embraces the dynamic of self with self without making the separations of traditional, patriarchal thought. It is within this awareness that the energy of conversation as a mutual narrative can be powerfully experienced. Griffin (1995) explains that as a story is shared there is something in the narration that changes both the hearer and the teller of the story. She notes that such change can happen both interpersonally, in the private sphere, or politically, within public discourse. As societies repeat the stories of their communal experience, they construct the reality by which they continue to live and grow (often it is the loudest experiential narrative that informs the direction of a society and the historical construction of it). The power of mutually sharing both individual and group narratives lies in the ways that such sharing informs the direction in which even groups of people eventually grow. Griffin reflects on such power: "Perhaps some strange unexplained physics exists, the physics of narration, by which stories are drawn together, like atoms with a positive charge. It is after all only when they are assembled that stories can partake in that alchemy by which one common account will be made. A story we will all hear, and that, as it moves through our bodies, will change us" (p. 277).

COMMUNION: A MORAL PERSPECTIVE

In trying to frame the perspectives of literature having to do with what is "moral," it is difficult to not add the words "thought," "reasoning," "logic," or even "development" to this work. This pairing of the moral with that which is logical or linear or even thoughtful is what lies at the heart of traditional, even liberal modes of grappling with the moral. In the psychological and spiritual literature the concepts of morality and agency are intricately linked, as if one could not have one without the other. From Kant to Erikson to Kohlberg and the modern-day authors of virtue and character, the height of moral progression lies in the ability to independently discern the good, the right, and the true. While these constructs help trace the movement of moral dictum to moral dialogue to moral conversation, the moral dimensions of conversation that are rooted in communal experience focus on the dialectic between the concrete and the generalized other.

Immanuel Kant (Paton, 1961) stands among the most influential contributors to contemporary moral and ethical theory. His deontological approach posits that an action has moral worth only if the actor has good will, and an actor has good will only if the sole motive for action is moral duty based on a valid rule. Kant's test of validity for moral rules is the "categorical imperative," considered by some to be a philosophically improved version of the Golden Rule. It states that rules of conduct must be categorical or universalizable, being absolutely binding and admitting no exceptions; that is, to be valid a moral rule must be valid for everyone. The process by which one arrives at these valid moral rules for conduct is rational critical reflection.

The problem with Kant's imperative is that reasoning happens within the solitary, rather isolated, and independent view of the individual. Like Decartes, the mind turns inward on itself to refine appearances and thus to achieve truth. Habermas's philosophy moved from the subject-centered reason of Kant and Decartes to a more communicative reason. In this his hope was to rescue the Enlightenment project of human emancipation through reason with a reason centered not in solitary critical reflection and logic, but in related conversation and language. Gadamer's (1989) critique of the Enlightenment concept of universal reason is based on the historicity of knowledge, that what is defined as reasonable is always determined by culture, context, and historical tradition. For Gadamer, "Conversation is a process of coming to an understanding" (p. 385). But this understanding is not that of the information-processing model of communication—that is, where two individuals process what each other is saying—but that conversation is large and deep. Understanding in conversation results when partners in the conversation come to a common viewpoint, a "fusion of horizons" about the subject of the conversation. In such conversation, both parties as well as the conversation itself are transformed by the experience of the conversation.

In this movement from the rational, individualistic notions of the moral dimensions of conversation to the relational and mutual ones, Seyla Benhabib (1987) poses the dichotomies of early modern moral and political theory by discussing the two concepts of self–other relations as the "generalized other" versus the "concrete other." Drawing on the work of contemporary moral theorists from the field of psychology and moral development, such as Kohlberg and Gilligan,

Benhabib (1987) posits the generalized other as autonomous, independent, public minded, and justice oriented. She describes the concrete other in terms such as "nurturing," "bonding," "domestic," and "good life." The following outlines the dichotomies that she sees in the work of these two contemporary theory fields:

Generalized Other	**Concrete Other**
Individuals	
Rational beings entitled to the same rights and duties we ascribe to ourselves.	Rational beings are individuals with a concrete history, identity, and affective-emotional constitution.
Abstracting from	
The individuality and concrete identity of the other. What constitutes moral dignity is not what differentiates us from each other, but what we have in common.	What constitutes our commonality; we seek to comprehend the needs of the other, their motivations, what they search for and desire; our differences complement rather than exclude one another.
Norms of Relating	
Formal equality and reciprocity; norms are primarily public and institutional. I confirm your rights of humanity and I have a legitimate right to expect you will do the same in relation to me.	Equity and complementary reciprocity; norms are private and noninstitutional. Friendship, love, and care as important. I confirm not only your humanity but your human individuality.
Moral Categories	
Right, obligation, entitlement.	Responsibility, bonding, sharing.
Moral Feelings	
Respect, duty, worthiness, dignity.	Love, care, sympathy, solidarity.

Benhabib (1987) joins others who are moving the conversation about the moral from the standpoint of the individual over the communal to the individual as part of an intricate communal web that depends upon the mutuality of self and other, be it human, ant, or mountain. Stephen Rockefeller (1992) points to the number of philosophers and social scientists who see the history of moral conversation as "a story of a developing a sense of community that begins with the family and tribe and then gradually extends outward embracing the region, the nation, the race, all members of a world religion and then all humanity" (p. 144). He goes on to explain that unless we extend our moral sensibilities beyond a human perspective to a perspective that involves all life forms, we are involved in a crisis that impacts all of life itself.

NATURE'S CONVERSATION: A UNIVERSE IN COMMUNION

In the last thirty years a growing number of feminists, contemporary moral philosophers, and those who engage in spiritual reflection have shared the perspective that the conversation in which we are involved impacts environments far beyond the distance between two people. For example, Albert Schweitzer (1933) came to a definition of the moral person as one who promotes life, who "raises life to its highest value." He explained that a person is ethical only when life, as such is sacred . . . that of plants, and animals as that of his fellow man, and when he devotes himself happily to all like that is in need of help" (pp. 159–160). While Schweitzer still poses the moral conversation from an androcentric point of view, he joined others of the time who clearly articulated a more organic view of the human–nature relationship. Others, like Leopold, embedded a broader, environmental perspective into the enterprise of human ethics. His point was that the "land ethic" intricately interweaves human experience with that of animal, rock, and soil (Rockefeller & Elder, 1992).

With the articulation of the interrelatedness of human to human, and of the even more holistic connection that includes the conversation of bird song, whale song, and wind song, it is evident that the communal nature of conversation is present within and among all that lives. The meanings held within this realization go deeper than our simply saying, "Ok, ok, we all are one." Our authentic comprehension of how such a stance changes the meaning and quality of our interactions has very specific and concrete implications for how we develop and evolve as human beings. David Abram (1996) describes such implications as follows:

> As we grow into a particular culture or language, we implicitly begin to structure our sensory contact with the earth around us in a particular manner, paying attention to certain phenomena while ignoring others, differentiating textures, tastes and tones in accordance with the verbal contrasts contained in the language. We simply cannot take our place within any community of human speakers without ordering our sensations in a common manner, and without thereby limiting our spontaneous access to the wild world that surrounds us. Any particular language or way of speaking thus holds us within a particular community of human speakers only by invoking an ephemeral border, or boundary between our sensing bodies and the sensuous earth. (pp. 255–256)

In other words, how we see ourselves on the planet, in the galaxy, and within the universe influences how we interact and converse, which in turn influences how we see ourselves and so on. Eco-feminist Charlene Spretnak (1991) reiterates that we need not "invent a ground of connected-ness but only realize it" (p. 188). She wonders how our true realization of the connection might influence our educational process. "What if," she says, "we were educated to nurture awareness of our inseparable relatedness?" (p. 188). What if, indeed.

Seeing ourselves as necessarily related to all who dwell in the biological network that we call life stands us within a very different conversation than that of the individual mind looking out for individual interests. Such a standpoint takes us beyond even that of the beneficent earth dweller who is steward of everything on the planet. The place of communion with the other clearly recognizes the mutuality of life with life. Such recognition ultimately changes the very way we interact, which in turn changes the experience of our living. This conversation is nothing short of a profound communion with life itself.

REFERENCES

Abram, D. (1996). *The spell of the sensuous.* New York: Vintage Books.

Bakan, D. (1966). *The duality of human existence: An essay on psychology and religion.* Boston: Beacon Press.

Belenky, M., Clinchy, B., Goldberger, N., & Tarule, J. (1986). *Women's ways of knowing.* New York: Basic Books.

Benhabib, S. (1987). The generalized and concrete other: The Kohlberg–Gilligan controversy and moral theory. In E. Feder Kittay & D. Meyers (Eds.), *Women and moral theory* (pp. 154–177). Totowa, NJ: Rowan and Littlefield.

Benjamin, J. (1988). *The bonds of love: Psychoanalysis, feminism, and the problems of domination.* New York: Pantheon Books.

Erikson, E. (1982). *The life cycle completed.* New York: Norton.

Gadamer, H. G. (1989). *Truth and method.* New York: Crossroad.

Gilligan, C. (1982). *In a different voice.* Cambridge: Harvard University Press.

Griffin, S. (1995). *The eros of everyday life.* New York: Doubleday.

Jordan, J. (1991). The meaning of mutuality. In J. Jordan, A. Kaplan, J. B. Miller, I. Stiver, & J. Surrey (Eds.), *Women's growth in connection* (pp. 81–96). New York: Guilford Press.

Josselson, R. (1992). *The space between us: Exploring the dimensions of human relationships.* San Francisco: Jossey-Bass.

Levinson, D. (1978). *The seasons of a man's life.* New York: Alfred A. Knopf.

Miller, J. B. (1986). *Toward a new psychology of women.* Boston: Beacon Press.

Nouwen, H. (1975). *Reaching out.* New York: Doubleday.

Palmer, P. (1983). *To know as we are known: Education as a spiritual journey.* San Francisco: Harper and Row.

Palmer, P. (1990). *The active life: A spirituality of work, creativity and caring.* San Francisco: Harper and Row.

Palmer, P. (1998). *The courage to teach: Exploring the inner landscape of a teacher's life.* San Francisco: Jossey-Bass.

Paton, H. (1961). *The moral law: Kant's groundwork of the metaphysic of morals.* New York: Barnes and Noble.

Rockefeller, S., & Elder, C. (Eds.). (1992). *Spirit and nature*. Boston: Beacon Press.

Schweitzer, A. (1933). *Out of my life and thought: An autobiography* (C. T. Campion, Trans.). New York: Holt.

Spretnak, C. (1991). *States of grace: The recovery of meaning in the postmodern age*. San Francisco: Harper.

Surrey, J. (1991). *Relationship and empowerment*. In J. Jordan, A. Kaplan, J. B. Miller, I. Stiver, & J. Surrey (Eds.), *Women's growth in connection* (pp. 162–180). New York: Guilford Press.

Wilber, K. (1995). *Sex, ecology, spirituality*. Boston: Shambala.

3

Looking Back: Precursors to Conversational Learning in Group Dynamics

Ann C. Baker, Esther D. Wyss-Flamm,
David A. Kolb, and Patricia J. Jensen

> We must conclude that the psychology of groups is the oldest human psychology; what we have isolated as individual psychology, by neglecting all traces of the group, has only since come into prominence out of the old group psychology, by a gradual process which may still, perhaps, be described as incomplete.
>
> Sigmund Freud (1929)

CONVERSATIONAL LEARNING EMBEDDED IN A PRECOURSE

Renowned twentieth-century physician and founder of psychoanalysis Sigmund Freud's (1929) declaration of intellectual indebtedness to earlier works in psychology alludes to the importance of intellectual antecedents. In conversational terms, antecedents are the precourse that preceeds any important development in human thought. Indeed, every intellectual breakthrough is situated within a larger context or conversation that contains relevant ideas serving as precursors to accompany its evolution into the future. This chapter is devoted to examining such a precourse to conversational learning, residing specifically in group dynamics, a field of rich intellectual activity that emerged in the mid-twentieth century.

"Group dynamics" is a term that conjures up different images for different people depending upon their previous experiences. For the organizational-development specialist, it is part of an everyday vocabulary. Human resource specialists and effective managers consistently need to consider group dynamics in organizational decision making. For a person in a technical field, group dynamics is often perceived as a hindrance to getting tasks accomplished. In this chapter the term is used in two ways. First, it primarily recalls the infinite realm of human social behavior among people when they are together in groups in and beyond organizational settings. Second, as a field or discipline, the term encompasses a relatively new and rich area of study. The field of group dynamics can be traced to some pioneering thinkers, many of them deeply influenced by training in psychology, who began their work by intentionally focusing on human behavior in groups in the 1940s.

By its nature, conversational learning is a social process that implies the presence of others in the form of a group, team, organization, or other interpersonal setting. When people enter a group, they bring their own expectations and assumptions that influence and shape the conversations, how they behave, what they notice and pay attention to, and what they are likely to expect in the group in the future. These influences reside not only in the assumptions of group members, but also in the assumptions that many organizational-development experts, leaders, and managers are tethered to, often in unarticulated and unexamined ways. It thus seems pertinent to specifically explore the contribution of group dynamics to expand and develop our understanding of conversational learning.

Even when a person is not familiar with the classic writers and practitioners in the field of group dynamics, their influence has become so enmeshed in ways that mold conscious and unconscious assumptions that they still shape much group behavior, particularly within Western culture. These assumptions include, for example, the cues that influence what is considered acceptable group behavior, the norms about leadership, the appropriateness of beginning work immediately or initially spending time on social relationships, and what are considered appropriate or inappropriate responses to conflict.

This chapter provides some historical context about the origins of group dynamics, reviews some of its classic works and its continuing evolution, and explores its relationship to conversational learning. The primary purpose of the chapter is to heighten awareness of the influence of group dynamics on contemporary group behavior and thus contribute to a more comprehensive perspective on conversational learning.

The chapter begins with a brief overview of the origins and characteristics of group dynamics from the mid 1940s through the 1970s.

Against the vitality and tremendous variation that can be found in group dynamics, the chapter then identifies six themes nascent within group dynamics that serve as precursors to conversational learning. An exploration of each of these precursors includes a brief discussion of the relevant major contributions by leading theorists and practitioners.

While this chapter does not portend to be an exhaustive portrayal of the roots of group dynamics or conversational learning, it does offer insight into their evolution. It includes references to the classic works of W. R. Bion (1959), Philip Slater (1966), Robert Freed Bales (1950, 1970), William C. Schutz (1966), Kurt Lewin (1951), Theodore M. Mills (1967, 1979), Frederick Perls (1973), Elaine Kepner (1980), Irving Janis (1972), Carl Rogers (1970), Chris Argyris (1970), and Edgar Schein (1993). It also delves into related, more-contemporary writing by Amy Edmondson (1996, 1999), Ikujiro Nonaka (1994), John Seely Brown and Paul Duguid (1991, 2000), Leigh Star (1989, 1996), Etienne Wenger (1998), and Mary Fambrough and Susan Comerford (1998). To connect these early origins to the present, references to more recent points of view in related fields of organizational learning and knowledge management demonstrate further the evolution and profound influence of group dynamics. Taken together, these works form a vibrant body of literature that has strongly influenced not only the authors of this book but also the ways in which people throughout much of Western culture have come to think about groups.

A HISTORICAL PERSPECTIVE OF GROUP DYNAMICS

The story of the origin of group dynamics is intimately intertwined with both the darkest and the most euphoric intellectual and historical events of the twentieth century. As a recognizable field of study, group dynamics emerged simultaneously in several different locations in the United States and Europe during the mid to late 1940s, soon after the end of World War II. In many ways it is not surprising to see such a profound interest relating to groups develop at this time. Psychology and psychoanalysis had made enormous inroads in and beyond academia, fed by the frequent movement and migration—often forced, due to wartime conditions—among intellectual giants in and beyond continental Europe. This led to a cross-fertilization of new combinations of ideas and approaches that began to be applied from the intrapersonal to the interpersonal levels. In addition, the postwar period was marked by pervasive concerns that focused attention on the level of the group. The rise to and subsequent abuse of power by extremist political groups, the development of new potential for global destruction by small groups of scientists, the persecution and attempted extermination of certain population groups, the corresponding denial of responsibility by others, and, not least important, the experience of group camaraderie shared by thousands of people recruited into war all contributed to this shift in focus toward groups. In the words of Theodore Mills (1979),

> The visions were largely post World War II, coming during a period when it was clear that in shifting from war to peace, societies would reassemble, rearrange, and rebuild. The opportunity to participate in the reordering of our social structure probably contributed to the enthusiasm. . . . But why the small group? . . . Somehow, if the dynamics in the small group could be understood, then a lot of power might be released—power to understand, to heal, to teach, to lead. (p. 410)

This eruption of interest in "releasing the power of the small group" in the late 1940s and 1950s in the United States and Europe created a fecund milieu for new thinking.

Although group dynamics includes a wide spectrum of thought and approaches, the early efforts were attempting to create objective, positivist scientific theories and methodologies to explain and predict human behavior. Yet the emerging work was also feeling-focused, emphasizing the affective dimensions of the group experience, including primal emotions and behaviors such as inclusion–exclusion, intimacy–autonomy, and fight–flight.

On the surface these two descriptors—of objective scientific prediction and of affective feeling-focused dimensions—may seem contradictory. While cognitive, rational dimensions of human interactions are more often associated with the objective scientific paradigm, there was an increasing recognition during these years of the role of emotions and their associated behaviors in groups. An alternative to the positivist, scientific approach for inquiry into the relationship between these emotions and group behavior had not yet fully emerged and gained credibility.

Examples of this can be found in the work of W. R. Bion (1959), who suggested that there are basic assumptions about people's behavior in groups that would apply regardless of the context or cognitive content of the discussion. His attention was on primitive, raw behavior, about which he tried to develop a scientific perspective that would be predictive of future groups. The very name of Schutz's (1966) classic work, *The Interpersonal Underworld*, is an apt metaphor for the early group-dynamics work, describing fundamentally primal interpersonal behavior that drives a group with little awareness of or attention to how the content of the group's work, the context surrounding the group, or group membership would affect interactions. Early researchers in this tradition were trying to understand human communication without yet taking into account what was being said or who was present. The premise was that what is being said derives from what is happening, and thus is usually devoid of or at least unaffected by specific content or context.

One of the most notable aspects of this early tradition of group-dynamics research (for which it has been frequently criticized) is that the study of primarily white male group members in therapeutic settings, in alcohol treatment centers, or in mental institutions was assumed to be predictive for all people, regardless of mental health, cultural background, race, or gender. The behavior patterns of small homogeneous groups of people were extrapolated to universal principles that could be used to predict behavior across contexts. This approach seems entirely contradictory to conversational learning, which affirms difference and the relevance of the locally particular context. At the same time, this research tradition offers original thinking that has inspired conversational learning. What then are areas of congruence and connection between group dynamics and conversational learning?

IDENTIFYING PRECURSORS TO CONVERSATIONAL LEARNING ROOTED IN GROUP DYNAMICS

As suggested in the introduction to this chapter, there are intellectual threads originating in group dynamics that represent an important conversation that precedes conversational learning. While some aspects of group-dynamics research are antithetical to conversational learning, others serve as important theoretical footholds that significantly shape and undergird our understanding, particularly of the social aspects of conversational learning. Thus, the identification of precursors or themes residing in the group-dynamics literature begins with sifting through the many works associated with this tradition. It also means espousing a stance of valuing the tremendous variation that so clearly characterizes group dynamics as it is carried into the twenty-first century.

One way of illustrating the variation of perspectives identified under the broad rubric of group dynamics can be found in the work of Jack Gibb (1964), who traced evolving ideas across a continuum of assumptions. Gibb offered a frame of reference to help understand early traditions in group-dynamics research that still have influence today. He suggested that there were two opposing underlying sets of assumptions that contributed substantially to how groups developed: persuasive technology and participative technology. (The term "technology" to illustrate the two opposite approaches across a continuum of differing assumptions is revealing in itself and highlights a substantial difference from conversational learning that strives not to be a technology, method, or technique.)

Gibb's (1964) perception was that a leader develops a somewhat systematic set of "attitudes, beliefs, and assumptions about group formation, person formation and his relationship to such formation" (p. 293). These behaviors tend to cluster around a technology of persuasion on one extreme, with an opposite pole called a technology of participation. According to Gibb, leaders who tend to use persuasion technology are those whose behavior "is derived from fear, distrust, and lack of confidence in the capacities, attitudes, and maturity of the members of the group . . . tends to use command, persuasion, influence, guidance, or training in an effort to give motivations to members of the group and to influence productivity (learning, work, or growth)" (p. 293). Gibb goes on to describe the opposite pole characterized by "a 'Participative' technology, [where there is] . . . greater trust and respect in the group relationship—greater acceptance of self and others within the group. . . . Individuals in the group are allowed great freedom to assess their own goals, determine their own intrinsic motivations and decide their own directions for learning, productivity, and creativity" (p. 296).

In his work, Gibb (1964) employs a continuum to graphically represent this range (Figure 3.1). One extreme, the persuasive pole, is the psychoanalytic paradigm based on assumptions of a leader who has the answers and knowledge and who should remain distant from group members and in a position of authority. Along the participative pole is a more collaborative approach of nondirective peer facilitation that assumes each group member brings knowledge and valuable experience to the group interactions and assumes that new ways of knowing can be created relationally among peers.

Gibb's (1964) continuum can be used to demonstrate how early shifts within the original group-dynamics field have influenced organiza-

Figure 3.1
Variations in Assumptions Underlying Group Dynamics: An Adaptation of Gibb's Continuum

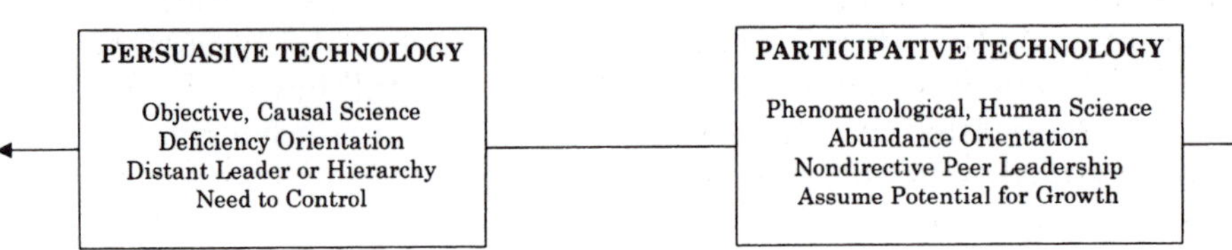

tional-development experts, leaders, managers, consultants, and academics of today. The perspectives across this continuum also lead to the identification of precursors to conversational learning that cover a wide paradigmatic range. This chapter identifies six precursors of conversational learning that can be traced to group-dynamics research. Each precursor is both deeply rooted in the origins of group dynamics and highly relevant for extending contemporary understanding of groups and conversational interactions. Each of them is intended to draw attention to a particular aspect of group dynamics that is fundamental to conversational learning:

- Interpersonal Underworld.
- Tension of Differences.
- Mutual Interdependence of the Whole and Its Parts.
- Capacity for Personal Growth.
- Acceptance and Trust.
- Nondirective, Peer Facilitation and Leadership.

The following pages offer descriptions, references, and explorations of each of the precursors, explicitly making connections between group dynamics and conversational learning. In doing so, the hope is to provide a sense of the historical evolution of these precursors across time, as well as to illustrate some of the major contributions of group dynamics. However, many of the influences on social behavior in group dynamics do not follow a strictly linear chronology or occur in a direct cause-and-effect relationship. These precursors and their sources do not do so either.

As is the case with any major intellectual contribution, group dynamics has spawned not only numerous followers in academia and among organizational-development practitioners, but also a significant number of critiques as well. In the descriptions of the precursors, occasional references to these more recent works will be included to round out our understanding of the precursor's relevance to conversational learning.

Interpersonal Underworld

Organizational thought in the 1940s and 1950s was marked by new attention drawn to group behavior, at least partially influenced by the World Wars and intellectual migrations already described. Earlier research had been focused on the individual (psychological) and organizational (mechanistic) levels. With this increasing interest in social behavior at the group level, a major shift gradually occurred away from structural explanations for organizational outcomes toward more emphasis on the interpersonal interactions among people in and beyond organizational settings. This one contribution alone cannot be overemphasized, as it opened a gold mine of new possibilities for a learning-centered perspective.

Among the first people to open this new arena was W. R. Bion (1959). For a time during World War II, Bion was in charge of the training wing of a military psychiatric hospital. Growing out of that experience, in 1948 he began to work with therapeutic groups of the Tavistock Clinic. Bion's approach is marked by a decidedly psychoanalytic orientation. It is embedded in assumptions, which come from working primarily with patients in mental hospitals, about the deficiencies and pathologies of group members and about the need for group leaders to maintain a distant stance vis-à-vis the members. Bion's predisposition toward hierarchy is not limited to the leader–patient relationship, but is also evident in his frequent references to his perceptions of hierarchies among group members.

Bion (1959) is most known for developing a set of three basic assumptions out of which he saw all group members acting: fight–flight (conflict and avoidance), pairing (joining and subgrouping), or dependence–counterdependence (support-seeking from others) behaviors. Throughout his writing, Bion uses anecdotal narratives and stories to illustrate his theory. These basic assumptions reflect a kind of primal undercurrent—a veritable interpersonal underworld—in groups that appear to be at least partially related to his hierarchical leadership style, and assumptions about the deficiencies of the members of the groups. Similar to others at the time, his work demonstrates a shift not only toward an increasing interest in interpersonal interactions but also toward a focus on the more primitive, instinctual behaviors often referred to as the "dark side" of human behavior.

In accordance with norms at that time, Bion (1959) initially worked with male patients in military mental institutions and developed a theoretical perspective based on such groups that he then extrapolated to be applicable to all groups. He looked for the causes of behaviors and sought to create a scientific approach predictive of group behavior without leaving much room for alternative explanations for the behavior of group members.

Other theorists and practitioners who were active and influential in similar arenas were Robert Freed Bales (1950, 1970), Philip Slater (1966), and William Schutz (1966). Bales began to develop his Interaction and Process Analysis (IPA) approach in 1942 and continued revising it over several decades. Initially, the IPA approach focused entirely on observable interactions; over the years, it was expanded into a methodology for analyzing attitudes, values, fantasy themes, and interpersonal perceptions. Bales eventually created an objective, empirical method for classifying direct interactions as they actually occur among group members, with a heavy emphasis on perceptual data. In keeping with the times, Bales (1970) said, "The pragmatic aim of observations and inferences is prediction and increased ability to control events" (p. 20). Bales's distinctively psychoanalytic background is evident in his perceptions about method: "Conceptions of good technique in the conduct of self-analytic groups are more or less direct adaptations of the classical Freudian approach to psychoanalysis, applied to the group situation" (p. xi). Yet he acknowledged that he avoided using psychoanalytic language because it interfered with the receptivity to his approach among academic psychologists.

As a former student and colleague of Bales, Philip Slater (1966) developed an approach that was also highly psychoanalytic. His classic book, *Microcosm*, grew out of his experiences with a university course, Analysis of Interpersonal Behavior, and its associated staff meetings from 1958 to 1961. Slater's work is especially well known for the vivid metaphorical images that he crafted regarding leader–member interactions around omnipotence, eating and feeding the leader, and sexuality. These images reflect a strong emphasis on the primal behaviors associated with the interpersonal underworld to understand group behavior.

Slater (1966) attempted to add to the scientific and empirical examination of small-group behavior using a male-centered orientation focused especially on issues of authority, separation, and independence. For example, Slater's strong advocacy for independence can be seen in this quote: "Independence cannot be conferred; it can only be seized. For independence . . . has become manifest in an individual or group when it no longer occurs to that group or individual to seek the solution of its problems by an agent outside itself" (p. 150). A keen implication is that working collaboratively with others is not valued as a desirable aspect of the group experience. This perception is profoundly contrary to more recent trends in groups research and the images of group interaction in conversational learning as envisioned in this book.

William Schutz (1966) shared with Bion, Bales, and Slater a primary focus on interpersonal interactions as distinct from behavior at the group level. Schutz developed an elaborate theory of interaction supported by postulates and theorems that are defined by mathematical expressions. According to his theory, people have preferences for patterns of interaction emerging out of what he saw as three universal interpersonal needs—inclusion, control, and affection—that people need to both receive (want) and need to give (express). Schutz developed numerous instruments that attempt to measure people's preferences for these needs (the FIRO series), many of which are still widely used. These measurements were designed to predict compatibility between and among people. Schutz's psychoanalytic background can be seen in the emphasis on childhood patterns in his earlier work, although his later work manifests a shift in interest toward actual behavior within groups.

The major contribution of this precursor to conversational learning is the emphasis on and attention to the often emotive aspects of the interpersonal experience among group members, even when those behaviors are unpolished and primal. Moreover, the validation of the potential power of what can be learned by studying behavior of small groups and identifying various patterns of interaction is profound. Thus, these early contributions began to lay the foundation for recognition of the potential that resides in conversational learning.

Tension of Differences

Deliberately introducing differences of perspective into the group experience was in some ways an inadvertent discovery that originated in the work of Kurt Lewin (1951), who is considered the founder of American social psychology (Kolb, 1984, p. 8). In the summer of 1946, a year before his untimely death, Lewin agreed to requests from group members in a training program he was facilitating for them to sit in on evening staff sessions. The evening sessions had previously been open only to staff members and were intended to analyze the group's experiences during that day.

As the group participants began to participate with staff in the evening sessions and became a part of the reflections, new perspectives were introduced to the conversations, often creating tensions that could also lead to new insights. This format came to be known as the T-group. Out of this experience came the "discovery . . . that learning is best facilitated in an environment where there is dialectic tension and conflict between immediate, concrete experience and analytic detachment" (Kolb, 1984, p. 9).

By the 1960s other noted organizational theorists, researchers, and practitioners focused on group behavior as it related to innovation and change in organizations. Influenced by Lewin, they identified the key role played by the tension of differences in the group process. Chris Argyris's work (1970) had already moved beyond striving for prediction toward the importance of the role of the intervener. Along with Donald Schön (Argyris & Schön, 1978), Argyris was among the first to coin the term "organizational learning," which advocated that differences were a fundamental element of innovation and learning. In his work, Argyris (1978, 1994, 1997) described how differing perspectives could become "undiscussable" in organizations and groups. Undiscussables arise when talk about differences brings tension and challenges prevailing assumptions, and there is reluctance to be vulnerable, to take risks, or to ask difficult questions. Undiscussables are those vast differences in organizations that are typically avoided, glossed over, or debated in ways that silence many voices (i.e., silence new sources of learning).

A parallel perspective on the effects of the absence of verbalized difference is found in the classic work, *Victims of Groupthink*, by Janis (1972). He describes "social pressures that typically develop in cohesive groups . . . to preserve friendly intragroup relations" (p. 8). His research analyzes the group process used in the political decision making that resulted in the disastrous Bay of Pigs invasion. Janis's work is a vivid illustration of the implications for poor decision making when there is a loss of vital sources of learning because group members do not express differing points of view to avoid creating tension that might threaten the group's cohesiveness.

More recently, Amy Edmondson's (1996, 1999) work on psychological safety continues to affirm both the importance of bringing up differences for learning in groups and the challenges inherent in doing so. Developing a context to support and provide enough psychological safety to allow for the tension associated with differences among group members to emerge is thus a vital element of learning.

As a precursor of conversational learning, the tension of differences highlights the vitality inherent in group members' abilities to recognize and work across their differences, a vitality that can enhance the learning process. Indeed, from this perspective, conversational learning without the explicit presence of differences and the tensions they entail becomes unthinkable.

Mutual Interdependencies of the Whole and the Parts

Frederick Perls and his wife Laura Perls (Perls, 1973; Perls, Hefferline, & Goodman, 1951) opened the doors of their therapeutic practices in New York City in 1947, during this early fertile period of group-dynamics activity. In the words of Polster and Polster (1973), who were also actively working in these areas, Perls was Gestalt psychology's "main proponent and developmental genius" (p. ix). Although what became known as Gestalt psychology began with the Perls and their colleagues, it evolved substantially over time. One of the most notable developments specifically relevant to the content of this chapter is a shift that began in the late 1950s and early 1960s through the work of the Gestalt Institute of Cleveland (GIC).

Elaine Kepner (1980), a faculty member at GIC, describes this evolution and articulates the more current philosophy. Early in Gestalt psychology, especially as practiced by people like Frederick Perls, the individual was figural, with intrapersonal development as the focal point. However, growing out of the emphasis on wholeness and a systems orientation, those associated with the GIC increasingly wanted to learn more about both interpersonal and group dynamics and were instrumental in developing these areas of Gestalt psychology. According to Kepner, the essence of Gestalt psychology is to develop the potential of people, to work from assumptions of health rather than pathology, to focus on the "here and now" concrete behavior, and to "consider the individual and the environment as a unified field or system, in which all parts are interdependent" (p. 7). The concept of a unified whole requires what she describes as one of the primary intentions of the Gestalt approach: "to 'heal the splits' within the personal subsystems. . . . Integration is defined as all parts being unified and available for contact with the environment" (p. 8). This attention to the mutual interdependencies of the whole and its parts brought critical new possibilities into understanding group dynamics.

A major tenet of Gestalt psychology as it is currently taught and practiced through the GIC and elsewhere is that group interactions have three simultaneous processes in motion: the intrapersonal level (growth of the individual), the interpersonal level (improvement in the interaction potential among people), and the group level (development of the group as a social system). The group facilitator and participants can engage around any one or a combination of the three levels to explore possible growth opportunities for the group and its members. A related development is that working patterns in Gestalt groups are increasingly developed more collaboratively among the group members and facilitators than with early Gestaltists.

Another influence that encouraged recognition of the mutual interdependencies of the whole and its parts can be found in Kurt Lewin's (1951) concept of "field theory," which foreshadowed developments that evolved after his death. Even though Lewin strived to establish a scientific approach for studying human behavior and relied heavily on scientific constructs, mathematical representations, and analytical language, he never lost sight of the practical application of his work to create social change. His personal style of working in groups was less distant than was typical at the time. Lewin focused on behaviors at the individual, interpersonal, and group levels, a practice that shows a "close relation to Gestalt psychology . . . [where] the various parts of a given life space are to some degree interdependent" (p. xii). Lewin said, "Structural properties are characterized by *relations* between parts rather than by the parts or elements themselves" (p. 192). The appreciation for these interdependencies in Lewin's work is particularly significant when contrasted with Slater's (1966) focus on independence discussed earlier.

Chris Argyris's work can be seen as similar for its focus on increasing the effectiveness of systems (the whole) by focusing on the behavior of people within the systems (the parts of the whole). His interests in group functioning and individual growth centers primarily around learning how these phenomena contribute to system effectiveness more than to changes at the individual level.

The influence of these early contributions can be seen in contemporary research. For example, the essence of Leigh Star's (1989, 1996) work is an emphasis on the interaction across all disciplines and professions to be responsive to the challenges of the current world. The inadequacy of either–or ways of thinking that attempt to isolate parts without consideration of more complex interdependencies is articulated in her writing. Star (1996) says, "All knowledge, including scientific, comes in many voices . . . is a negotiated, contested phenomenon . . . that local knowledge, as well as local error, partly determine the nature of all information, including the numerical" (p. 312). Her model of robustness of knowledge (Star, 1989) can be seen as growing out of this burgeoning root value of interdependency. The model recognizes that "each local truth is partial and flawed; no a priori specification can encompass any global truth, but when scientists and other actors join local truths they create a robust, emergent negotiated order" (Engestrom & Middleton, 1996, p. 303).

This precursor is relevant to conversational learning in its explicit recognition of the interconnected whole and its parts. Conversational learning represents a meeting point of multiple individual voices woven into an interconnected whole. Mutual interdependence resides at the heart of valuing the local truth of each of these voices for social learning through conversation.

Capacity for Growth

Theodore Mills's (1967) classic book, *The Sociology of Small Groups*, devoted considerable attention to understanding how groups grow and develop. Specifically from a sociological perspective, Mills focused on strategies that contribute to increasing the group's awareness and consciousness about their process and purpose to support generative growth and consideration of alternative goals. Therefore, an important theme in his work, despite an emphasis on experimental method, prediction of group behavior, and a hierarchical approach to learning, is the recognition of an individual's capacity for growth, learning, and development.

As a therapist and writer, one of the fundamental premises that undergirded Carl Rogers's (1970) approach to working with people was his confidence in the capacity of each person for growth, development, and learning. Unlike many of the early contributors to the field of group dynamics, Rogers did not try to create an objective, predictive science. Instead, he felt that a primary challenge for those like him who wanted to learn about human behavior was to "develop a phenomenological human science which will be realistic and illuminating" (p. 165). All his work grew out of his belief in the capacity of each group member to learn and contribute. This contrasted profoundly with the prevailing notion of seeing the facilitator as the expert, teacher, and researcher trying to measure and change others. To accomplish these intentions, one of his suggestions was to "enlist every 'subject' as an 'investigator'! Instead of the wise researcher measuring changes in his subjects, suppose he enlisted them all as co-researchers . . . wholeheartedly enlisted the intelligence and insight of the person involved" (pp. 165–166). Thus, his assumptions were grounded more in the health and wisdom of each person's experience as a source of learning about group behavior than in the position and expertise of the group's leader.

Rogers's (1970) influence can be seen throughout the organizational-learning and knowledge-creation literature. Both approaches assume and depend upon the individual's capacity for learning and potential value as a resource to the group. Eliciting participation, candid expressions, and reflective listening among people are seen as essential not only to sharing knowledge but also to creating new ways of knowing. Through the valuing of tacit knowledge that each person brings into a group, new opportunities for social learning are opened. In the words of Nonaka (1994), "A key way to build mutual trust is to share one's original experience—the fundamental source of tacit knowledge" (p. 24).

Additional contemporary group research and theory building reinforces this assumption of the value and capacity within each person. For example, the work of Fambrough and Comerford (1998), deeply influenced by feminist and ethnic literature, underlines an increasing awareness that every context embodies vital sources of learning and an understanding that each person's unique perspective has as much value as any other perspective.

This precursor is intimately linked with conversational learning because it affirms each group member's inherent ability to learn and develop, as well as to assist others in learning through conversational interactions. It asserts the vitality of conversation: the emphasis on the telling of stories and the sharing of experiences implicitly acknowledges the value of each storyteller.

Acceptance and Trust

Intimately connected to the preceding exploration of the capacity for growth in group dynamics is the theme of acceptance and trust.

Carl Rogers (1970) emerges as a preeminent intellectual force behind this precursor in his role as an early spokesperson for the importance of acceptance and listening carefully to build trusting relationships where people feel safe enough to speak freely. He worked extensively with encounter groups and was especially articulate about the role of listening and safety to foster personal growth, fundamental elements of our idea of conversational learning. Carl Rogers was preeminent in believing in people's inherent health and potential for growth, stressing the importance of trust and "unconditional positive regard" to nurture the development and growth of group members and the group as a whole.

For decades Edgar Schein's (1993) work as a researcher and consultant has emphasized many of these same themes. In his more recent writing, Schein talks about the "dynamics of 'building the group' [where] . . . issues of identity, role, influence, group goals, norms of openness and intimacy, and questions of authority all have to be worked on" (p. 47). By encouraging group members to "suspend" their positions long enough to try to accept and listen to others, Schein says, "the dialogue process speeds up the development of the group . . . [and] creates psychological safety and thus allows individual and group change to occur" (pp. 47–48).

Similarly, when there is congruence between what Argyris (1997) calls "espoused theories" (theories that are claimed) and "theories-in-use" (theories that are observed) in organizations, trust is built among people in ways that facilitate candor and learning. The word "theories" as Argyris uses it in this context is not a conceptual, abstract idea. He is referring to modes of action that describe concrete behavior. As an example using Argyris's words, the theory Rogers espoused (his talk) was highly congruent with his theory-in-use (his walk) in his work, enabling him to create safe and trustworthy relationships. However, when the theory-in-use (actual behavior) is incongruent with the espoused theory (claims about behavior), the message that gets communicated is that relationships among people in that setting are not safe and trustworthy. This lack of safety and trust impedes learning among people.

More recent proponents of organizational learning like Brown and Duguid (1991, 2000), Nonaka (1994), and Wenger (1998) emphasize the pivotal role that informal organizational groups, known as "communities-of-practice," play in new knowledge creation and their dependence on collaborative interactions, acceptance, trust, listening, and safety. Communities-of-practice are being encouraged in places where innovation and spontaneous learning are nurtured, as they bring together groups of like-minded people that are not usually the sanctioned, formal groups within most organizational settings. Instead, the memberships and boundaries of such groups tend to be profoundly fluid, and these emergent groups are responsive to changing needs and opportunities. The challenge for organizations is not to try to make the groups happen, but to get out of the way so that they can emerge. Such informal groups are illustrative of conversational-learning approaches that are rooted, consciously or unconsciously, in the works of Carl Rogers.

Creating collaborative environments that draw on these early messages of acceptance and trust and that support conversational learning are at the heart of this precursor. Such collaborative environments come about by affirming the importance of acceptance and trust in the group context and in the conversation itself. There are conversational interactions that build acceptance and trust (e.g., affirming other group members' contributions, listening and being open to each other's ideas, valuing the unique skills and perspectives of others), and those that can break it down (e.g., dismissing others' suggestions, insisting on adopting one's own ideas, dominating the talk). These behaviors have profound impact on the learning among group members.

Nondirective, Peer Facilitation and Leadership

Once again, the work of Carl Rogers (1970) is pivotal to developing our understanding of this precursor. Rogers was especially noted for his client-centered approach to therapy and his nondirective, peer-leadership style in groups. While some people criticized him for not intervening enough, he tried to avoid making interpretations and giving answers to minimize the likelihood of being seen as an authority figure. Instead, he artfully crafted a nondirective, peerlike approach that broke new ground. To reiterate, his work and philosophy are marked by a deep respect for the experiences and resources that each person brings to a group. He modeled an approach characterized by loosening group-leader control, allowing for more peerlike relationships and more fluid facilitation patterns to emerge. Rogers's approach, located at the heart of the group-dynamics tradition, has profoundly influenced whole generations of group facilitators practicing today using participatory approaches that engage them as peer learners.

Theodore Mills (1979) wrote an insightful historical overview of development in group dynamics that frequently alluded to the evolution of alternative styles of leadership and facilitation. He observed developmental trends that began in the 1940s with research assumptions that claimed it would be fairly easy and appropriate to use a scientific approach to study and predict group behavior. Yet he concluded that three decades later the complexity of group behavior left people more puzzled than ever. Mills attributed this evolution at least partially to the insufficiency of an objective scientific method, often associated with hierarchical group leadership. He saw that the application of such methods too often became more important than genuine attempts to understand group process. In Mills's words, "The scope of group phenomena tapped by these methods remained largely restricted to overt behavior and manifest content, categorized in highly abstract terms. For the most part their data were dissociated from the more subtle instinctual, emotional, evaluative, and symbolic processes" (p. 412).

Specifically regarding the leadership of groups, Mills (1979) suggests, "To do things *to* the group rather than *with* it, or *for* it, is an act which in itself embodies a primordial issue; as an act of 'using the other,' it claims ultimate authority and requires subjugation" (p. 416). Thus, he also represents a moderating of the authoritative and distant leadership style.

Conversational learning picks up on this theme by espousing an approach where everyone in the group, including the authority figure or facilitator, takes a stance of engaging in genuine conversation that emphasizes listening along with talk. Conversational learning breaks down the hierarchy of leadership even further by suggesting that the facilitator is another peerlike participant in the larger conversation that has brought the group together.

CONCLUSIONS: MOVING FORWARD

In the prophetic words of Mary Parker Follett (1965), who spoke and wrote extensively about human organizing and enterprise in the 1920s and 1930s, "Group activity . . . should aim: to incorporate and express the desires, the experience, the ideals of the individual members of the group: also to raise the ideals, broaden the experience, deepen the desires of the individual members of the group" (p. 275). This kind of complex interaction is at the core of group dynamics, and can only be fully realized through an essentially conversational process.

The six precursors explored in this chapter are all rooted in the rich history of group dynamics and provide an important platform for developing our understanding of the social dimensions of conversational learning. Conversational learning can be seen as taking some of the best, most durable aspects of group dynamics, bringing them into the present, illuminating the vast potential residing within them, and pushing them a notch further into the future. Forces from these origins, joined by the critiques and reactions these approaches have engendered, can be seen as contributing to the need for fundamentally new forms of learning socially in groups. These forces have broken away from paradigmatic assumptions like linearity, technique, prediction, and rightness toward new ways of anticipating and being in conversation that will be developed throughout the remainder of this book.

Many bodies of literature have been influenced by these works, including feminist studies, ethnic studies, conflict resolution, organizational learning, knowledge management, communities-of-practice, self-organizing systems, distributed artificial intelligence, computer-supported cooperative work (CSCW), activity theory, and information-system development. Awareness of the importance of collaborative group interaction and communication has soared in the current knowledge-intensive era. As conversational learning gains currency in our understanding of group and organizational interactions, examining the assumptions from these origins contributes to more insightful and conscious approaches to interpersonal behavior. Exploring the ideas and practices of these original thinkers in the field of group dynamics ultimately provides a broader context for developing understanding of the heart and spirit of conversational learning.

REFERENCES

Argyris, C. (1970). *Intervention theory and method: A behavioral science view*. Reading, MA: Addison-Wesley.

Argyris, C. (1994, July–August). Good communication that blocks learning. *Harvard Business Review*, 77–85.

Argyris, C. (1997). *On organizational learning*. Oxford: Blackwell Business.

Argyris, C., & Schön, D. A. (1978). *Organizational learning*. Reading, MA: Addison-Wesley.

Bales, R. F. (1950). *Interaction process analysis: A method for the study of small groups*. Chicago: University of Chicago Press.

Bales, R. F. (1970). *Personality and interpersonal behavior*. New York: Holt, Rinehart and Winston.

Bion, W. R. (1959). *Experiences in groups and other papers*. New York: Basic Books.

Brown, J. S., & Duguid, P. (1991). Organizational learning and communities-of-practice: Toward a unified view of working, learning and innovation. *Organization Science*, 2 (1), 40–57.

Brown, J. S., & Duguid, P. (2000). *The social life of organization*. Boston: Harvard Business School Press.

Edmondson, A. (1996). Learning from mistakes is easier said than done: Group and organizational influences on the detection and correction of human error. *Journal of Applied Behavioral Science, 32*, 5–28.

Edmondson, A. (1999). Psychological safety and learning behavior in work teams. *Administrative Science Quarterly, 44*, 350–383.

Engestrom, Y., & Middleton, D. (1996). *Cognition and communication at work*. Cambridge: Cambridge University Press.

Fambrough, M., & Comerford, S. (1998). Changing epistemological assumptions of group theory. Under revision for publication.

Follett, M. P. (1965). *Dynamic administration: The collected papers of Mary Park Follett*. London: Sir Isaac Pitman and Sons. (Original work published in 1941).

Freud, S. (1929). *Civilization and its discontents*. New York: J. Cape and H. Smith.

Gibb, J. R. (1964). *Climate for trust formation*. In L. P. Bradford, J. R. Gibb, & K. D. Benne, (Eds.), *T-Group theory and laboratory method: Innovation in re-education* (pp. 279–309). New York: John Wiley and Sons.

Janis, I. L. (1972). *Victims of groupthink: A psychological study of foreign-policy decisions and fiascoes*. Boston: Houghton Mifflin.

Kepner, E. (1980). Gestalt group process. In B. Feder & R. Ronall (Eds.), *Beyond the hot seat: Gestalt approaches to group* (pp. 5–24). New York: Brunner/Mazel.

Kolb, D. A. (1984). *Experiential learning: Experience as the source of learning and development*. Englewood Cliffs, NJ: Prentice-Hall.

Lewin, K. (1951). *Field theory in social science*. New York: Harper Torchbooks.

Mills, T. M. (1967). *The sociology of small groups*. Englewood Cliffs, NJ: Prentice-Hall.

Mills, T. M. (1979). Changing paradigms for studying human groups. *Journal of Applied Behavioral Science, 15*, 407–423.

Nonaka, I. (1994). A dynamic theory of organizational knowledge creation. *Organization Science, 5* (1), 14–37.

Perls, F. (1973). *The Gestalt approach and eye witness to therapy*. Ben Lomond, CA: Science and Behavior Books.

Perls, F., Hefferline, R. F., & Goodman, P. (1951). *Gestalt therapy*. London: Souvenir Press.

Polster, E., & Polster, M. (1973). *Gestalt therapy integrated: Contours of theory and practice*. New York: Vintage Books.

Rogers, C. (1970). *Carl Rogers on encounter groups*. New York: Harper and Row.

Schein, E. (1993). On dialogue, culture, and organizational learning. *Organization Dynamics, 22* (2), 40–51.

Schutz, W. C. (1966). *The interpersonal underworld*. Palo Alto, CA: Science and Behavior Books. (Original work published 1958).

Slater, P. E. (1966). *Microcosm: Structural, psychological and religious evolution in groups*. New York: John Wiley and Sons.

Star, S. L. (1989). *Regions of the mind: Brain research and the quest for scientific certainty*. Stanford, CA: Stanford University Press.

Star, S. L. (1996). Working together: Symbolic interactionism, activity theory, and information systems. In Y. Engestrom and D. Middleton (Eds.), *Cognition and communication at work* (pp. 296–318). Cambridge: Cambridge University Press.

Wenger, E. (1998). *Communities of practice: Learning, meaning, and identity*. New York: Cambridge University Press.

4

Conversation as Experiential Learning

David A. Kolb, Ann C. Baker,
and Patricia J. Jensen

> Truth [is] being involved in an eternal conversation about things that matter, conducted with passion and discipline. . . . Truth is not in the conclusions so much as in the process of conversation itself. . . . If you want to be in truth you must be in conversation.
>
> Parker Palmer (1990)

Grounded in the theory of experiential learning, this chapter proposes a theoretical framework for conversational learning, a process whereby learners construct meaning and transform experiences into knowledge through conversations. Experiential learning theory (ELT) provides a holistic model of the learning process and a multilinear model of adult development, both of which are consistent with what we know about how people learn, grow, and develop. The theory is called "experiential learning" to emphasize the central role that experience plays in the learning process, "the process whereby knowledge is created through the transformation of experience" (Kolb, 1984, p. 38). Another reason the theory is called "experiential" is its intellectual origins in the experiential works of Lewin, Piaget, Dewey, Freire, and James, forming a unique perspective on learning and development.

The ELT model portrays two dialectically related modes of grasping experience—apprehension (concrete experience) and comprehension (abstract conceptualization)—and two dialectically related modes of transforming experience—intension (reflective observation) and extension (active experimentation). A closer examination of the ELT learning model suggests that learning requires individuals to resolve abilities that are polar opposites, and that the learner must continually choose which set of learning abilities he or she will use in a specific learning situation. In grasping experience, some of us perceive new information through experiencing the concrete, tangible, felt qualities of the world, relying on our senses and immersing ourselves in concrete reality. Others tend to perceive, grasp, or take hold of new information through symbolic representation or abstract conceptualization, thinking about, analyzing, or systematically planning, rather than using sensation as a guide. Similarly, in transforming or processing experience some of us tend to carefully watch others who are involved in the experience and reflect on what happens, while others choose to jump right in and start doing things.

The four learning modes illustrated in Figure 4.1 constitute a four-stage experiential learning cycle, whereby learners resolve the tension of two dialectically opposite learning dimensions in a cyclical fashion. The cycle begins with immediate or concrete experiences that serve as the basis for observations and reflections. These reflections are assimilated into abstract concepts from which new implications for action can be drawn. These implications can be actively tested and serve as guides in creating new experiences.

Drawing from the theory of experiential learning, in this chapter we propose conversational learning as the experiential-learning process as it occurs in conversation. Learners move through the cycle of experiencing, reflecting, abstracting, and acting as they construct meaning from their experiences in conversations. As such, a theoretical framework based on five process dialectics will be proposed as the foundational underpinning of conversational learning. As participants engage in conversation by embracing the differences across these dialectics, the boundaries of these dialectics open a conversational space.

In the sections that follow we will explore the role of the five dialectical processes, beginning with a discussion of what is meant by a dialectical approach in the context of conversational learning. Our elaboration of these dialectics begins with the dialectic of the knowing dimensions of experiential-learning theory: apprehension and comprehension. Next, the dialectic of praxis that incorporates the integration of intention–reflection and of extension–action is explored, followed by an examination of the dialectical tension between the epistemological, discursive process and the ontological, recursive process.

Figure 4.1
The Experiential Learning Cycle of Development

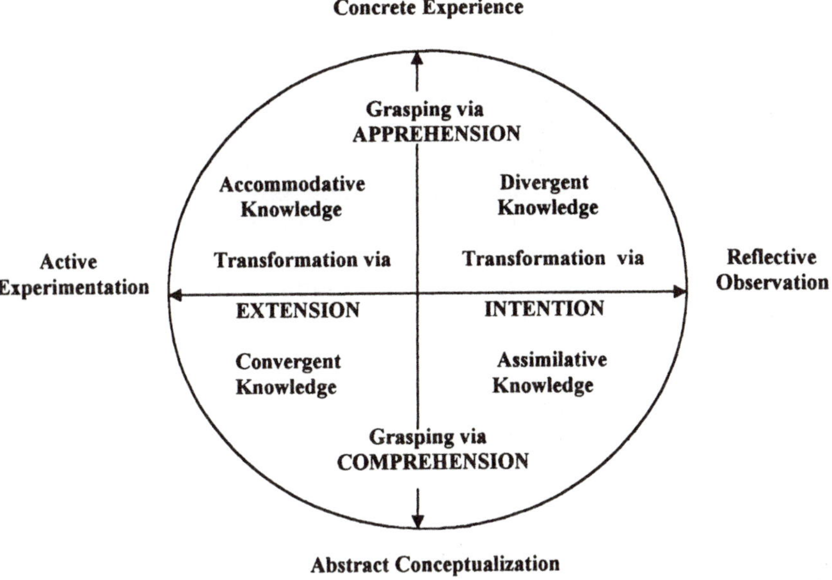

Source: From *Experiential Learning: Experience as the Source of Learning and Development* (p. 141), by D. A. Kolb, 1984, Englewood Cliffs, NJ: Prentice-Hall.

The fourth is the dialectic of individuality and relationality that contrasts conversation as inside-out and outside-in experiences. Finally, the dialectic of status and solidarity describes the ranking and linking dynamics that shape the social realm of conversation. The simultaneous interactions among these five dialectics will ultimately guide and sustain the act of learning through conversations. The description of the five dialectics will be followed by an exploration into the nature of conversational space that holds and sustains the conversation across these dialectics.

A DIALECTICAL APPROACH TO CONVERSATIONAL LEARNING

The proposed dialectical stance on conversational learning suggests that conversation is a meaning-making process whereby understanding is achieved through interplay of opposites and contradictions. Traditionally dialectics have been viewed as a linguistic process that leads to generation of new ideas and concepts by one's awareness of a tension and paradox between two or more opposites. It involves stating a point of view and questioning it from other points of view, eventually seeking consensual agreement that in turn is ultimately questioned from still other perspectives. As the opening quote by Parker Palmer (1990) suggests, truth thus lies in the journey, not in an ultimate destination or having the final word.

Dialectical inquiry aspires to holism through the embracing of differences and contradictions. It begins with contradictions, or literally opposing speeches. By taking the most opposite imaginable point of view, one increases the chance of encompassing the whole situation. Thus, inquiry into the dialectics of conversation is a means of uncovering the assumptions and frames that cause a "tunnel vision" of the whole (Mitroff & Emshoff, 1979). An inviting attitude about differences in opinion and perception is key to the process. Peter Elbow (1986) affirms this view as follows:

> Since perception and cognition are processes in which the organism "constructs" what it sees or thinks according to models already there, the organism tends to throw away or distort material that does not fit this model. The surest way to get hold of what your present frame blinds you to is to try to adopt the opposite frame, that is, to reverse your model. A person who can live with contradiction and exploit it, who can use conflicting models can simply see and think *more*. (p. 241)

John Van Mannen (1995) critiques paradigmatic organizational science as excessively focused on establishing a ruling discourse that obliterates or subsumes opposing ideas. He proposes a new brand of theorizing based on ongoing conversations that "plant, nurture and cultivate" and not on contentious and defensive debates that lead to polarization of differing views. The five dialectics presented here are an attempt to describe similar dialectical contradictions at the level of the process that creates the content of the conversation. This dialectical process can open a conversational space within which opposing ideas can be explored, resolved, or embraced through conversations.

The making of a conversational space can be equated to the autopoietic (self-making) process of a living system. The term "autopoiesis," first coined by Maturana and Varela in 1987, refers to a mechanism whereby a living organism, whether physical, mental, or social, becomes a self-organized, autonomous system by specifying its laws and determining what is proper to its existence. An autopoietic system is organized as a network of processes with two primary tasks: to regenerate and realize the network of processes that enables its existence through their continuous interactions and transformations, and to specify the boundary of its realization as a concrete unity in the space where they exist. It is important to notice that these are not separate sequential processes, but two different dimensions of the same phenomenon. On one hand, the dynamic interaction of network processes is essential for the creation of the boundary of the system; on the other hand, a boundary is essential for the processes to operate as a unified system. As Maturana and Varela put it, "The organization of an autopoietic system is such that their only product is themselves, with no separation between producer and product. The being and doing of an autopoietic unity are inseparable, and this is their specific mode of organization" (p. 49).

The conversational space defined by the five dialectics is similar to an autopoietic organism. On one hand, the five dialectics serve as a network of dynamic processes that opens up a conversational space where multiple conversations are generated; on the other hand, conversational space can be seen as a boundary that preserves the integrity of the dialectical processes that create those conversations.

A variety of external factors that act upon the internal dynamics of the dialectical relationships may disturb or support the integrity of the conversational space. It is also true that the nature of the five dialectical interactions will largely determine the pattern and quality of conversations that are generated within the conversational space. These dynamic external and internal interactions and their impact on conversations will become clear as we proceed to discuss the five dialectics as a network of processes that opens a space for conversational learning.

APPREHENSION AND COMPREHENSION: CONCRETE KNOWING AND ABSTRACT KNOWING

The dialectic of apprehension and comprehension is at the heart of dual-knowledge theory, whereby reality is grasped through two distinct but inseparable modes of knowing: concrete knowing and abstract knowing (Kolb, 1984). Concrete knowing is called apprehension—an immediate, feeling-oriented, tacit, subjective process largely based in older regions of the human brain that serve as physiological and emotional gatekeepers that monitor the emotional dimensions of learning. Abstract knowing is called comprehension—a linguistic, conceptual, interpretative process based in the relatively newer left cerebral cortex of the brain (de Bono, 1969; Gazzaniga, 1985). Learning is based on the complex interrelationship of these two knowing processes. Thus, integrated learning occurs when learners engage simultaneously in these two complementary modes of knowing.

William James articulates the conceptual underpinning of the dual-knowledge theory in his philosophy of radical empiricism (Hickcox; 1990; James, 1890). James's philosophy was based on two coequal and dialectically related ways of knowing the world: "knowledge of acquaintance" based on direct perception (apprehension) and "knowledge about" based on mediating conception (comprehension). In his own words, "Through feelings we become acquainted with things, but only by our thoughts do we know about them. Feelings are the germ and starting points of cognition, thoughts the developed tree" (p. 222).

In radical empiricism, direct perceptions have primacy, since all concepts derive their validity from connection to sense experience. Concepts, however, have priority in guiding human action because they often enable us to predict the future and achieve our goals. James (1977) further draws attention to the importance of this coequal relationship as follows:

> We thus see clearly what is gained and what is lost when percepts are translated into concepts. Perception is solely of the here and now; conception is of the like and unlike, of the future, and of the past, and of the far away. But this map of what surrounds the present, like all maps, is only a surface; its features are but abstract signs and symbols of things that in themselves are concrete bits of sensible experience. We have but to weigh extent against content, thickness against spread, and we see that for some purposes the one, for other purposes the other has the higher value. Who can decide off hand which is absolutely better to live and to understand life? We must do both alternately, and a man can no more limit himself to either than a pair of scissors can cut with a single one of its blades. (p. 243)

For James, conversation is more than an exchange of concepts; it is perceptual process as well. That is to say, conversation is a sensual experience. Conversation is typically thought of as speaking and listening, but James would enlarge the realm of conversation to conceiving and perceiving that involves all the senses, including emotions and feelings, touch, taste, and smell. His observation that rationalism and discursive thought are intrusive on the conversational experience is a warning to those who would study conversation as a solely discursive process that is unaffected by the experiential context in which it occurs. Different conversational experiences that take place in varied contexts enhance or restrict different senses and hence affect what is heard and perceived in the conversation. As many communication theorists have said, most of the meaning in communication is nonverbal. From the speaker's perspective, this means that conversation is as much about showing as it is about telling. From the listener's perspective, this means that conversation is as much about perceiving as it is about hearing.

INTENSION AND EXTENSION: REFLECTION AND ACTION

Kolb (1984) articulates the central idea of experiential learning theory as follows: "Simple perception of experience alone is not sufficient for learning; something must be done with it. Similarly, transformation alone cannot represent learning, for there must be something to be transformed, some state or experience that is being acted upon" (p. 42). This view is crucial to understand the synergistic nature of the dialectic of apprehension–comprehension and the dialectic of intension–extension as they represent two distinct but interconnected learning processes. Learning is like breathing; it follows a rhythm of taking in and putting out, of incorporating ideas and experience to find meaning and expressing that meaning in thought, speech, and action. Extending this idea by using a somewhat different metaphor, Elbow (1986) identifies two sources for what he calls real learning, a process of applying concepts and inventing new concepts:

> These two roots of cognitive processes are complementary and the basis of real learning from the most primitive to the most sophisticated. The reason they are so crucial is that they represent the two directions of traffic across the border between verbal and nonverbal experience. Where the first consists of constructing new experience from words, the second, sensing functionally, consists . . . of constructing new words from experience: searching for felt relationships among experiences in order to bring to birth new implied concepts. (p. 33)

Elbow's concept of verbal and nonverbal experience corresponds to the comprehension and apprehension modes of "grasping" experience, while the two modes of traffic between them represent the transformative dimensions of extension (action) and intention (reflection).

Freire (1992) describes the dynamic interplay of the dialectic of action and reflection as follows:

> As we attempt to analyze dialogue as a human phenomenon . . . within the word we find two dimensions, reflection and action, in such radical interaction that if one is sacrificed—even in part—the other immediately suffers. . . . When a word is deprived of its dimension of action, reflection automatically suffers as well; and the word is changed into idle chatter, into verbalism, into an alienated "blah." . . . On the other hand, if action is emphasized exclusively, to the detriment of reflection, the word is converted into activism. The latter action for action's sake negates the true praxis and makes dialogue impossible. (pp. 75, 78)

Freire's (1992) metaphor for traditional education, the "banking concept of education," where the main focus is to deposit ideas in the heads of students, describes a relationship between teacher and student that scarcely can be called a conversation. The dialectic is so polarized toward the student only taking in that very little emphasis is given to the student's expression of his or her meaning-making process through intentional action. Too many courses spend fifteen weeks inputting information to students and then asking them to express themselves by answering "A, B, C, D, or none of the above" in an examination. Experiential-learning approaches to education, on the other hand, seek to develop a conversational space where the praxis between reflection and action is fully recognized (Baker, Jensen, & Kolb, 1997).

EPISTEMOLOGICAL DISCOURSE AND ONTOLOGICAL RECOURSE: DOING AND BEING

Conversational learning occurs within two distinct but interconnected temporal dimensions: linear time and cyclical time. The discursive process is guided by linear time, whereas the recursive process follows a rhythm of cyclical time. The discursive process is an epistemological manifestation of individuals' ideas and experiences that are made explicit in conversations. As such, epistemological discourse is a linear process of naming and describing individuals' ideas and concepts generated in conversations from past, present to future in a continuous flow of activities.

The recursive process, on the other hand, is an ontological and subjective manifestation of the desire to return to the same ideas and experiences generated in conversation. In this sense, ontological recourse is cyclical in nature, where ideas and concepts acquire new meaning as individuals return to the same conversation to question and inquire about their experiences anew. As such, learners' abilities to simultaneously engage in these two temporal dimensions will largely determine the depth and quality of learning generated in conversations.

A closer look at the interplay of epistemological discourse and ontological discourse will throw light upon how these two processes manifest themselves in conversations. We shall discuss these processes individually, beginning with epistemological discourse.

As illustrated in Figure 4.2, the discursive process follows a linear time progression from precourse, to discourse, to postcourse. Precourse is a manifestation of previous conversations, which sets up the assumptive frame of the discourse. In this sense, precourse serves as the "fore-structure" of the conversation (Hans, 1989) or "prejudgments" (Gadamer, 1989) that individuals bring into the conversation. Simply stated, in anticipation of joining a particular circle of conversation, individuals have assumptions and expectations about the experience they will embark on. These assumptions and expectations will ultimately influence and shape the discourse they are about to join and establish their positions in the conversation.

The discourse takes the sets of assumptions generated through precourse and begins a process of "framing" and then proceeds to elucidate the implications of those assumptions, a process of "nam-

Figure 4.2
The Discourse–Recourse Dialectic in Conversation

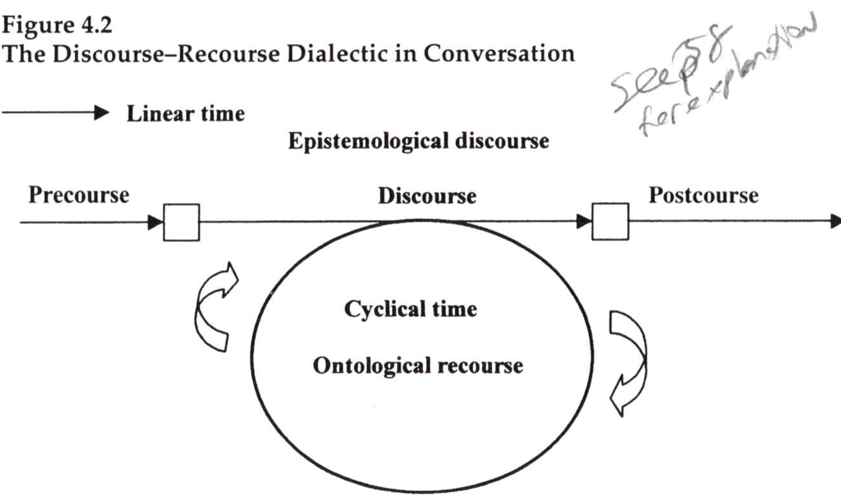

ing." A point to be highlighted here is that the framing of a discourse is a tacit, apprehensional process, while naming is a verbal, comprehensional process. Thus, the assumptions that make up the frame are often unconscious and tacit and are made explicit only through the naming process (Schon & Rein, 1994).

Robert McNamara (1995) reports in *In Retrospect: The Tragedy and Lessons of Vietnam* a tragic example of how difficult frame reflection is. He points out that while there were many policy debates, the assumptions that framed these debates (e.g., the domino theory, that this was a war to contain Communism, or the idea that the war could be won with European warfare tactics) were never seriously questioned.

Returning back in time and questioning the framed assumptions afresh can avoid this situation. This is when ontological recourse makes its appearance in the conversation. In his philosophical inquiry into the human conception of time, Hans (1989) offers an insightful argument as to why humans often fail to equally engage in discursive and recursive processes in a given situation. According to Hans, humans tend to be primarily driven by the linear, epistemological dimension of the dialectic and shy away from the recursive, ontological end of the dialectic. The accentuation of the linear time dimension, says Hans, is caused by the fear of the "return of the same." In returning to the same, one stands face to face with one's being, an ultimate ontological state that manifests itself in the cyclical passing of time. This fear of being evoked by the cyclical, recursive process drives humans to embrace the epistemological, sequential progression of events where they find comfort in the absence of repetition.

Yet the regular return with a difference is at the core of all understanding and it ultimately guides humans to attain a higher level of consciousness. Freire (1992) describes the understanding that is achieved through simultaneous engagement in the epistemological and ontological dimensions of the dialectics as follows: "To exist, humanly, is to name the world, to change it. Once named, the world in its turn reappears to the namers as a problem and requires of them a new naming" (p. 76).

As such, the discursive process is at work when learning is grounded through the naming of the world, whereas recursive process enters the scene as learners return to the subject that reappears anew, claiming an in-depth questioning and inquiry. In their studies of the recursive process in adult learning, Sheckley, Allen, and Keeton (1994) similarly describe the manifestation of the dialectic of discursive and recursive in the adult meaning-making process: "Simply stated, what learners 'know' influences what they 'experience' and conversely what they 'experience' influences what they 'know'" (pp. 60–61).

Finally, the end of the conversational discourse leads to postcourse. Here there is a process of sorting what to keep from the conversation and what to throw away. The resulting story of the conversation becomes precourse for future conversations, thus transporting the discourse into other contexts and the future. Thus, any conversational discourse is embedded in a complex network of previous and future conversations.

What has been described thus far illustrates the dialectical relationship of the discursive and recursive processes that drives conversation. Conversational learning occurs within such distinct yet intertwined linear and cyclical time dimensions that ultimately come together as a flux of spiral movement as new ideas are grounded through the discursive process and questioned from different perspectives through the recursive process of conversation.

INDIVIDUALITY AND RELATIONALITY: INSIDE OUT AND OUTSIDE IN

The tension between individuality, where a person takes in life experience as an individual process, and relationality, where life is an experience of connection with others, can be described as an intersubjective process whereby an individual maintains a sense of self while at the same time is aware of and open to the influence of others (Hunt, 1987; Jordan, 1991).

According to evolutionary biology, humans have two biological prime directives: to preserve the self as an individual and to preserve the species as a whole. Guisinger and Blatt (1994) argue that these two orientations are dialectically related: "Individuality (or senses of self) and the sense of relatedness to others develop in a transactional, interrelated, and dialectical manner, with higher levels of self-development making possible higher levels of interpersonal relatedness and vice-versa" (p. 111).

Carl Rogers's (1961) reflection on his professional and personal life is an insightful example of someone whose selfless act of extending oneself to others is drawn from his very capacity and willingness to be himself:

> Yet the paradoxical aspect of my experience is that the more I am simply willing to be myself, in all this complexity of life and the more I am willing to understand and accept the realities in myself and in the other person, the more change seems to be stirred up. It is a very paradoxical thing—to the degree that each one of us is willing to be himself, then he finds not only himself changing; but he finds that other people to whom he relates are also changing. At least this is a very vivid part of my experience, and one of the deepest things I think I have learned in my personal and professional life. (p. 22)

Similar views are articulated by various scholars from the Stone Center devoted to the understanding of human development with a particular focus on the experience of women. Surrey (1991) proposes a self-in-relationship as follows:

> The notion of the self-in-relation involves an important shift in emphasis from separation to relationship as the basis for self-experience and development. Further, relationship is seen as the basic goal of development: that is, the deepening capacity for relationship and relational competence. The self-in-relation model assumes that other aspects of self (e.g., creativity, autonomy, assertion) develop within this primary context. That is, other aspects of self-development emerge in the context of relationship, and there is no inherent need to disconnect or to sacrifice relationship for self-development. (p. 53)

In *Women's Ways of Knowing*, Belenky, Clinchy, Goldberger, and Tarule (1986) approached intersubjectivity through the concepts of separate and connected knowing. According to their study, separate knowing operates in a primarily comprehensive mode, assuming autonomy, reciprocity, extrication of self, and doubt, whereas connected knowing assumes relatedness, empathy, use of self, and connection. Their research further revealed a more intersubjective way of knowing where learning is a process of "weaving together the strands of rational and emotive thought and of integrating objective and subjective knowing. Rather than extricating the self in the acquisition of knowledge, these women used themselves in rising to a new way of thinking. As Adele described it, '*You let the inside out and the outside in*'" (pp. 134–135; emphasis added).

Finally, Gadamer (1989) articulates the value of this kind of approach to conversation as follows: "When one enters into dialogue with another person and then is carried along further by the dialogue, it is no longer the will of the individual person, holding itself back or exposing itself, that is determinative. Rather, the law of statement and counterstatement in the end plays them into each other. Hence, when a dialogue has succeeded, one is subsequently fulfilled by it, as we say" (p. 104).

STATUS AND SOLIDARITY: RANKING AND LINKING

The dialectical tension of status and solidarity opens a hospitable space where individuals engage in conversation with mutual respect and understanding toward one another. Relationships among human beings, as well as other social animals, can be portrayed on a two-dimensional, interpersonal space of status and solidarity (Schwitzgabel & Kolb, 1974). Status here refers to one's positioning or ranking in the group, while solidarity refers to the extent to which one is linked interpersonally with others in a network of relationships. The interplay of this dialectical relationship will ultimately define and create a hospitable space conducive to conversational learning. The underlying premise here is that some measure of both status and solidarity are necessary to sustain conversation. Without status, where one or more participants take initiative or lead, the conversation can lose direction. Without solidarity, where participants build upon and link to each other, conversation can lose connection and relevance and not benefit from the multiple perspectives and diverse expertise of each person. When one person dominates rather than the fluid spontaneity of participants' voices dynamically shifting, the potential for learning is impeded. When one dialectical pole dominates to the exclusion of the other, conversational learning is diminished. At the extreme, ranking leads to an unanswered monologue from the top. With total solidarity, talk can be aimless and repetitive.

Wilber (1995) offers an insightful discussion on this matter. In his mind, a living system is made whole by a healthy interaction of hierarchy (ranking) and heterarchy (linking) of its components. A normal hierarchy contributes to the wholeness and integrative capacity of a living system. Its ultimate goal is the actualization of each individual member as a valuable contributor. A normal hierarchy turns pathological when its functioning is based on force or threat that results in a suppression of individual actualization, undermining the good of the whole.

In a normal heterarchy, no element is given special importance or dominant position; each element strives to equally contribute to the wholeness of the system. A normal heterarchy becomes pathological when an individual element "loses itself in others—and all distinctions, of value or identity are lost. . . . Thus pathological heterarchy means not union but fusion; not integration but dissociation; not relating but dissolving" (pp. 23–24).

A similar view is offered by Miller (1986), who identified two fundamentally different types of inequality in relationships: temporary and permanent inequality. Temporary inequality permeates the relationship when the lesser party is socially defined as unequal for a limited period of time. In such a relationship, the superior party will assist the lesser party to develop. This development from unequal to equal is the primary purpose of the relationship. For example, parents assist children to become adults, teachers assist students to become capable graduates and colleagues. The ultimate goal of this type of relationship is to end the inequality. In the second type of unequal relationship, permanent inequality, the goal is to enforce the inequality. Here, individuals or groups are permanently defined as unequal by ascription into categories such as race, sex, class, or religion, and by positional power. The nature and range of this unequal relationship are seen as being a "birthright," and it is implicitly assumed by the dominants to be permanent.

Critical to the understanding of the dialectical tension being suggested here is the dynamic nature of status and solidarity as they unfold in conversations. For example, a teacher or a leader may hold expert status on a particular area of expertise in a given moment during conversation; however, his or her position is only temporary, in that the expert role is equally shared by other participants of the conversation as the need for different expertise and knowledge arises during conversations.

Freire (1992) writes about this balancing act of status and solidarity among individuals engaged in conversation as follows: "But while to say the true word . . . is to transform the world, saying that word is not the privilege of some few men, but the right of every man. Consequently, no one can say a true word alone—nor can he say it for another, in a prescriptive act which robs others of their words" (p. 76).

This exploration of several strands of scholarly thought brings us to the understanding of the nature of the dialectic of status and solidarity as it shapes the conversational learning space. A receptive space does not favor extreme status or extreme solidarity; it simply acknowledges their qualitative distinction as they bring life to conversations by virtue of their own distinctiveness.

THE CONVERSATIONAL LEARNING SPACE

Making space for conversation can occur in many dimensions: making physical space, as when a manager gets up from behind the desk to join colleagues around a table; making temporal space, as when a family sets aside weekly time for family conversation; or making emotional space through receptive listening. It is so easy to get focused on the structure of conversation, on what is said and how speech flows from one participant to another, that one fails to notice the bounded space that holds the conversation and allows it to occur.

The process dialectics described thus far create a receptive space that holds the conversation. As noted earlier, the extreme poles of these five dialectic dimensions define the autopoietic boundaries of the space within which conversational learning occurs. When one pole of any of the dialectics dominates, learning through conversations is impeded and may cease to exist. Some semblance of boundaries is necessary to preserve and make space for structures, just as the process of structuring creates boundaries. The dual-knowledge dialectic opens a space where speaking and listening creates conversation. Speaking without listening or listening without speaking is futile. Similarly, as Freire (1992) points out, reflection without action turns into "idle chatter" and activism by itself becomes action for action's sake. Discourse without recourse is brute force. Recourse without discourse, of course. Extreme individualism—"I touch no one and no one touches me"—can result in alienation, while total relatedness can lead to conversations that go nowhere. Totalitarian authority crushes other voices, while laissez-faire egalitarianism can produce aimless talk.

Hence, conversational learning space can be viewed as a product of the dialectic of boundary and structure between boundaries that define and protect a space where conversation can occur and the internal processes and norms that shape the conversational interaction. Conversational learning as a self-organizing entity cannot exist without a receptive space to hold it. The conversation can be killed from within, as when, for example, an authoritarian monologue crushes the spirit of other participants. Or it can be destroyed from without by strong rhetorical precourse, prejudice, or prejudgment.

In conversation, the autopoietic process can be seen in the development of norms. As conversations progress, a normative value core that structures the conversation develops and at the same time creates boundaries that define the conversational learning space. These norms determine what can be said and not said, who has voice and who does not have voice in the conversation. At the same time, these norms create boundaries that define who is in and out of the conversation. Those who do not know or refuse to abide by or participate in changing the normative rules of the game are excluded from the conversation.

There is a paradoxical quality to conversational boundaries. Initially, it seems that boundaries inhibit or block conversation, and indeed conversation across boundaries is often difficult. However, the space created by the boundaries can create a space that is safe and open enough for the conversational exploration of differences across various dialectical continua. "From this perspective, boundaries are not confines but 'shape-givers' that can provide us with healthy space to grow. . . . Boundaries are not prisons, rather, they serve an essential function to make our existence more alive and vibrant" (Wyss, 1997, p. 4). Creating this kind of healthy receptive conversational leearning space is the focus of Chapter 6.

REFERENCES

Baker, A. C., Jensen, P. J., & Kolb, D. A. (1997). In conversation: Transforming experience into learning. *Simulation & Gaming, 28* (1), 6–12.

Belenky, M., Clinchy, B., Goldberger, N., & Tarule, J. (1986). *Women's ways of knowing*. New York: Basic Books.

de Bono, E. (1969). *The mechanism of mind*. New York: Simon and Schuster.

Elbow, P. (1986). *Embracing contraries: Explorations in learning and teaching*. Oxford: Oxford University Press.

Freire, P. (1992). *Pedagogy of the oppressed*. New York: Continuum.

Gadamer, H. G. (1989). *Truth and method*. New York: Crossroad.

Gazzaniga, M. (1985). *The social brain: Discovering the networks of the mind*. New York: Basic Books.

Guisinger, S., & Blatt, S. (1994). Individuality and relatedness: Evolution of a fundamental dialectic. *American Psychologist, 49*, 104–111.

Hans, J. (1989). *The question of value: Thinking through Nietzche, Heidegger and Freud*. Carbondale and Edwardsville: Southern Illinois University Press.

Hickcox, L. (1990). *An historical review of Kolb's formulation of experiential learning theory*. Unpublished Ph.D. diss., University of Oregon, Corvallis.

Hunt, D. E. (1987). *Beginning with ourselves*. Cambridge, MA: Brookline Press.

James, W. (1977). Percept and concept: The import of concepts. In J. McDermott (Ed.), *The writings of William James* (pp. 217–247). Chicago: University of Chicago Press.

James, W. (1890). *The principle of psychology*. New York: Holt, Rinehart and Winston.

Jordan, J. (1991). The meaning of mutuality. In J. Jordan, A. Kaplan, J. B. Miller, I. Stiver, & J. Surrey (Eds.), *Women's growth in connection* (pp. 81–96). New York: Guilford Press.

Kolb, D. A. (1984). *Experiential learning: Experience as the source of learning and development*. Englewood Cliffs, NJ: Prentice-Hall.
Maturana, H., & Varela, F. (1987). *The tree of knowledge: The biological roots of human understanding*. Boston: Random House, New Science Library.
McNamara, R. (1995). *In retrospect: The tragedy and lessons of Vietnam*. New York: Times Books.
Miller, J. (1986). *Toward a new psychology of women*. Boston: Beacon Press.
Mitroff, I., & Emshoff, J. (1979). On strategic assumption-making. A dialectical approach to policy and planning. *Academy of Management Review, 4,* 1–12.
Palmer, P. (1990). Good teaching: A matter of living the mystery. *Change, 22,* 11–16.
Rogers, C. (1961). *On becoming a person*. New York: Houghton Mifflin.
Schon, D., & Rein, M. (1994). *Frame reflection: Toward the resolution of intractable policy controversies.* Cambridge: MIT Press.
Schwitzgabel, R., & Kolb, D. A. (1974). *Changing human behavior: Principles of planned intervention*. New York: McGraw-Hill.
Sheckeley, B., Allen, G., & Keeton, M. (1994). Adult learning as a recursive process. *Journal of Cooperative Education, 28* (2), 56–67.
Surrey, J. (1991). Self in relation: A theory of women's development. In J. Jordan, A. Kaplan, J. B. Miller, I. Stiver, & J. Surrey (Eds.), *Women's growth in connection* (pp. 51–66). New York: Guilford Press.
Van Mannen, J. (1995). Style as theory. *Organization Science, 6,* 133–143.
Wilber, K. (1995). *Sex, ecology, spirituality*. Boston: Shambala.
Wyss, E. (1997). *Exploring boundaries: A personal journal of culture-crossing*. Unpublished working paper, Case Western Reserve University, Cleveland, OH.

5

The Evolution of a Conversational Learning Space

Alice Y. Kolb

> The more genuine conversation is, the less its conduct lies within the will of either partner. Thus, a genuine conversation is never the one that we wanted to conduct. . . . [It is] more correct to say that we fall into conversation, or even that we become involved in it. . . . A conversation has a spirit of its own, and the language in which it is conducted bears its own truth within it—i.e., that it allows something to "emerge" which hence forth exists.
>
> Hans Georg Gadamer (1994)

This chapter is a case history of knowledge creation through conversational learning. It describes the journey from tacit, intuitively felt notions of conversational learning to the explicit development of theory and practice of conversational learning reported in this book. The purpose of the case study is to show the evolution of conversational learning from the traditional discourse model of education to a conversational approach to education. To understand the emerging process of such a learning space, this study will explore the evolution of a conversational learning space and the emergence of principles of conversational learning. The context of the conversational learning space was a required first-year Ph.D. seminar on learning and development in the

Organizational Behavior Department at Case Western Reserve University. This study traces the evolution of the conversational space by examining the process and content of the conversations among participants over twelve years from 1988 to 1999. The concept of conversational learning grew out of David Kolb's aspiration to explore a new approach to teaching and learning based on the theory and practice of experiential learning.

Unlike a traditional method of learning that places primary emphasis on abstract and conceptual dimensions of knowledge, conversational learning equally values the learner's emotional, sensual, and physical engagement in the learning process. While there have been many studies conducted on a particular course within a period of one semester (e.g., Mazen, Jones, & Sergenian, 2000), there is no study that traces the evolution of conversational learning longitudinally across multiple years of a course.

This evolutionary process can be seen as experiential learning in conversation as learners in a given class move through the learning process of experiencing, reflecting, conceptualizing, and acting to create new experiences. Through this process each class became a self-organizing system by focusing on certain ideas and trends and turning away from others. The way each group organized itself was passed onto future generations of the course through several means: through modifications of readings in the syllabus to reflect and accommodate changes in participants' interests as well as the instructor's need to introduce new ideas and concepts; through conversation starters, a one-page summary of thoughts and reflections voluntarily written and shared by participants in the class on a rich array of topics and experiences of a particular interest to them; through introduction of various artifacts in the class that served as reminders of previously discussed topics and ideas; and, finally, through Kolb's position as transmitter of previous ideas, perspectives, and experiences over the course of twelve years in the life of the seminar.

Thus, one can distinguish between the personal knowledge that grew out of participants' personal experience and the social knowledge that grew out of explicit ideas generated through texts and experiences shared in conversations. This process can be equated with Nonaka's (1994) concept of explicit and tacit dimensions of knowledge creation and transmission. Hence, we can trace the evolution of the larger conversation by the analysis of the explicit records of participants' conversation starters. We can also see how the experience of a given class session was shaped by the social knowledge of the preceding years. As the personal knowledge and the social knowledge continued to influence and shape each other through conversations, we can witness Gadamer's (1994) idea of "the conversation as larger than the consciousness of any single player" (p. 104). The conversation generated by a group of individuals in a given year is passed onto the next generation of players, perpetuating a dynamic flow of conversations over time. As the personal and social knowledge continued to be integrated and externalized thorough conversations, participants' deep interests also gained clarity and focus. Participants' pursuit of their personal interests led ultimately to substantial knowledge creation, as a significant number of doctoral dissertations were produced over the years as offspring of the multiple conversations conducted over time (e.g., Baker, 1995; Banaga, 2000; Fambrough, 2000; Hazelwood, 1999; Jensen, 1995; Kayes, 2001; Kolb, 2000; Mainemelis, 2001; Park, 1996; Steingard, 1997; Sullivan, 1997; White, 1993).

The twelve yearly course sessions can be describe in three broad phases: phase I (1988 to 1989), phase II (1990 to 1996), and phase III (1997 to 1999). Phase I can be described as the exploratory period, in which both content and process of conversational learning were yet to be created and defined. A seven-year phase of a rapid growth in which the scholarly conversations explored by the readings increased in breadth and depth begain in 1990. Phase III can be characterized as a stable phase, as the scholarly readings and ideas remained relatively unchanged but gained further depth and elaboration in conversation. These phases can be illustrated by the growth of the syllabus over time, as shown in Figure 5.1.

The overall characteristics of the phases will be described within the five process dialectics discussed in Chapter 4: the dialectics of concrete and abstract, inside out and outside in, status and solidarity, discursive and recursive mode, and action and reflection. Overall, the learning

Figure 5.1
Growth of the Syllabus over Time

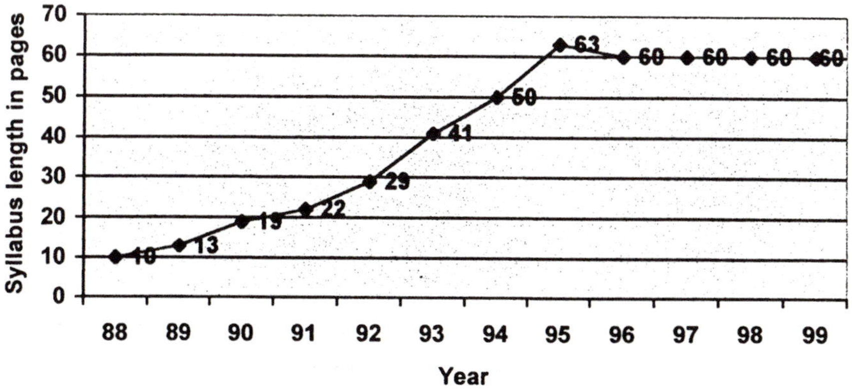

space transitioned from a traditional discourse mode of learning to a conversational mode of learning. This transition will be described by analysis of the conversation starters voluntarily written by participants in each year. The analysis will focus on how explicit principles of conversational learning emerged through conversations, and not on the specific content topics covered and discussed in the seminar.

The analysis of the conversation starters will be conducted within the frame of hermeneutic text interpretation, a critical and intersubjective approach to understanding "the familiar world in which we stand and the strange meaning that resists assimilation into the horizons of our world" (Gadamer, 1976, p. xx). According to Gadamer, "Like all genuine dialogue, the hermeneutical conversation between the interpreter and the text involves equality and active reciprocity. It presupposes that both conversational partners are concerned with a common subject matter—about which they converse, for dialogue is always about something" (p. xx). By critically reflecting on the individual text at hand and recursively coming back to the experience afresh, I will attempt to elucidate how knowledge is created through conversations and how the five process dialectics open up a conversational learning space.

COURSE DESCRIPTION

The seminar on learning and development was created in 1988 to introduce Ph.D. students to experiential learning and adult development perspectives on organizational behavior. The course description of the seminar is as follows:

> This course provides an exploration of the learning and development paradigm underlying the human potential development approach to human resource development. The origins of this approach in the naturalist epistemologies—John Dewey's pragmatism, Kurt Lewin's gestalt psychology, the works of James, Follett, Emerson, Piaget, Maslow, Rogers, and others—and the current research in adult development, in biology and brain/mind research, artificial intelligence, epistemology, and adult learning will be considered. The course will focus on applications of these ideas to current issues in human resource development such as adult learning in higher education, advanced professional development and organizational learning and development. (Kolb & Kolb, 2001)

Participants in the seminar were adult learners with diverse professional backgrounds, nationalities, and life experiences, and between twenty-five and sixty years of age. Prior to joining the organizational-behavior department, many of the participants had held leadership and managerial positions at various for profit and not-for-profit organizations, as well as at several educational institutions nationally and internationally, with an extensive knowledge and expertise in their professional areas. The diverse and unique composition of the seminar participants mirror the long-held Organizational Behavior Department tradition and philosophy grounded on life-long learning and fostering of the unique human potential of the individual learners.

In the first year, the course was designed as a typical doctoral seminar covering interdisciplinary topics related to learning and development in psychology, philosophy, biology, neuroscience, and education. The primary text, *Experiential Learning* (Kolb, 1984), provided an intellectual backbone for the course, with readings selected to explore current developments in topics covered in the book. The other text, *The Tree of Knowledge* (Maturana & Varela, 1998), described the biological roots of human understanding and the essence of life. In addition, there were readings specifically related to the topic of each week.

Only two components of the seminar were explicitly related to conversational learning. The first was a classic book, *The Tao of Conversation*, by Michael Kahn (1995) that described four dysfunctional metaphors for exploring ideas in a seminar: the free-for-all, the beauty contest, the distinguished house tour, and the barn raising, a fourth metaphor that served as a guide for functional intellectual conversation. The concept of the cooperative Amish barn raising was to become a normative ideal for the seminar process. The second component was the one-page conversation starter, an idea borrowed from Ronald Reagan, who insisted on one-page summaries of major issues, stating that no idea was so complex that it could not be summarized in one page. Seminar participants prepared a one-page conversation starter on the readings, their personal reflections, summaries of related topics, comments on the group's process, or anything else on their mind. On average, five to six conversation starters were voluntarily turned in during each seminar session. Copies of the conversation starters were passed around at the beginning of each seminar session and were discussed one by one during the course of conversation.

THE DIALECTIC OF CONCRETE AND ABSTRACT

The dialectical relationship between concrete knowing and abstract knowing in the learning process is one of the central concepts of the experiential learning theory. Concrete knowing involves experiencing the world primarily through feelings in an immediate, tacit, and subjective way, whereas abstract knowing is centered in a conceptual, linguistic, and objective interpretation of the world. Integrated knowing is achieved when learners equally engage in both dimensions of knowing in a given learning context. Individual learning as well as conversational learning are based on the complex dialectical interrelationship between these two knowing dimensions. In conversational learning, concrete knowing manifest itself as learners engage emotionally in conversation, whereas abstract knowing is the manifestation of the learners' abstract and conceptual mode of engagement in conversation.

The gradual unfolding of a conversational space was largely dependent upon how safe participants felt in fully engaging their physical, intellectual, emotional, and sensual experiences in conversation. For the most part, participants' past experiences in the classroom were shaped by the traditional model of learning, where the primary emphasis was placed on the intellectual and abstract dimensions of learning.

Common to all conversation starters of phase I is a strong sense of commitment to produce a detailed, well-thought-out analysis and reflection on the assigned reading materials. A typical conversation starter would begin with a definition or a brief description of the main concept of the reading, followed by a summary of propositions and ending with several questions drawn from personal reflections. The preferred writing style tended to be very conceptual and abstract, taking up the full length of a page and, in many instances, far exceeding the one-page norm established early in the semester.

Participants tended to emphasize the reflective and abstract dimensions of the experiential learning cycle, for the most part shying away from the emotional and active side of the learning cycle. One participant expressed his struggle to engage his emotions in his intellectual endeavor, as his former socialization processes prevented him from doing so: "I thought how a formal education process constantly reminded me of the importance of separating emotional or personal aspects from the rational thought process. Especially in an intellectual setting, we were told time and time again that there would be no room for emotionalizing or personalizing. In this respect, experiential learning seemed to me anti-intellectual" (1989).

One of the marked characteristics of phase I was the acknowledgment of the importance of emotions and feelings in learning, and yet there is reluctance to embrace them fully at the personal as well as the group levels. In many instances the attempt to express emotions and feelings tended to be disguised in the form of vague questions, as if they were addressed to an unknown audience: "How do (1) sharing subjective observations and reflections of concrete experiences and (2) fitting subjective experiences into conceptual generalizations aid the learning process? During the process of reflection, we often become emotional (smiling, crying, etc.). Does this mean reflection involves something more than a cognitive process of languaging?" (1989).

In the early years others are rarely mentioned in the conversation starters. The reflections are primarily drawn from individual readings and rarely from unique experiences of others or from interaction with other participants. The experience with others takes place in a somewhat unique way. In several instances over the course of the semester, several participants wrote a joint conversation starter on a particular topic of interest. The composition of the group varied, from mixed-gender groups, to male groups, to female groups. The end product was generally a high-quality in-depth critique and discussion drawn from a particular reading assignment that supposedly had generated strong interest among participants. An example is a conversation starter jointly written by four female participants based on *Women's Ways of Knowing* (Belenky, Clinchy, Goldberger, & Tarule, 1986). One can immediately sense from their writing how serious and close to their heart this topic was. The questions raised at the end of the conversation starter in many ways symbolize what came to play a substantial role in opening up a space for feminist voices to be explored and heard in subsequent years:

> I sometimes wonder what it would be like to have more women role models in our field. I'll never "live up to" the male role models; what does that do to my self-esteem? I like being female. I don't want to be pushed into acting like "men" in order to survive. It scares me to think that women may be tempted to give up femininity to compete in a more masculine environment—like the woman Gloria works with who is only having a child to please her husband, has her C-section date all planned and knew in her third month what date she would be returning to work. What kind of monster are we creating? (1989)

It is clear from the questions that an intense conversation was exchanged among four women with unique views and perspectives on this topic. However, although the name of the contributors appears at the top of the page, the identity of each individual contributor in the conversation starter is unknown. The entire conversation starter is written in the first person, making it impossible to recognize the uniqueness of individual voices. As an indication of great sensitivity and effort exerted to keep the anonymity of the participants' identities, in one particular instance the name of a participant is carefully disguised by means of pseudonym. The feminist perspective was the first of several emotion-laden, controversial topics introduced in the seminar that came to play a significant role in expanding the conversation from a primarily abstract and intellectual mode to an emotional, personal, and passionate mode of conversation.

As the conversational learning space entered phase II there was a marked increase in the number of topics and reference materials discussed in the seminar. In addition, a significant change was witnessed in the language style of the conversation starters. During this phase the carefully measured words wrapped in highly abstract language of phase I gradually receded into the background and were replaced by emotional, highly charged tone of voices of men and women who were unafraid of being known for who they are. The conversation starters were no longer without a face. Participants' willingness to bring their diverse personal experiences and styles into the public life of the classroom further added to the richness and diversity of the conversation. The language became increasingly informal and personal, as an indication of participants' willingness to move from the realm of the cognitive and the abstract to the realm of emotions and feelings. Graphics, drawings, and poetry became an integral part of the writing, and the overall length of the conversation starters saw a substantial reduction during the growth period: "Kohlberg was great. Love the man. Though Marcus Aurelius misses the boat on the universe, Spinoza is sixties groooovy" (1992).

In his conversation starter entitled "I am what I am—Popeye the Sailor (among others)," one participant expressed his confusion and discomfort as he delved into the readings: "I sit here at my desk having finished most of the reading—particularly on individuality (i.e. the 'self contained' self vs. the 'ensembled' self or the 'eco' self) and I realize that I am still having a quite *visceral* reaction to what I have read! I am upset, disturbed, no more than that. I am *angered* by what I have been reading! As I read it, it challenges most of the basic foundations that I have built my life upon. Where do I start?!?" (1993).

Similarly, a female participant opened her conversation starter in a somewhat defiant tone as she struggled with the unfamiliarity of the newly acquired knowledge:

STAND BACK! It's a (yes it is, for real) CONVERSATION STARTER

Bill Cosby once spoke at length about where a thought goes when it's forgotten. His logic, impeccably punctuated with cigar jabs into the air, confirmed a deep-seated suspicion of mine—forgotten thoughts end up in your butt. Now all this talk about experiential learning has got me wondering—where does what I have learned go when it disappears? How is it that one moment I can understand (Grok) something only to lose that understanding in the next moment? Do you know what I mean? (1994)

The collaborative effort to create a safe and welcoming learning space had a significant impact on the manner in which participants opened themselves up to different ways of being in conversation. As participants grew more comfortable in engaging their feelings and emotions in conversation, the learning space was enriched in a way that thought alone could not have achieved.

It is important to mention at this point a number of initiatives taken by the instructor and participants that contributed to the significant shift in the tone of the conversation starters from an abstract to emotional mode of expression. To enumerate a few, in 1993 the instructor introduced music in the seminar as an acknowledgment of the sensual dimension of the learning space. In the same year, a Korean student brought flowers and placed them in the center of the circle as a way to honor nature. On another occasion the instructor distributed shells to the seminar participants as gifts from his winter retreat in the Pacific Islands, a practice that became ritualized in the seminar during subsequent years. This invited a host of initiatives by students, who at different times brought various artifacts that symbolized concrete manifestations of seminar topics. One student brought a small doll as a souvenir from her trip, whereas on a different occasion a Turkish student brought a small tapestry from his home country. As a part of an ongoing effort to create a hospitable space for learning, the instructor placed the books, articles, handouts, and reading materials on the floor to allow participants to easily walk in the circle and reach out for the readings of their own choosing.

In 1995 the instructor introduced the Amish wagon in the circle. The strong communal bond embedded in the Amish tradition was a reminder to all participants of the value of the equality and solidarity in the conversational space. In addition, the books, artifacts, and various objects stacked in the colorful wood wagon were an invitation for the participants to adopt a spontaneous and playful stance toward learning. Participants shared their experiences of the learning space in many ways: "In reflecting on the sessions, I am aware that much that 'stuck' in my mind, has to do with the presence of flowers, plants, feathers, talking stick, puka shells, music, bell, prayer wheel, and animal images. . . . What a wonderful rich learning environment! Is there a way to make learning about symbols and sound more explicit in the classrooms?" (1995).

In a letter to the instructor, a participant shared her experience with the physical space of the seminar as follows:

> I love flowers and books, and it made me feel warm and comfortable to have them around. It also gave me something to look at while I was deep in thought so the rest of the class did not know how far gone I was. The various objects that you passed around were interesting, and continued to remind me how little time I take to physically feel things. They allowed me to get in touch (no pun intended) with senses that are underutilized. I would always think to myself, I have to take more time to really explore things in depth. I see shells all over the beach but never really studied them, or pick them up. It's like taking time to really to get to know something. I realize that I know a little about a lot of things, but I miss out on the richness of knowing something really deeply. (1995)

As the conversational learning space entered phase III, the physical, sensual, emotional, and intellectual dimensions of knowing were more integrated as learners grew more comfortable with moving across the concrete–abstract continuum in a more flexible way. Learners' highly abstract and conceptual orientations of phase I, or the emotional and affect orientation that dominated phase II, was replaced by a dynamic blend of these two dimensions of knowing. The atmosphere of the learning space as depicted in the conversation starters of phase III was dynamic, receptive to diversity of experiences and views, with attention and care devoted to the integration of the intellectual, sensual, and emotional dimensions of the learning process. The unique physical arrangement and design of the learning space that mirrored the multifaceted dimensions of the learning process encouraged learners to be adventurous, playful, and multidimensional in pursuit of their deeply held interests: "In the center of our human circle there stood the wagon (fire?), a symbol of the mobilization and dynamism that learning involves. The flowers were there to remind us of the nature, its diversity, and its ability to (re) create life, harmony, and beauty. The feather and the stick were the metaphors for the mystery of life, whereas the books on the floor created an atmosphere of play—the Lila [free play] path to our original nature" (1997).

At the end of the semester a participant summarized her memorable experiences of the conversational learning space as follows:

> Sharing David's coffee and drinking it from a wagon mug. The consistency of the family room setting. The Tibetan bells (did we first ring then for Joanna's mother?) The grandfather spirit who joined us for the spirituality session. The support and encouragement to be honest and respectfully direct. David's books, being in the section of his library relating to the week's topic. Other people's conversation starters (people willing to trust me and others with their thoughts and opinions). (1999)

In stark contrast to the early phases, what emerged from the conversational starters of phase III was the profile of learners who are attracted to the idea of integration of opposites as they pursue their interests, balancing the dialectical tension between the objective and subjective, the conceptual and emotional dimensions of knowing:

> The readings for the week, especially the reading from "Free Play", brought to mind many things. But what I immediately thought of was the musician Wynton Marsalis. Wynton is an extraordinary musician. He freely flows between jazz and classical musings seemingly without much effort. The regimental approach of classical music and the freedom of expression found in jazz seem diametrically opposed, but yet he finds freedom and enjoyment in both. I believe that jazz provides the *temenos* (play space) for Wynton. The

main thing that I notice about Wynton's music is the ability to cross the boundaries of jazz and classical and yet maintain the integrity of both styles. (1998)

Must we function with either/or choices? Why not, instead, chose to utilize the most positive aspects for a wider band of options? Qualitative and quantitative evaluations? The scientific approach coupled with a constructionist science? If there are questions, why not find answers in a variety of ways? (1998)

Each syllabus topic is a distinct facet of the social forces that influence me and other individuals. . . . For example, I now see myself as being at a stage of moral development, in the conflict between women and men, of a style of learning and conversing, with multiple meanings of adultness, and aboard the boat of spiritual self in the organizational world. I learned that I am of many things and all can be held simultaneously. (1999)

The evolutionary process of the dialectic of concrete and abstract illustrated thus far opened up yet another window of opportunity for participants to explore a new realm of learning experience that required a significant shift in their previously held basic assumptions and beliefs: the balancing of the inside-out and outside-in approaches to learning.

THE DIALECTIC OF INSIDE OUT AND OUTSIDE IN

The inside-out learning mode challenges learners to return to their reservoirs of life experience and stand face to face with their own deeply held values, feelings, and thoughts, and make them the starting points of their learning process. Inside-out learning finds its roots in the ideas of humanists thinkers such as Maslow (1968), Rogers (1961), Freire (1992), and Hunt (1987), for whom the process of individuation toward becoming a whole person cannot be achieved without valuing or owning one's own experience as who we are, regardless of what others construe of what we are or should become. The path toward becoming an authentic individual, however, is met with a paradox along the way, the outside-in process to learning that challenges the very process of inside-out learning.

Outside-in learning refers to the external ideas and events that act upon us and shape our knowing. Often we find ourselves caught between the conflicting demands of the external world and the need to follow our true voices from within. Nonetheless, how one integrates the paradoxes and conflicts generated by the tension between inside out and outside in ultimately determines one's success in becoming a whole person. If the journey toward becoming an authentic individual requires one to resist conformity to outward expectation and conceptions bestowed upon oneself, what is one to become at the end of the journey? As much as we may exert our own individuality and even claim the victory of having achieved it, the fully independent self will always remain one step ahead of us, for contrary to our perceptions our individuality is very much shaped in relationships with others. Paradoxically, the awakening of our own individuality or the affirmation of who we are grounded in our own experiences is achieved by entering into conversation with others who in turn reinforce and acknowledge our freedom and existence as individuals. As participants venture into the new realm of learning experience holding the tension between individuality and relationality, inside out and outside in, the learning space continues to evolve and expand.

When the inside-out approach was first introduced in the seminar the idea was received with a mix of hesitation and anticipation. In one of the conversation starters of phase I a participant expressed her dilemma in integrating herself as a whole person to pursue her own growth as well as that of others:

> What am I doing/thinking/feeling when I'm pursuing my own growth and that of my classmates? To what, to whom do I look to evaluate how I'm/we're developing skill in learning how to learn? Hunt suggests that we start with ourselves, that we take an inside-out approach. What do I/we know/think/feel/believe about learning? . . . How am I/are we shaping ways of interacting with one another that respect individual differences, challenge growth and create an environment that invites participation by all? (1989)

In phase II the hesitation and tentativeness of phase I were replaced by a passionate gesture of full acceptance of the inside-out approach, as participants eagerly shared their experiences of the encounter with the newly found idea:

> "Inside out Psychology" is most intriguing, and I should admit, a relatively new life value for me. . . . I believe so strongly in the concept that I have come to believe that an inside out approach can arm one with the potential for overcoming *any* difficulty if he or she chooses and is able to fully connect with his or her inner self. (1993)

> When I read Rogers "A Modern Approach to Values", I said, "Yes, here it is!!!" (Not the first, and I'm sure not the last time that that will happen). I was one those "usual adults" (slugs) running around corporate America in search of love, acceptance and esteem. I operated on a variety of introjected organizational values, which were in conflict, and which ultimately proved unsatisfactory and untenable . . . the "Is that all there is?" scene. (1996)

As liberating as the discovery of the inside-out approach was, this idea clashed with an apparently conflicting set of values that permeated the diverse topics introduced in the course over the semester. The course readings were structured and designed to introduce participants to a wide range of ideas and concepts beyond the confines of the Western concept of development. The broad reading assignments, which ranged from Eastern religion and spirituality to the communal lifestyle of the primitive societies to the postmodern philosophy that questions the capitalist and individualist way of modern life, challenged participants to venture into the unfamiliar territory of a new learning experience and see their familiar world anew. These ideas stirred heated discussions and lively exchanges of diverse views and beliefs among participants. A male participant expressed his strong reactions and concerns as Western values come under intense scrutiny in conversation:

> During last week's class I felt that the class had a growing movement/willingness/need to attack "Western culture." Whether it is capitalism, individualism, competition, rationality, functionalism, intellectualism, etc. . . . I know that I tend to take all this personally (probably too personally), but my personal values and beliefs are very closely tied to some of these concepts, and I often feel as if others are trying to change those beliefs so that I will be more closely aligned with some status quo. (1993)

In a different voice, another participant expressed her longing for relational values as she found herself moving toward a community-oriented life philosophy:

For some time, I have been playing with the word "communitarian" as a descriptor for the lifestyle I tried to create for myself and encourage in others before coming to Case. . . . Over the past few years, I have emerged from a career cocoon to become aware of, develop attitudes about (prize), and invest in the community around me. . . . For me, that amorphous need for valuing, beauty, connectedness, however you wish to describe it, leads us to communitarianism. (1993)

As the inside-out learning rooted in the awakening of the individual values and beliefs met a host of concepts that redefine the conception of self, participants were challenged to reexamine their previously held conceptual frame. As the conversational learning space entered phase III, a shift was witnessed in the way learners approached the concepts of inside out and outside in. As learners delved into this dialectical dilemma with a deeper sense of reflection, the bipolar stance many participants exhibited in the early years toward diverse views gradually shifted to a more balanced conception of the self that coexists with one's surrounding environment. The following conversation starters reflect the gradual shift that took place in conversation during phase III. The conversation transitioned from a reflective stance toward deeply held issues to that of a desire to actively transform the ideas and concepts gained through reflections into a greater purpose in benefit of a larger community.

What I found most intriguing about the readings for today was the variety of different ways in which the concept of "self" was presented. What is the self? Am I really an individual with unique properties, an intrinsically valuable, self-contained, self-determined unit? . . . Personally I think a concept of self that can encompass all of these thoughts makes the most sense. That is, I am unique, but my existence is intimately and inextricably tied to the people and world around me. Coming from a culture that stresses individualism, where we feel that if we can just get people to value themselves, everything will work out well, I find it very tough to avoid dwelling on the individual aspect of "self". Which makes me wonder, do I really need more self-esteem training? Maybe what I need is to have more esteem for others! (1997)

I think there is more to be gained in "work" realms by taking in concepts from the outside. . . . I'd like to explore the balance further, the balance between inside out and outside in. (1999)

The illustration of the conversational space thus far has focused on the process whereby conversations continued to evolve and transform as participants gravitated around the dialectical movement between feeling and thinking, inside out and outside in. It is important to emphasize, however, that the evolution of the conversational learning space did not follow a linear progression, as the descriptions seem to convey. Rather, it evolved in an organic and recursive fashion as each year the learning space was influenced by the distinct composition of participants with multiplicity of views, interests, and unique life experiences. The focal point of the conversation would gravitate around topics and issues participants had strong energy and passion invested in, reaching a deeper understanding and sharing their knowledge and experience with others. In a given year, feminism was the topic that gained prominence in conversation, whereas in the following years topics that ranged from postmodern philosophy, deep ecology, and spirituality were received with equal passion and interest as they gained central focus in the conversation. The impact of such topics was substantial in the life of the seminar. The more passionately participants engaged in conversation on a topic of great interest, the deeper they reached into their reservoir of feelings and emotions. The emotional turn of the conversation gradually changed the landscape of the conversational space. As participants delved into their deepest interests and passions, the dialectical horizons of feeling and thinking, inside out and outside in of the conversational space saw further expansion over the years.

STATUS AND SOLIDARITY

The equality of status between the instructor and participants was a pivotal, albeit controversial issue in the seminar. The idea of "conversation among equals" that is at the crux of conversational learning could not go unexamined if the conversational space was to strive and continue to flourish. Before proceeding to the illustration of the dialectical relationship between status and solidarity, it would be helpful to briefly recall the profile of the seminar participants described early in the chapter. It is safe to say that the unique and diverse composition of the seminar participants played a significant role in creating and making the conversational learning space possible. Participants' rich lives and professional experiences further contributed to the richness and complexity of the learning process in the seminar. It is interesting to notice, however, how participants perceived themselves as learners upon entering the classroom setting. Regardless of their prior status as accomplished and autonomous individuals, lingering somewhere inside their minds was the idea Freire (1992) described as "internalized oppression," a process whereby learners relinquish the valuable experience and knowledge they already possess in the name of the expert knowledge of the teacher. By surrendering their power to the teacher, learners relegate themselves to the position of passive recipients of information and knowledge. Perhaps a typical classroom scene commonly shared by most of the traditional educational institutions is the one in which, in a classroom of thirty students, only one person, the teacher, does most of the talking while the rest are left in silence. In the conversational learning space, however, the status of the teacher as the sole authority had to be reconsidered as the instructor deliberately shifted his position as a power figure to that of an equal participant in the seminar. Although the instructor provided syllabus and reading assignments early in the semester, he set no learning agenda or specific direction in the class discussions throughout the semester. The stance he maintained over the course of the semester was that of an equal participant who encouraged learners to have their voices, in stark contrast to the traditional lecture format, where the instructor dominates most of the airtime in the classroom. In a recent interview in a European journal, the instructor voiced his conversational learning philosophy as follows:

> One of the key concepts behind the conversational model of learning is the idea of a learning process where teachers and students come together as equal learners. When learning is viewed as a dialogue among equals, the teacher is no longer viewed as the sole provider of the expert knowledge. The status of the expert is equally shared among learners who actively take responsibility in offering expert knowledge when needed. . . . Paulo Freire writes that you can't deny the fact that teachers know more in some regard. I think that it means that knowledge is a dynamic process which changes all the time. While I may know a lot about management, the others may happen to know a lot about engineering or some kind of expert knowledge. Dialogue among equals

doesn't mean that in any single conversation there isn't a point in which one person is an expert and the other person is not. (Kolb, 1998, p. 51)

Inevitably, participants faced a period of adjustment in order to become familiar with the new seminar concept and configuration. The lingering "internalized oppression" would resurface from time to time in the seminar, as participants looked to the instructor and asked for his voice and direction at crucial points during the conversation.

Particularly during phase I of the seminar, the shift in perspective from a lecture format to the conversational mode was met with hesitation. By and large, the instructor appears to have been viewed as the primary purveyor of knowledge, as evidenced in the way he is portrayed in the conversation starters:

Kolb defines learning as a holistic adaptation to the social and physical world. We would like to look further into the meaning of the word "social" in reflection. (1989)

The first sentence of Kolb: Human beings are unique among all living organisms in that their primary adaptation lies . . . in identification with the process of adaptation itself.

The last sentence of Kolb: The dawn of integrity comes with the acceptance of responsibility for the course of one's own life. For in taking responsibility for the world, we are given back the power to change it. (1989)

David Kolb pointed out in his chapter on lifelong learning and integrative development that many people follow a life path of highly focused specialization. (1989)

The instructor is frequently personified as quotes, his physical presence far removed from the conversational space and for the most part clouded by an unspoken expectation participants attributed to him: the role of an ultimate knowledge provider.

In 1989, one event occurred several weeks into the seminar that was to give a new shape to the conversational learning space. An Asian student mentioned on several occasions that he was having trouble hearing and understanding what was being said. Finally someone suggested that the room be rearranged to bring the group closer together. However, eighteen people seated around a circle of tables placed people far away from each other. The tables were pushed away and the group sat in a circle inside the tables. This created a more informal and intimate conversational space. In addition, the group's action to improve members' ability to listen to and understand each other served to remind speakers that conversation is not just about speaking, but about being understood. Particularly in this larger group this required some effort and discipline. In subsequent years this room arrangement was to become a norm and ultimately led to the physical arrangement and design of the learning space described in the previous section.

Coming together in circle not only brought the participants closer physically but also challenged the hierarchical mentality embedded in the traditional classroom setting. It is safe to say that the change in physical configuration of the room played a significant role in promoting an egalitarian atmosphere in the learning space. As the conversational learning entered phase II, participants began to openly voice the need for a learning environment where all voices were equally heard and valued: "A hierarchical approach to learning undermines the very concept of process and the prospect for dialogue among equals. It interferes with the spontaneous confrontation of different perspectives" (1990). For the first time, the instructor is acknowledged and challenged as an equal member of the group: "Ok Dave . . . How is this course a demonstration of experiential learning?" (1990).

In 1990 the instructor introduced the Native American "talking stick" and the "feather" as a way to manage the flow of conversation in the group. The talking stick was used in tribal meetings as a form of parliamentary procedure, being passed from one speaker to the next as others listened and concentrated their attention on the holder of the stick. At the end of his speech, the speaker would hand the feather to a specific tribal member as an invitation to voice his opinion. A participant described her first encounter with the talking stick and the feather as follows:

> As David passed around the Native American talking stick and the response feather I imagined the differences in the type of dialogue that our desks and the stick/feather allowed. The stick, with its jagged edges and short branches, looked at first glance to be a weapon. But then as David spoke of its use the stick began to look like a hand—each little branch represented the individual fingers that come together into the collective unit. I saw it as an outstretched hand that at one time may offer assistance in the dialogue, and another time may slam down on the desk to strengthen the authority of the speaker. The feather, in contrast, offered a gentler and freer expression. I saw the bearer of the feather bringing a delicate and soft touch to the act of listening. Yet by its very function, assisting in flight, I also saw the feather helping the respondent to hover with the discussion or to lead the group into heights beyond normal reach of the hand. (1993)

Although the practice of the talking stick and the feather generated a certain level of discomfort and awkwardness, it helped participants to shift their focus from speaking to attentive listening. Over the years the greater emphasis placed on deep listening further enhanced solidarity among participants who equally shared the privilege of speaking and being listened to. An example of such acknowledgment of the group solidarity is metaphorically expressed in the following conversation starter:

To make music (knowledge) beautiful and whole we need to understand the various positions that are out there and be able to appreciate them not just sing our verses and over. When we nurture and support each other a much more complete outcome is possible. We can't sing all the parts, and we have to recognize that there are other parts. Solos can be beautiful, but their beauty is enhanced if they are a part of a greater group piece. (1992)

It is important to emphasize, however, that the awakening process of group solidarity did not happen overnight. To better understand this process it would be helpful to look into some patterns that kept resurfacing in the conversations starters over the years. Around the third to fifth weeks into the semester several participants began expressing frustration and discomfort as a reaction to their new experience of conversational learning. In a given year a participant expressed her growing frustrations and anger directed toward the process and content of the seminar:

I'm not sure whether I want to continue being part of this class. Maybe if I just do the readings, discuss these with one or two other people, and then space out during our Wednesday morning together . . . but then I can't really handle sitting in class anymore. I left class yesterday feeling emotional, followed by feeling increasingly angry at my fellow classmates, our professor, and most of all (inevitably) myself. I played with the idea of dramatically walking into David's office during break announcing my desire to be excused from the class . . . or just getting up and stomping out of our cooped up place on the 5th floor of Sears. **Drama . . .** I wish I could convince myself that I wouldn't come across as too self-indulgent, egotistical, and morally superior by doing just that! Because a good kick in the butt may be just is needed. . . . Why get so riled up? After all, it's only a class! But I have better ways of spending my time, I think, than watching us toy with ideas. . . . I am accusing all of us flirting . . . with very complex and meaningful concepts in a cursory self-indulgent way, leaving our comments to a level of superficially befitting of a talk show, but not of a group of students committing themselves to questioning in depth. (1995)

During phase III the same frustration resurfaced in the seminar, as described in the following conversation starter:

I don't know about you, but I am really frustrated with this class. I have reflected on the experience and developed a theory for how to make it more interesting for me.

Experience: I've experienced frustration for 3 consecutive weeks during this class only.

Observations: We come together in a room for 3 hours each week. There is lots of commentary on personal experiences. Our content has fleeting references to the reading and even fewer insights drawn about the personal experiences that are shared. 80% of the talking is done by 20% of the people. David has very little verbal involvement in the discussions. My experience of being in that circle is intensely frustrating for me; I feel like I'm missing out on the theoretical insights, the intellectual ah-ha's and David's experience for which I came to this doctoral program.

Concept/Theory: I've tried on several theories, and 2 emerge as useful for me.

1. Content—If we *(everyone!)* anchor our insights and discussions in the core concepts and theory of the readings, then the theoretical insights and intellectual "ah-ha's" will emerge. David's choices about how he shares his experiences and insights are his decision, although I think more input would help my process.
2. Process—If we *(everyone!)* were conscious of being concise, of listening and thinking before speaking, and of being mindful of the thrust of the speaker's point (rather than their tangents), then I could more easily pay attention and more easily learn from everyone's ideas. (1999)

This insightful snapshot of the learning space offers a glimpse of critical moments in the life of the seminar as participants struggle to redefine and reexamine what is to be a self-organizing learning group and what it would take for a group of adult learners to create a learning space that is hospitable enough to welcome everyone's expectation yet tight enough for rigorous learning and deep thinking to occur. Here the self-organizing nature of the conversational learning space is put to an ultimate test, as its survival is dependent upon how well the group will steer the oars of status and solidarity in a balanced fashion if they are to guide the conversation to a right course. In this regard, participants were left with several conflicting issues. The welcoming of personal experiences creates a sense of belonging in the learning space, yet an overdose of those moments runs the risk of neglecting the readings by only touching them in a cursory and superficial way, thus sacrificing the valuable learning one can gain from them. Enthusiasm and passion toward one's interest leads to powerful learning; however, too much of it will leave others powerless, sitting in silence.

Adding more frustration to an already complex situation, the instructor seemed as though he had totally surrendered his authority as the ultimate power figure and did not show any inkling in coming to the aid of the group and steering the course of the conversation. The following comment by a student reflects the instructor's persistent attitude and stance in the seminar: "David wants us to be a self-organizing class—he doesn't want to be a typical lecturer" (1999). Such was the atmosphere of the seminar that the group seems to have been practically left with no choice other than discovering the way on their own if they were to make their learning experience valuable and meaningful.

It is worth mentioning here yet another revealing pattern that emerged over the years that sheds an important light on the group's self-organizing process. During phase I the crisislike outburst expressed in response to the uncertainty and ambiguity of the learning space did not surface in the conversation starters. During phase II a clear emotional outburst made its appearance in the conversation starters eight to nine weeks into the seminar, whereas in phase III its occurrence was evidenced as early as three weeks into the life of the seminar. During phase I participants' concerns seem to have been explicitly shared outside the seminar and only in an implicit way mentioned during the seminar. During phase II, however, participants seemed to have gained enough confidence to cast off any restraint and inhibition in voicing their concerns. As the learning space transitioned to phase III, not only did participants became more vocal in expressing their mounting frustrations, they also seemed to become keenly aware of the fact that it was up to them to make the learning space a productive and valuable place for all. As evidence of such awareness, participants began actively searching for ways to make the learning a meaningful experience to every member of the seminar by proposing detailed courses of action and inviting others to experiment with different processes and ways of being together in the classroom:

> Whether we do it implicitly or explicitly, we are developing through experiential learning during our class. I suggest—regardless of what we choose (or don't choose) to do during each class—that we make our mode of learning more explicit. I suggest that we explicitly do the following—we actively reflect on what works and what doesn't. We actively theorize. We actively propose new experiments. At a macro level, this is the essence of experiential learning. (1999)

A final observation of the dialectic of status and solidarity points to the emergence of a rather unique phenomenon that surfaced over time in the conversational learning space: the awakening of the gift cycle of conversational learning. Recall for a moment how the dialectic of status and solidarity evolved over time from phase I to phase III. In the early phase, when the conversational learning space was skewed toward the status end of the dialectic, the learners' overall tendency was to be primarily recipients of knowledge generated in the seminar. Their primary focus was on receiving rather than giving. As the conversational learning space transitioned to phase II and phase III, giving and receiving became reciprocal processes as the balancing of the dialectic of status and solidarity became more apparent in conversations. Participants' increased awareness of their own unique expertise and knowledge encouraged them to actively influence the process as well as the content of the conversation by means of sharing new concepts and ideas in the group. Many ideas and concepts offered in the seminar were eventually incorporated in the syllabus over the years in a continuous gift cycle of new knowledge that was passed on to the next generation of learners. The gradual increase in the syllabus page numbers portrayed in Figure 5.1 is the manifestation of such a gift cycle in the conversational learning space.

We now turn to another key element that had a significant impact in the life of the conversational learning space: the combination of discursive and recursive processes embedded in the conversational mode of learning. In the next section we will uncover the meaning of discursive and recursive processes of learning and inquire into how they manifest themselves in conversations.

THE DIALECTIC OF DISCURSIVE AND RECURSIVE

The discursive and recursive processes are very much a part of the conversational learning process, where learning occurs simultaneously within two intertwined time dimensions: linear time and organic time, the former being connected to the discursive process and the latter to the recursive process of learning. As learners engage in conversation they situate themselves within two qualitatively distinct, though closely interconnected, experiences specific to each temporal dimension. The discursive process unfolds progressively from the past, present, to future in a continuous flow of activities. The weekly topic outlined in the course syllabus serves as the underlying structure that allows for these activities to unfold over time. Through the discursive process, learners become aware of what they know by explicitly voicing and sharing their thoughts and ideas related to their subject of interest to the larger group. What happens after the ideas and thoughts are voiced and heard is largely influenced and shaped by the recursive process of learning. During the conversation learners arrive at choice points where they are faced with the decision to move on to a new topic of discussion or return to the previous subject that continue to intrigue, disturb, or capture their attention.

Learners' choices to return to their topics of interest is largely dictated by the intrinsic interest as well as emotional investment they have in the subjects of their choice. In this sense the recursive process is closely related to the concrete and inside-out dimensions of the dialectics of concrete–abstract and inside-out–outside-in. The intrinsic as well as emotional engagements with the topic operate as primary motives for learners to go back in time and attend to the subject of their interest in a deeper way. In the absence of this recursive process, the discursive process would take over and drive the conversation in a predominantly linear fashion. In this sense the discursive process is closely related to the active dimension of the active–reflective dialectic of conversational learning. The discursive process is a manifestation of learners' desire to move on and drive the conversation forward in an active way. In order to clarify the relationship between the discursive and recursive dialectic of conversation, let's return for a moment to the dialectical manifestations of the concrete–abstract and inside-out–outside-in processes illustrated early on. Recall that as learners migrated from the abstract to the concrete and from outside-in to inside-out poles of the dialectics the conversational learning space was dominated by an emotional, personal, and passionate tone of conversations.

A similar phenomenon manifested itself in the discursive and recursive process of learning. During phase I, with some rare exceptions, conversations were predominantly discursive, as learners tended to stick to the agenda assigned to the particular class and methodically follow the topics of discussion outlined in the syllabus throughout the semester. This phase coincided with the strong abstract and outside-in approaches learners preferred during the early years. Learners tended to have an intense intellectual engagement with the preassigned topics, come to closure at the end of the session, and moved on to the next subject of discussion. During phase II, as learners began to gravitate toward concrete and inside-out dimensions of the dialectical poles, the recursive process made its first appearance in the conversational learning space. Learners began frequently to regress in time and revisit the subjects discussed during the previous sessions:

> Last week Paul related how his experiences made him angry with Habermas for using two-bit words too much. I agree, though I suspect it has to do with Germans semantics and word forms more than Habermas trying to show off. Although Emerson uses normal words and writes in English, my experiences make me mad at him. Emerson shows off by using ornate metaphors to make a mundane point sound richer than it is. (1992)

> During last week's class, I realized a long-growing concern of mine. I sense that orthodoxy of thought seems to have crept into many of our class discussions. While this orthodoxy affects me in particular because I disagree with it, I hope that I would be concerned about it under any circumstances. (1993)

A closer look at individual conversation starters points to the rich array of trigger points, spontaneous and visceral reactions, that prompted learners to return to a particular topic or experience in a deeper way. Furthermore, learners' inquiry and interests were triggered not only by personal reflections on the reading materials, but from experiences largely drawn from class interactions. The urge to go back in time and revisit the subject of the previous conversation can be attributed to the emotional impact learners experienced through assigned readings or through memorable group interactions. To a great extent what drives the recursive process during this phase is the learners' tendency to rely heavily on the concrete dimension rather than the abstract dimension of the dialectics and to engage an inside-out approach as opposed to outside in as their predominant modes of conversation. It is worth pointing out that learners' preference for frequently going back in time and revisiting their topics of interest or their tendency to digress the conversation based on their personal motives undermined the discursive process of learning during phase II. The accentuation of the recursive process of learning often kept learners from exploring new topics of discussion and moving the conversation forward in a timely manner.

Toward the end of phase II, however, the discursive and recursive processes of learning faced a significant turning point in the life of the conversational learning space. In a particular year the discursive and recursive processes of conversational learning were for the first time explicitly acknowledged and voiced in a conversation starter:

> What about the act of coming back again and again to the same bench in the same park to feed the sparrows—can this be called experience? Is the repetition of the same act indicative of experience or the denial thereof? Does the comfort of knowing the park, the bench, and the sparrows cover up a fear of venturing further into deeper and perhaps "unsafe" knowledge areas (i.e. Maslow) and becoming "stuck" in a place where we end up denying our talents and creativity? Or, is the repetition of the same act (leading perhaps to new understanding of the behavior of sparrows in their park environment) an attempt to probe more deeply, to deal head-on with the "shallowness that everyone threatens the true and the good" (Ken Wilber), an act of bravery, perseverance, and of appreciation of subtlety? I wonder. (1995)

In her metaphorical inquiry into the discursive and recursive processes of learning, the learner described her experience of tension and conflict as she inquired deep into the subject matter. The deeper one probes into the phenomenon at hand, the more heightened becomes one's awareness of the back-and-forth movement of these two distinct temporal dimensions of learning. The recognition of the discursive and recursive processes of conversational learning marks the transition from phase II to phase III of the conversational learning space.

During phase III the acknowledgment of the discursive and recursive process of learning became more deliberate and explicit as learners actively sought to pause and return to the subject of their interest by consciously redirecting the course of the conversation. The following sample conversation starters illustrate the state of the discursive and recursive processes of learning in phase III:

This class is called Learning and Development and it is based on the Experiential Learning Theory. Last week, we had the chance to learn more about our Learning Styles but, somehow, we did not. Instead, we thought that the LSI was a generalization, a classification, a labelization, and, in general, anything else ending in –ation. Moreover, we found LSI to be "culturally insensitive." Not everybody expressed such view, of course, but, as far as I recall, no one said anything different. In any case, the fact is this: We did not learn much about and from the LSI, because we never gave it a chance. Why? I am taking advantage of today's topic to introduce the following questions:

1. How our values may paralyze our quest for scientific thought and knowledge?
2. How our values may create a barrier to any kind of learning experience?
3. How our values may assassinate any spark of creativity?
4. How our values may limit our opportunities for becoming better researchers and professionals? (1997)

Last week I learned several lessons while observing and reflecting both about class content and about class members. Forgive me for a moment while I digress with an excerpt from my class notes and reflections. . . .

Lessons about others and myself:

- Joanna likes to experiment.
- Paul likes to experiment and he likes to discuss ideas through pictures.
- Jane likes to think before he [*sic*] talks.
- Tina sees this "unstructured" time as a release from her more structured work environment.
- Tangents take air time—sometimes inappropriately.
- Its is [*sic*] good to take time to get in touch with one's inner self.
- Sometimes its [*sic*] hard to tell when a tangent is a tangent or a good idea.
- Carol & Helen feel like we need "something" more from class.
- Sometimes we aren't always interested in the line of conversation and it is easy to tune out.
- Its [*sic*] OK to let Joyce know when I've gotten the idea.
- David wants us to be a self-organizing class—he doesn't want to be a typical lecturer.

Lessons about the process of experiential learning:

- Experiential learning is all about learning through processes.
- If we are going to self-organize, we need to examine our PROCESS of learning.
- If we choose to focus on process, our approach needs to be loose enough to accommodate everyone's needs, yet tight enough to accomplish something of value to the members of the class. (1999)

These two conversation starters highlight a distinct portrait of the conversational learning space of phase III. In contrast to the previous phases, much of the learners' deliberate attempt to return to past class experiences was geared toward actively redirecting the course of the conversation for the purpose of urging and often challenging the group to inquire deeper into the subject or dynamics that emerged during the conversation. It is also true of this phase that participants often expressed a sense of weariness and concern toward tangential discussions that might have diverted the course of the core subject of the conversation. From this perspective, learners were also operating under the pressure to move forward by stressing the discursive mode of learning, thus emphasizing their need to engage in conversation in a more focused and meaningful manner. In order to balance this tension, there is a concerted effort to balance the recursive and discursive processes in conversation. When learners chose to refer back in time to a particular topic or group process, they consciously bridged the subject of their interest to the core topic of the ongoing conversation in the seminar.

As we turn to the last principle of conversational learning, the dialectic of action and reflection, the dynamic evolutionary trend described thus far becomes even more accentuated as the five dialectics diverge at times and converge at another in a highly organic manner.

THE DIALECTIC OF ACTION AND REFLECTION

Central to the theory of experiential learning is the idea that the creation of knowledge and meaning occurs through the active engagement in ideas and experiences in the external world and through internal reflection about the qualities of these experiences and ideas (Kolb, 1984). Thus, learning occurs through the dialectical movement of action and reflection as learners move outward into the external world and inward into themselves.

The same principle applies to conversational learning. Knowledge is created through conversation as learners actively voice their ideas and experiences in conversation and make meaning of the experiences and ideas through reflection. The balancing of action and reflection is crucial to conducting a meaningful conversation, since suppression of one dimension will automatically hurt the other. When learners engage in conversation primarily through the reflective mode, conversations are turned into frivolous chatter. Conversely, if action is overemphasized to the detriment of reflection conversation is turned into mere activism, denying learners the possibility of engaging in a meaningful conversation (Freire, 1992).

This tenuous relationship between action and reflection is captured in one conversation starter written early in the life of the seminar:

Boud, Keogh and Walker emphasize reflection as necessary to formulating informed action. Emerson emphasizes action as liberation: "The preamble of

> thought, the transition through which it passes from the unconscious to the conscious, is action." For BKW reflection precedes action, reflection implies action, for Emerson action precedes reflection but reflection is not in the drivers seat. What is the proper linkage between action and reflection? (1989)

The question posed by the learner, "What is the proper linkage between action and reflection," marks the beginning of the twelve-year exploration into what constitutes the nature of conversation and how it generates knowledge and shapes human understanding. The question regarding which comes first, reflection or action, or what connects the two was given focused attention during phase I of the seminar, as learners engaged in a series of reflective exploration into the evolutionary process of human consciousness and inquired into how language and the human's innate desire to communicate and dialogue ultimately gave meaning to human existence.

> What connects—in an admittedly sketchy fashion—for me at this point is that new perceptions enter our awareness, and create new knowledge, when there exists an urge to know, and a capacity for empathy which allows dialogue, and there are others with whom we can engage in dialogue who can help us to "grasp, name and share" new ideas. In order to create new knowledge, it is necessary to overcome, not only the fear of knowing which Maslow discusses, but the active hatred of learning from experience which Bion suggests is present in most adults. . . . Perhaps learning occurs when we are able to transcend that fear in a dialogue with others where we let empathic understanding have free reign. (1989)

What comes through the early writings is a highly reflective stance that dominates the conversation starters of phase I. Much of what emerges from their writings is the acknowledgment of the process of dialogue and communication that is grasped and named but shared only in a tacit way. For the most part, learners' reflective tendencies and preferences appear to have kept the actual conversation within the confines of each individual's internalized monologue.

It is important to pause for a moment and reassess why learners' reflective and tacit tendencies became a predominant pattern in the early phase of the seminar. This phenomenon coincided with learners' tendency to be conscious of the status of the instructor. The idea of solidarity between the instructor and the seminar participants was not readily embraced during the birth phase of the conversational learning space. Learners' perceptions of the instructor as the primary purveyor of knowledge and thus the one who possibly would be the dominant voice in the conversation might have kept learners inclined toward the reflective side of the dialectic of action and reflection. As the instructor maintained his nondominant and nondirective posture over the years, the conversational learning space transitioned to phase II, where the idea of solidarity was explicitly verbalized in the seminar.

This also marks the transition of the learning space from the reflective to the active mode of conversation as learners searched for the meaning of conversation among equals amidst their struggles and confusions to make sense of the process of the seminar, perceived at that time to be unclear, ambiguous, and without a specific goal. The following conversation starter illustrates the learners' awakening process to conversational learning as they slowly emerged out of the reflective, internalized mode of dialogue and transitioned to a collective mode of exploration into the meaning of learning through conversations.

Somehow education as learning needs to provide an environment where students and teachers both discover new realities that get beyond the current zero sum game between systems. Is the new curriculum doing this? Or is it just indoctrinating a different value set that makes the faculty feel better? How can we evaluate the dialogue about learning that we have here? Is this really a dialogue, or a multilogue, or a collection of monologues and dialogues? Is connectivity a multilogue, dialogue or a distributed monologue? How could we possibly tell the difference? (1992)

It is worth mentioning here yet another event that influenced the transition of the conversational learning space from a tacit and reflective mode to an active mode of conversation. In 1993 a significant event took place early in the semester that in many ways had a substantial impact in setting the course of future Learning and Development seminars on the path to conversational learning. During that year, Ann Baker and Patricia Jensen had begun their dissertation work on the topic of conversational learning, and the entire class of 1993 was invited to participate in their studies as part of the data-collection process. Both Ann and Patricia were present in the seminar during the entire semester as participants in the conversation. As part of their data collection, each conversation session was tape recorded in addition to all participants being asked to participate in individual interviews at the beginning and at the end of the semester. The purpose of the interviews was to understand how participants learned through conversations by inviting them to explore and reflect on their learning experiences gained through conversation with someone at some point in their lives.

The simultaneous experience of being in conversation with one another in the seminar and being a part of a larger study on conversation learning appears to have had a significant influence on the life of the group. The scenario described in the following conversation starter mirrors the atmosphere of the seminar of that particular year:

Last week I thought I saw a pattern emerging that seems very familiar to me from other classes, seminars, and workplace meetings: In class some people were very vocal and spoke often. Others spoke rather less often or almost never. I wondered about this recurring dynamic. . . . I am intrigued by the power of silence and of listening. The gift of silence and listening is a great gift to a group. For starters, quiet creates the possibility of conversation; otherwise there is merely a free-for-all of competing voices. In addition, when I am speaking and I realize that my words are not just vanishing into thin air, but are being listened to with care by another human being, I am deeply moved and feel increased connection to the listener and to myself. Also, when I'm able to still my interior monologue and listen, truly listen to others, there is the pleasure of being taken outside my monologue and, paradoxically, I feel more centered. The gift of speaking is also a great gift to give to a group. Words are as fundamental to dialogue as quiet. However, as someone who tends to be pretty vocal, I wonder at my own need or tendency to be vocal. No doubt, my excitement and excitability play a part. I feel passionate about ideas and there is a pleasure to thinking out loud about them with others. Yet I sense there is another side to it: Am I afraid to be quiet? Am I afraid to give up control of the conversation for fear that my ideas will not be heard? Am I afraid to trust that my colleagues will take the conversation in promising directions? The gift of listening and the gift of speaking are necessary gifts for group function. But I wonder what will happen if we specialize in these gifts rather than each of us giving both to the group. Do we not run the risk of all specialization: lop-sided development, strong in one area, weak in another. Aren't we all tired to some extent of being specialists? (1993)

The clear articulation of the key elements and processes that ultimately would lead the group to conducting a meaningful conversation is the first indication that conversational learning left the realm of the tacit and reflective and entered the realm of the explicit and active side of the conversational dialectics. In this process conversation was acknowledged as a legitimate language and an active way to engage in learning. This trend continued through subsequent years during phase II as learners continued to explicitly articulate the meaning and values of different forms of conversations and how their learning experiences were impacted and shaped through conversation.

This is a conversation starter about . . . conversation starters, and some reflections about our semester together. We began many conversations with each other during the past several months—some were in written form, and most were begun verbally. There were calm conversations, rational conversations, emotional conversations, exciting conversations and more exciting conversations. There were long periods of silence, too. Yet isn't silence a form of communicating? We talked about epistemology, biology, naturalism, education, morality, spirituality, learning and development. And we received many gifts each week—flowers, seashells from Hawaii, books, learning and development. I anticipate that all those "unfinished" conversation starters will continue on and on . . . and they will evolve into many new conversation starters. Thanks for the new beginnings. (1995)

The conversation starters reviewed thus far are illustrative of how the conversational learning space transitioned from a primarily reflective and tacit mode to an explicit and active mode of conversation over the years. It is important to note, however, that knowledge creation through conversation does not occur without simultaneous engagement in the active and reflective modes of the conversational dialectic. The movement from the tacit mode of the birth phase to the explicit mode of the growth phase was a substantial development in the seminar; however, it still left unfinished the integrative work of the dialectic of action and reflection that ultimately would result in generation of knowledge through conversations.

The following poem serves as the prelude to what marks the transition of the conversational learning space to phase III, where learners engage in conversation with a clear sense of purpose and intention to integrate action and reflection and the tacit and the explicit dimensions of the dialectic:

Shared separate loneliness
Days left me
I sit alone in person
Sharing only a passive life
Filled with lonely ideas
That few apprehend
And none will know
Share my loneliness? !
Come and listen to my ravings? !
Take a seat by half cooked ideas
And the solitude of knowing
I too will listen to your loneliness
So that you will not remain,
Silently
Confined to ideas
We may not share love
Nor even resonation
But seldom do singing birds harmony
Always your children will cry
May we hear? Together different sounds
May we share? Separate loneliness

Born from the proposition that we are always infinitely alone, that others can never completely know what we feel, this poem asks what might be gained from the activity of conversation. What might be gained from sharing this loneliness? It is actually an optimistic piece, both extending an invitation and asking the questions. (1996)

The question, "What might be gained from the activity of conversation?" expressed in the poem continued to be articulated throughout phase III, as conversation increasingly gained in complexity and richness. Learners chose to approach conversational learning from multiple perspectives and personal interests. For some participants conversation triggered in them a desire to act in the service of a cause they deeply cared about: "Many times I leave class wondering how we can translate these great conversations into some action that will make a change for the better in some way, whether it's the academic world, the natural world, my world as a parent, or my world as a member of this department and this program" (1997).

Yet for different learners conversation is experienced as the manifestation of the gift cycle of the learning process as the selfless exchange of giving and receiving among learners promotes solidarity, understanding, and authenticity in the learning space:

> Yet, what better way truly depict the exchange of miracles between two human beings; miracles, which ignite the mind, enliven the spirit and awaken, rejuvenate, and touch the soul. You tell me something. I tell you something. Together we enrich our existence, our space and our "being" in that moment of space and time. The conversation starts, grows and unfolds. The gift (the conversation) takes on a life of its own. It spreads its wealth all around the universe. (1988)

Other times learners resorted to the exploration of the theoretical and conceptual side of conversation as they inquired into the connection of the theory and practice of conversational learning:

> Conversational learning: Learning occurs in many ways for many situations and for many people. I wish that I felt confident with when and how conversational learning is a good idea. Short of that, I am confident that it is a powerful learning mode. Now seeing myself as a lifelong learner, I can probably find more opportunities than I ever expected to learn through conversation with others. In so doing, I am inherently valuing what others have to offer me short of books, empirical findings and codified "knowledge." What actually is a conversation anyway? (1999)

The dynamic movement of the dialectic of action and reflection illustrated in the ebb and flow of the conversation starters reviewed thus far is indicative of how conversation evolved from the reflective to the active mode of learning during phases I and II and became more balanced during phase III. As the conversational learning space evolved, learners' distinct perspectives, interests, and styles shaped their integrative effort to make sense of the idea and the act of learning through conversations. Action-oriented learners were drawn to the active side of the conversation as a potential source of influencing change in the world, whereas philosophically and ideologically oriented learners chose to inquire into the meaning and impact of the conversation as they saw it manifest in life situations at large. Learners with a pragmatic orientation fell somewhere in the middle, as their interests were geared toward balancing the conceptual and theoretical framework of the conversational learning model against the practice of conversation.

SUMMARY

The evolution of the conversational learning space described thus far illustrates how the five process dialectics that make up the foundation of conversational learning manifested themselves in the Learning and Development seminar over the course of twelve years. From phase I to phase III, the evolutionary process of the conversational learning space took a highly unpredictable and nonlinear path. The manifestations of these dialectics in each evolutionary phase were interdependent and organic, adding to the complexity and richness of the conversational learning space over time. At one time conversations were highly abstract and discursive; at other times predominantly emotional and recursive. The five dialectical processes evolved in a highly interconnected manner, as one dialectic triggered another in an almost chainlike reaction. An example of such movement can be seen in the dialectical process of feeling and thinking as it ultimately influenced the dialectic of inside out and outside in. As learners moved toward the feeling end of the dialectic, there was also a gradual awakening and movement toward the inside-out approach to learning.

The overall pattern identified throughout the three evolutionary phases within each of the five dialectics is the learners' tendency to move from one extreme of a dialectic continuum to the other during phase I and phase II, until finally they settled somewhere in the middle of the dialectic during phase III upon reconciling the two extreme ends in a flexible manner.

The overall processes and factors that ultimately guided the conversational learning space deserve closer attention. From the perspective of the course content and structure, the syllabus served as a guide to the destination; however, learners made their own choices as to how to proceed and what to focus and attend to. The manifestation of such a process can be witnessed in the dynamic change in topics and subjects over time, as topics that gained prominence in one particular generation were overshadowed by others in the generation that followed. The feminist voice that had a prominent place in conversation during one year receded into the background as postmodernism gained the central focus in the following year. In another year, naturalism and spirituality were the learners' choices, until they were replaced by deep ecology in the subsequent generation. Learners' self-organizing tendencies became more accentuated over the years as the instructor maintained his nondirective posture and stayed away from a discursive, lecture format of class delivery throughout these years. Another key factor that appears to have impacted the evolutionary process was the instructor's choice in including the conversation starters of previous years in the syllabus as part of the weekly focus readings. The knowledge and experience passed on to the next generation of learners through conversation starters gained significant historical value in the seminar over the years. The content as well as the process may have gained clarity and focus in the seminar as a result of the accumulated past experience and knowledge.

The combination of processes and factors that guided the conversational learning space throughout the evolutionary process brings to focus yet another phenomenon that emerged during phase III of the learning space. Learners' increased awareness of the past appears to have contributed to their confidence in making conscious choices with regard to the content and process of the class. What comes through in the conversation starters of the pioneering generations is a collective experience of frustration and confusion, punctuated with moments of breakthroughs and excitement amidst their struggles to make sense of the novel undertaking they have embarked on. Toward phase III, the novelty factor loses its power, as learners appear to have more or less gained control over the course of the conversation.

One may argue that the fusion of horizon, an ultimate state to be arrived at by individuals engaged in conversation, also poses a significant challenge to the conversational learning space in that it may eventually stagnate the conversation as a result of the shared sense of understanding and agreement jointly achieved by the learners. The challenge therefore resides in keeping the dialectical tensions alive thorough ongoing conversations in a hospitable and safe manner. As such, the creation of a safe conversational learning space becomes pivotal to promoting learning thorough conversations, a topic that will be covered in the next chapter.

REFERENCES

Baker, A. C. (1995). *Bridging differences and learning through conversation*. Unpublished Ph.D. diss., Case Western Reserve University, Cleveland, OH.

Banaga, G. L. (2000). *A calling to work, a labor of love: A phenomenological study of work as calling*. Unpublished Ph.D. diss., Case Western Reserve University, Cleveland, OH.

Belenky, M., Clinchy, B., Goldberger, N., & Tarule, J. (1986). *Women's ways of knowing*. New York: Basic Books.

Fambrough, M. (2000). *Forming and reforming gender identity: The experience of discovering and following one's calling*. Unpublished Ph.D. diss., Case Western Reserve University, Cleveland, OH.

Freire, P. (1992). *Pedagogy of the oppressed*. New York: Continuum.

Gadamer, H. G. (1976). *Philosophical hermeneutics*. Berkeley and Los Angeles: University of California Press.

Gadamer, H. G. (1994). *Truth and method* (2d rev. ed.). New York: Crossroad.

Hazelwood, D. (1999). *The utilization of expertise: Conversational analysis of software systems analysts and clients working together*. Unpublished Ph.D. diss., Case Western Reserve University, Cleveland, OH.

Hunt, D. E. (1987). *Beginning with ourselves*. Cambridge, MA: Brookline Books.

Jensen, P. J. (1995). *Streams of meaning making in conversation*. Unpublished Ph.D. diss., Case Western Reserve University, Cleveland, OH.

Kahn, M. D. (1995). *The tao of conversation*. Oakland, CA: New Harbinger Publications.

Kayes, D. C. (2001). *Experiential learning in teams: A study in learning style, group process and integrative complexity in ad hoc groups*. Unpublished Ph.D. diss., Case Western Reserve University, Cleveland, OH.

Kolb, A. (2000). *Play: An interdisciplinary integration of research*. Unpublished Ph.D. diss., Case Western Reserve University, Cleveland, OH.

Kolb, D. A. (1984). *Experiential learning: Experience as the source of learning and development*. Englewood Cliffs, NJ: Prentice-Hall.

Kolb, D. A. (1998). Experiential learning: From discourse model to conversation. *Lifelong Learning in Europe, 3*, 148–153.

Kolb, D. A., & Kolb, A. Y. (2001). *ORBH 570—Learning and development*. Cleveland, OH: Case Western Reserve University, Department of Organizational Behavior.

Mainemelis, C. (2001). *When the muse takes it all: A conceptual and empirical investigation of timelessness and its effects on creativity in organizations*. Unpublished Ph.D. diss., Case Western Reserve University, Cleveland, OH.

Maslow, D. (1968). *Toward a psychology of being*. Princeton, NJ: Van Nostrand.

Maturana, H., & Varela, F. (1998). *The tree of knowledge: The biological roots of human understanding*. Boston: Random House, New Science Library.

Mazen, A. M., Jones, M. C., & Sergenian, G. K. (2000). Transforming the class into a learning organization. *Management Learning, 31*, 147–161.

Nonaka, I. (1994). A dynamic theory of organizational knowledge creation. *Organization Science, 5* (1), 14–37.

Park, C. (1996). *Our place in nature: Naturalism, human mind and professional practice*. Unpublished Ph.D. diss., Case Western Reserve University, Cleveland, OH.

Rogers, C. (1961). *On becoming a person*. Boston: Houghton Mifflin.

Steingard, D. (1997). *Values integration in socially responsible business: From separation thesis to spiritual relationality*. Unpublished Ph.D. diss., Case Western Reserve University, Cleveland, OH.

Sullivan, H. G. (1997). *Creating common ground for collaborative learning: A Gestalt perspective for experiential learning*. Unpublished Ph.D. diss., Case Western Reserve University, Cleveland, OH.

White, J. (1993). *The role of individual characteristics and structures of social knowledge on ethical reasoning using an experiential learning model*. Unpublished Ph.D. diss., Case Western Reserve University, Cleveland, OH.

6

Receptive Spaces for Conversational Learning

Ann C. Baker

> The natural human tendency to resolve conflict by choosing between two opposing positions may relieve internal turmoil, but it doesn't reveal the deeper truth. . . . Truth is not static, like an answer, but *dynamic*, like a relationship. It is not an outcome, but a process. Awakening was the realization that reality is neither *this* nor *that*, but the living interaction between them both. . . .
> We are not entirely in charge of the process of reconciling ourselves to our enemies or the world at large. It seems to have a sense of its own time. We need only hold the door open, or at least keep it unlocked.
> Brian Muldoon (1996, p. 240, 248)

IMAGINATION

Imagine yourself in the following brief scenarios, taking a minute to consider each one before reading on to the next:

- A parent has learned that his or her teenage child recently began taking Ecstasy (a current popular, illegal mind-altering drug) sometimes on the weekends with friends. The parent is scared and angry. The child sees no reason to stop participating with friends doing something that seems harmless and that everyone else is doing.

- Members of a top-level management team (with a record of working productively together) in a medium-size company have just learned about an impending merger of their company with another similar-size company. There is sharp disagreement among the team members about whether, how, when, and how much information about the merger should be passed on to company employees.
- In a university-level management class of diverse races and ethnicities, employment practices and policies are the class topic. Intense disagreements begin to be expressed about the meaning of affirmative action, historical patterns of discrimination, issues of fairness, reverse discrimination, and institutionalized racism.
- A major company has announced intentions to build a large facility with possible negative environmental implications in a medium-size community that has high unemployment rates. The community is beginning to divide into factions among those in favor and those opposed to the development.

What came to mind as you read these scenarios? Is there one truth, one path to reconciliation? What are the "next steps" to be taken if the situation had relevance for you? Would conversations play a role in those next steps? While individual responses are likely to vary noticeably, most people would agree that conversations were part of the activities leading up to each situation. Ideas about what would be the appropriate next steps are influenced at least in part by previous experiences and cultural origins, natural inclinations in times of conflict, a personal sense of competence in dealing with conflict, and how much passion a particular scenario (or real-life situation) generates. In any case, these kinds of situations are ripe for learning conversationally.

When candid and respectful conversations among people involved in similar situations can be an ongoing norm, increased insights and understanding of the perspectives of others are much more likely. If these kinds of conversations do not occur or are infrequent, the impact can be dramatically different. What contributes to conversations that offer ongoing opportunities for learning and for seeing perspectives never imagined before? What makes this kind of conversational learning difficult and far too rare? Exploring these two questions is at the heart of this chapter.

Feeling passionate about something in situations similar to these stories can at times create seemingly unlimited energy. To paraphrase Parker Palmer (1990), the need to combine passion with discipline in search of some sense of the truth is one of the challenges that influences whether conversations open new doors of understanding. Unbridled passion without discipline in conversations can bring painful hurt and embarrassment, sever communication and sometimes relationships, block the possibility of hearing how other people see the same situation quite differently, and block learning.

Palmer's (1990) interpretation of the word "truth" is especially relevant in this context. Each person in these opening stories—as is true in life—has a "part" of the truth, a legitimate and valuable perspective to bring to the process of conversation, that Palmer says is the road to "being in the truth" (p. 12). Gadamer (1994) similarly talks about the value of ethical reflective conversations, not to find a universal truth, but to gain understanding from multiple viewpoints to create a "fusion of horizons" (Gadamer, 1994, p. 374). The parent and the child, each member of the executive team, each person in the university class, and the members of the community and company representatives have a legitimate part of the truth in these opening scenarios. Understanding each situation is directly related to including those diverse voices in the conversations to move forward.

Bringing multiple, diverse perspectives into conversations with an intention of inquiry and learning, more than for advocacy and control, requires a safe supportive context and receptive conversational space. Receptive spaces that support ongoing, sustained conversational engagement, with passion and discipline to promote learning, take preparation and time. Creating receptive spaces means thinking of space in new ways that are uncommon in Western cultures.

As a way to reframe the meaning of space, a case study from the empirical study that inspired this chapter gives an illustration of an actual conversation that occurred when a faculty member in a university setting cultivated a receptive conversational space. Drawing on a series of conversations among several people grappling with their differing perspectives on race, the case study helps to give life to the ideas explored in this chapter. Although the opening scenarios are hypothetical, this case study is similar to the scenario about the university class that begins to talk about the controversial issues of affirmative action, discrimination, and race. After the case study, the results of the empirical study are given, describing the characteristics that are associated with receptive conversational spaces using quotes from study participants. The chapter closes with practical guidelines for how to use the findings of this research to create these kinds of spaces. The characteristics and guidelines here are offered out of a primarily Western cultural experience and empirical study, requiring appropriate adaptation accordingly. Before the case study, considering varied cultural notions of space may help create more contextual understanding.

RETHINKING SPACE

Perceptions of space are primarily shaped and communicated culturally. If a person's entire cultural exposure is in one context, there may be no recognition that others do not share the same perceptions.

While each person is brought up with certain spatial elements emphasized and well developed, the process of focusing on some things means that others are screened out. There are cultural differences in how much personal space feels comfortable, for example, for someone in a conversation. In some cultures, such as Arab cultures, being close enough in conversations to feel another person's breath is often preferred. Yet in many Asian cultures people standing and talking would more likely prefer having about an arm's length distance from each other.

Edward Hall (1969) writes beautifully from an anthropological perspective about how Westerners learn to focus more on the objects within a space and to see the space between objects as "empty." He explores how some cultures focus more on the space "between." Hall articulates a way of rethinking the meaning of space that is relevant to the conversational context: "The study of Japanese spaces illustrates their habit of leading the individual to a spot where he can discover something for himself" (p. 154). In a Japanese garden the design centers on giving people opportunities for multiple ways to experience the space. While "the Japanese garden is designed to be enjoyed from many points of view" (p. 154), Hall illustrates how in Western art or design there is often more emphasis on a single or fixed point within the space. The emphasis in Western cultures tends to give less meaning or value to the space than to the objects or focal points within the space.

Even within Western cultures there are differences. Europeans often schedule fewer events within a certain period of time than people from the United States. Hall (1969) again illustrates how the concepts of time and space, for example, are interpreted differently from culture to culture. These differences are particularly reflected in the way scheduling of events shapes the pattern of human relationships in each culture. People from the United States are often seen as constantly "pressed" for time and not very interested in taking time to become acquainted with people before getting down to business. Hall says, "By overemphasizing the schedule Americans tend to underemphasize individual space needs" (p. 132). Thus, space in U.S. culture is typically perceived as having less meaning and value when it is not filled up. On the other hand, when space is perceived as a precious commodity, behavior vis-à-vis one's use of space shifts.

To illustrate, rethinking the meaning of space in conversation changes perceptions of silence. Rather than perceiving silence as "empty" in a negative way, silence can be experienced as an open space for people to move into, such as holding "the door open," as Muldoon (1996) says. This new frame of reference expands the possible images of quiet, reflective conversational spaces. Instead of being empty, space can be seen as full of the potential for individuals, who "can discover" what they need to know for themselves and what they can discover with each other.

This reframing of space has profound implications for how to prepare and create conversational space. It means not rushing in to fill up the space with speaking and with answers, and at times allowing whatever is present to emerge. It means trusting that each person brings his or her own legitimate memory, perspective, and imagination into the space as potential resources for learning. Preparation of such conversational space extends far beyond what is generally thought of as planning.

GLORIA AND NICK: AN ILLUSTRATION

Similar to the opening scenario about a university class talking about race and discrimination, a case study from the research project will be used as an illustration. This qualitative empirical study was designed to learn how differences among people could more readily become sources for learning. The twenty-three participants in the study included adults in doctoral degree and nondegree seminar programs. A series of three interviews with most of the participants were completed during one year. These adults ranged in age from mid-twenties to mid-sixties, were about 50 percent male and 50 percent female, and all had considerable work experience in industrial, business, educational, religious, and health care organizations. Approximately half of the group were either African Americans or were born in or had lived for extended periods in eight countries representing all continents. Thus, there was a rich diversity of race, ethnicity, and nationality among the participants. Throughout this chapter are quotations drawn from the fifty-five interviews and extensive ethnographical observations in the study.

This case study is drawn from one specific conversation that took place in the group seminar setting and a follow-up conversation among two of the participants, Gloria and Nick. Perhaps a good way to begin telling the story is with a quote. Nick said that at a break in the seminar Gloria approached him. She wanted to continue the previous group conversation with him one on one. He said that much to his surprise,

I realized that it was not a confrontation. And then my whole feelings about the conversation changed. And that I think opened me up so that we could actually, you know, share our opinions with each other, share information with each other. And listen to what the other person was saying. And at that point, I realized that neither of our opinions had to change and that was okay. We could just hear where the other person was coming from.

To set the scene, during one of the graduate seminars the conversation began to focus on people's very different perspectives about race, about what equality looks like, and how opportunities for jobs, education, and so on are related to race, discrimination, and issues of access. Many people in the conversation felt that affirmative action efforts are essential because of the inequities of the past and present, while others felt that there is equality of access now and that affirmative action is reverse discrimination. In this illustration the conversation was among people in an ongoing group who had known each other for several months, were building relationships with each other, and had a context that allowed them to talk about these issues if they were open to that possibility. These people were beyond the point of polite lip service and surface comments.

In this seminar session there were a lot of facts and data shared about different issues, along with very personal and emotional stories. During the intense group conversation, a young man, who will be referred to here as Nick, shared his personal experience of jobs he felt he had not gotten "simply" because he was a white male. In the follow-up interview with Nick as a part of the research, he repeated much of what he had said in the group. He recalled the conversation in detail:

> *There seems to be a double standard . . . recruitment of racial minorities, women . . . almost seems to be a discouraging force against white males. . . . If it was the other way around, in this current political climate, people would be screaming . . . if you were recruiting white males over other people. . . . One of the things that I brought up specifically . . . was black fraternities which I was under the impression that they actually restricted [open only to black members].*

Nick talked about feeling like he had been expressing a "contrary viewpoint" that was different from the prevailing norms of the group conversation, and that he felt somewhat like a heretic or outsider as he talked. Needless to say, he felt emotional and talked about feeling defensive and uncomfortable. Unlike many similar groups, as a white male Nick was in the minority. In this seminar of sixteen people, 50 percent were male and only 38 percent were Caucasians from the United States. The prevailing opinions expressed in this conversation leaned fairly strongly toward concern for inequities in society, institutionalized racism, and the importance of vigorous measures to address unequal access.

Perhaps supported by the diversity of the group and the support that she may have felt among her peers, during a break in the seminar one of the young African-American women in the group, Gloria (also not her real name), came up to Nick to continue the conversation. His immediate reaction was "for it to be antagonistic." But what happened was not at all what he expected and offers insight into how to create receptive space for challenging conversations.

In spite of his expectation, Nick described how Gloria came up and began calmly explaining her point of view. He said he began to hear things that "had never occurred to me before." What was Gloria doing—or not doing—that made this space more receptive?

I realized that she was not trying to attack me or change me. And I was able to calm down and just sit and listen . . . just the absence of tension. . . . She was able to let me have my own opinion without attacking it and just explain her opinion on the same issue. . . . [She] explained her viewpoint, and she was not really asking me to say it was right or wrong or even to accept it. She was just saying, this is how it is seen from the other side of the fence.

For Nick, feeling like she was not trying to change him and that she could let him have his own opinion seemed critical to him becoming more receptive to Gloria's point of view.

In their one-on-one conversation one of the things that Gloria specifically talked to him about was the question of black fraternities in the MBA program, saying, "The white MBA is pretty much the same as *the* MBA group and that is why black people feel that they need to start their own sub-group within it." As Gloria talked to Nick, he said that he

became more aware of the fact that different people perceive situations differently. The fact that I had never thought that someone would consider student government to be white student government . . . made me more aware of a different point of view, but it did not change my own raw viewpoint of the situation. I think it might have made me more accepting of different viewpoints of the topic that we were discussing.

Note here the value of realizing that really hearing and accepting another person's viewpoint does not mean having to give up or change one's own point of view. Gloria was articulate and unwavering in expressing her perspective. Nick did not change, in his words, his "own raw viewpoint." But Nick could listen to and understand this other perspective and then integrate it into his framework, leading to less judgmental, reactive behavior in future conversations and interactions. When people can listen reflectively, they "may not change their own opinions about an issue, but they are quite likely to change their opinions of other people's opinions" (Mathews, 1995, p. 28).

Having the follow-up one-on-one conversation with Gloria seemed to make a big difference to Nick, especially since it was such an emotional and volatile topic. Nick said the group conversation had "felt like it was almost a combat situation," with people "taking one side or another or purposely staying neutral and silent." He described how his own heart had been racing and his adrenaline going, and others seemed agitated and emotionally involved because these racial discussions touch "lots of people emotionally and from various perspectives." Yet during the break the combination of Gloria being calm and not attacking him and the conversation being just between the two of them seemed to make the space more receptive and less combative and enabled him to hear in new ways.

What contributed to each of these two relatively young people having the self-confidence and assertiveness to speak their "truths," both in the group and in their follow-up conversation? While there is no way of knowing for sure, several factors almost certainly contributed. Because this group was an ongoing one that was beginning to develop some history and relationships among themselves, challenging the status quo may have felt somewhat less risky. The deliberate efforts of the faculty member in this group to create and support a safe environment for in-depth exploration of controversial topics among peers were almost certainly crucial. The diverse nature of this group was another factor. The group membership created for each person at least a small critical mass of people who shared some common experiences. In the group of sixteen people there were four African-Americans, six white people from the United States, and six people who were not from the United States. Generally, in groups where the representation from similar diverse populations is limited to one or two people, there is not the critical mass needed for mutual support (Kanter, 1986), making it more difficult for "minorities" to speak up effectively. All these factors can be instructive about how to encourage more nontraditional voices and differences to stimulate conversational learning.

What does this story reveal? Unfortunately, this case is another example of the person of color being the one to "educate" the white person about issues that many whites are blind to because of privileges that are taken for granted (McIntosh, 2001). For most people it is difficult to recognize their "privilege" when it has always been a given in their lives, unless it has been taken away from them.

Generally, the more a person feels they have opportunities to speak and to be heard, the more they can listen to others. The more a person feels he or she has a genuine choice about whether to blindly accept or disagree in conversations, the less is the need to hold the unfamiliar at arm's distance, react, and defend against "hearing." Thus, people can consider (hear) the unfamiliar more fully if they know they can *choose* to discard what does not fit for them. In a conversation where there is ample receptive space to listen, reflect, and consider, it is possible to hear and speak more freely.

CHARACTERISTICS OF RECEPTIVE SPACE

The preponderance of the results of the study suggests a strong relationship between conversational context and the capacity for recognizing differences as resources and catalysts for learning conversationally. This interdependence is illustrated in the words of one participant: "The more I am able to actually hear what is being said, the easier it is to find my own voice. The more I tend to be reacting to what is being said, the more I tend to be just making noise." For this person there was a creative tension in the dialectical experience of finding the voice to speak through the listening to others. When reacting, it was just "making noise," rather than being receptive to hearing something new.

Drawing from both the positive and negative experiences of participants in the research, the following five contextual conversational characteristics are most strongly associated with being able to remain engaged with and learn from differences of perspective:

- Creating and sustaining a safe, receptive conversational space and context.
- Listening reflectively to give voice to others, especially those who seem different.
- Recognizing differences and conflict as resources for learning.
- Recognizing and valuing both the cognitive and the emotional dimensions of learning.
- Making a concentrated effort to simultaneously attend to all of these characteristics while maintaining a moderate pace in the conversation in ways that are appropriate to the situation.

The following are examples in the words of the participants to help bring each of these characteristics to life.

Creating and Sustaining a Safe, Receptive Conversational Space and Context

A safe, receptive conversational space is one where nonthreatening, nonjudgmental, and accepting attitudes prevail without a fear of embarrassment or recrimination. People are consistently treated with respect and acceptance, and offered verbal and nonverbal acknowledgment by their peers and people in leadership positions, such as faculty or managers. A spirit of openness to hear differences is associated with a sense of increased opportunities for learning. One participant described this kind of space as a "non-threatening environment . . . a feeling that you can offer your opinion and you are not going to get penalized for it in any way, shape or form. And the feeling within the group that we don't know the answer, so let's throw some ideas out . . . and come up with an answer. There is no right or wrong . . . no predetermined answer."

Feeling safe, nonjudgmental acceptance in relationships seemed to help people to speak and listen better. This feeling of acceptance was expressed by someone who began to "think about trust. Kind of unconditional friendship . . . taking a person for who they really are . . . understanding where the other person is coming from and not judging. And understanding their point of view and who they are."

This capacity to accept differences without necessarily agreeing increased for a person who said that a group discussion with others "clarified my own stance. I did not necessarily agree with what others were saying, but what I found at the end of the discussion was where do I stand, or where do they stand. And I tried to put myself in the shoes of the other person and tried to look at people in their perspective. . . . Now I understand why people would have this train of thought." The value of not feeling afraid was described this way: "Fear is one of the obstacles . . . it just came to my mind that whenever I don't have any fear, I can give myself totally to a particular thing that I am doing."

There were many comments from people who talked about the implications for their learning when they did not feel safe. One person talked about a lack of acceptance and openness, saying the conversation is inhibited "when some people become sort of belligerent or militant. . . . Whenever a conversation would turn that way, whenever it seems you are forced to defend a particular position . . . I noticed that the conversation would stop. . . . The person would be pushed against the wall . . . when you force them to buy your ideas."

The role of leaders, facilitators, or faculty members emerged as an important influence on whether group members were able to take risks and openly share opinions. One participant expressed concern about the behavior of a faculty member:

> *I think one of the faculty people has a way of handling the group by interjecting with sarcasm. . . . One of the evenings in which I thought there was really good conversation . . . one of the members of the group really took a position . . . and was teased by one of the faculty members. I think that person probably has been to only one or two sessions since . . . [and] has said very little when [he has] been back.*

Teasing and sarcasm can undermine feelings of safety and receptivity for conversation. In a more positive example, several participants talked about another faculty person who had a quite different effect on the creation of a receptive space for conversation. For example, when asked if he or she noticed anything in the conversational context that contributed to good conversations, one person said, "Yes, I think [the faculty member]'s characteristic of not dominating or lecturing. . . . I forget almost that [the faculty member] is sitting there. . . . The fact that [he is] able to do that or allow that to happen, I think that is good and allows for good conversation. . . . There is I think more constraint in . . . the other classes."

In this example, the group members are recognizing their shared resources for peer learning without having to depend on an external expert figure such as a member of the faculty. Another person sees this same process of the group becoming a self-organizing system. He or she described how this same faculty person's approach played such a positive role in creating a receptive space that the group was able to grow in ways they did not anticipate: "I am finally beginning to understand the strength of [the faculty member] as a teacher. . . . There is a great deal of grace in [her/his] awkwardness. And that is creating space where we can go into directions, go into areas that we may not have otherwise."

Listening Reflectively to Give Voice to Others, Especially Those Who Seem Different

A precursor to learning from diverse perspectives is including people who bring different, often nontraditional perspectives into conversations. Physical presence is not enough. Even when diverse others are included in the group, moments of silence and reflective listening are often needed to enable these people's voices to be heard. The artistry of bringing diverse voices fully into conversations means delicately holding the extremes of speaking and listening in carefully crafted receptive spaces. When both the active and receptive dynamics in conversation are in rhythmic symmetry with each other, the quality of the conversation is enhanced. This interplay seems to underlie the experience of one person, who said, "When you are speaking, you speak with the other person as a consideration in mind. . . . And listening, you have to listen to hear what is said, rather than having a preformed opinion which does not allow change." Listening to hear and speaking with consideration for the other embodies the interplay of speaking and listening, of action and reflection.

Another element of this rhythmic symmetry involves the reframing of the idea of space. When silence does not seem like an empty space that needs to be filled quickly, it can become a welcoming invitation to infrequently heard, often silent voices. The value of this space for silence was described when a participant was asked what helped him or her listen: "A brief moment of silence. . . . I either speak or listen to someone and think . . . and then respond. It is a give and take. You can't take at the same time and give at the same time. It is almost the same motion. . . . The flow is very important to me in conversing with anyone, either in a group or . . . one-to-one."

Some people are uncomfortable with silence. Talking about the value of silence and how it can be like a fertilizer for a richer kind of conversation can help people move beyond the initial discomfort, as described by one person: "I am becoming more comfortable with silence. I am not totally comfortable yet, but I use it as an insightful period. It is a period for reflection."

Another example of reflection and use of silence was described by someone talking about a conversation on the telephone. In the conversation, he or she was helping another person make a decision. During the first part of the conversation he or she thought the decision was clear and had been made, and then after listening more and speaking less, "about halfway through the conversation, we started together re-evaluating that. . . . I was brought around to say well wait a minute, let me back off a little bit. Let's re-evaluate whether or not we made the correct decision." There was a newfound willingness in this individual to slow down, reflect, and reconsider. The willingness grew out of this person's previous and ongoing efforts to listen more carefully and to speak in response to the other person rather than just speaking out of his or her own immediate thoughts and feelings.

Recognizing Differences and Conflict as Resources for Learning

The way people talk about differences and engage in conflict can vary dramatically and have a distinct effect upon the conversational space. Yet it is important to consider whether people allow differences to surface at all. When people begin to explore differences in conversations, can they continue to talk through their differences in spite of difficult and challenging issues they may have to face?

An increasing capacity to be open to those differences was described by one person: "I am just beginning to understand that [he or she has] different needs and [has] clearly been through a lot more than I have . . . so I am willing to accept that and I am becoming more receptive to that." The group's interactions and readings for a seminar contributed to someone else's observation that "I have learned that it is important to try to understand differences on their own terms and not to bring too much judgment to it initially. . . . It is worth trying to understand how cultures arrive at such very different ways of dealing with the same situation and factoring that into how I understand the person."

At the core of creating an environment in which it is safe enough to talk about differences is building relationships of trust with an appreciation for people's differences. A research participant who articulated this need said, "It is only after we have made a sort of strong relationship with a person, that we can tell the person that we disagree or agree . . . without fear of breaking that bond." Spending time together and having experiences and conversations together make it easier to let differences come to the surface.

Giving and receiving feedback can be an especially delicate kind of difference to talk about. To increase the likelihood that feedback can be heard and considered, the intentions that motivate it and the way it is expressed are both critical. One participant shared a conversation where he or she had received feedback that was difficult to hear, but said that it was given in a way that made it possible to hear:

[He] just very directly told me. . . . But there was a quality in the way [he or she] gave me that feedback that was very easy for me to listen to. I did not feel attacked, devalued, dismissed, made a problem of . . . so although the feedback and the information . . . was upsetting . . . I was able to hear it. . . . [He or she was] so direct and so non-judgmental . . . there was no good or bad attached to anything.

When the space was not receptive and the energy in the conversation was "suppressed," one person described how the conversation was hindered and led to "misunderstanding [that was] not healthy and not helping people to understand each other and to open up."

Too often difficult topics are talked about in ways that impede people from being able to listen and learn from the conversation. One person said, "There is something in [him or her] that needed to try to change me, needed to try to persuade me, and be something that I did not want to be instead of just hearing me and just acknowledging that [he or she] heard me." This inability to listen and acknowledge the legitimacy of differences interferes with people being able to continue the conversation in ways that contribute to learning.

Recognizing and Valuing Both the Cognitive and the Emotional Dimensions of Learning

People in the study reported that when they drew upon both their cognitive *and* emotional resources simultaneously they were better able to hear and learn from each other's differences. Recognizing the interdependence of these two aspects of learning involves considering the feelings of others while also analyzing the rationales they offer. It means not choosing one part of this dialectic as the way to learn. Yet concern was expressed by some people that too much emotionality would interfere in the conversation, especially around sensitive issues in the workplace. For example, one person said,

I . . . was trying to intellectualize my emotional reactions in part because I was afraid of . . . what might happen if the emotions started getting played around with. I was afraid I would get out of control because . . . it is a sensitive issue. And my gut feeling was that several other people were doing the same thing. . . . I think people were trying to talk about them in a detached way . . . to bring them to light without actually being overwhelmed by them.

Someone else expressed a similar idea, saying, "In a conversation there is some kind of fear of people going lower than [the] cognitive level and touch really the heart of their problem, what that means to you. Sometimes it happens, but not often. . . . Because I think going below, means revealing yourself more. Revealing your mind is not as hard as revealing your heart."

On the other hand, another person talked about how the conversation he or she was describing had resulted in him or her thinking about how critical the inclusion of both the cognitive and the emotional dimensions are in his or her consulting work:

It helped me think more about . . . the importance of relating on an affective level, before you can understand on a cognitive level. . . . One thing that definitely became even more clear for me . . . [was] the impossibility of understanding each other at the cognitive level, without working also on how we are working as a group and relating.

Making a Concentrated Effort to Simultaneously Attend to All of These Characteristics While Maintaining a Moderate Pace in the Conversation in Ways That Are Appropriate to the Situation

Receptive conversational spaces do not just happen. When they do occur, sustaining them after strong differences are discovered creates challenges. Sometimes people avoid talking about the issues. Sometimes people react and argue about them and may say things that interfere with feeling safe enough to talk openly in the future. Sometimes people make an effort to stay in conversation, without avoiding or reacting, in ways that open new paths for learning. The following accounts reported by several people in the study offer insights into how such a receptive space can be created and sustained through a collaborative effort.

Several people actually described the space as one that was "between" the people talking, as in this comment: "I was able to actually put stuff out in between us. And it was not my construction of you, or your construction of me, but that we did something together, that we made some meaning together as opposed to hanging our own on the other." This kind of learning is similar to the fusion of horizons that Gadamer (1994) describes, where what people create collectively is something that no one of them could have created alone.

Such interaction and learning usually requires intentional effort, such as in the difficult conversation about race, when someone said, "We searched and really delved deeply to make sure that when we were hearing people, we really heard what they were saying. . . . We tried to speak in ways that allowed other people to hear us [because there was a] desire for a better understanding among us."

When these characteristics began to emerge in conversation, people began to learn from their differences, such as in this person's experience: "I continued to push them, and they continued to push me. I got a sense of where they were coming from. . . . It became clear to me. . . . I learned some things that changed my mind on some things based on the conversation that we had." Another person described this same kind of interaction, saying, "It was not an easy conversation. It was not a pleasant one, but I do think it was a good one . . . because I learned . . . [and] could see the possibility that they were the way they were for reasons other than what I had thought."

The pace of the conversation also has an impact on how people are able to juggle complex interpersonal interactions. Among the participants, highly divergent preferences for conversational energy level were expressed. While some people both spoke and processed conversational interactions rapidly, others needed more time to listen and absorb what was being said. Thus, there is a need for people in conversations to pay attention to and respect people's naturally differing paces. One person verbalized the effect of the energy level on the quality of the conversation:

> *Some of the conversations where you really learn about the other person or about the topic is when it is more of a medium range energy level. The higher the energy level gets, the more it tends to be just your own personal . . . stuff that I am just slinging out there. . . . I get too involved in the conversation to really be a good listener. . . . The really low energy conversations tend to just not produce any reactions whatsoever and the conversation dies.*

Especially when there were feelings associated with tension, fear, or pain, such as around controversial issues, if the conversation was too fast paced people described a narrowing or shrinking of the conversational space. When this happened people tended to be less likely to bring up differences, or to react to them in ways that jeopardized their feelings of safety.

As people were more able to stay in conversation with each other to learn from their mutual differences, they often became more aware of the impact of their behavior on others, as expressed in these comments:

> *I will be more aware, what I do in answering and not spontaneously spring up and saying, "that is not true" . . . but also to show others . . . what I appreciate . . . [and] to show that I understand what the other person . . . feels. . . . The most important thing is . . . understanding the impact of what this kind of spontaneous reaction can have . . . especially when there is an atmosphere with a lot of tension.*

In another conversation the safety that was created in the context enabled the exploration of differences, demonstrating again the interdependence of the findings. This person began to see that their perceptions were only a small slice of the possibilities leading to new learning, saying, "I . . . became aware of how complicated . . . how complex a particular topic is . . . can be looked on from several angles. . . . After the conversation, because I heard some other perspectives, I began also to widen my horizons . . . perhaps . . . there is another way of looking at this."

Literature Related to Differences and Safety

The work of Jean Baker Miller (1986) emphasizes differences as assets. She says, "Growth requires engagement with difference and with people embodying that difference" (p. 13). She proposes that because historically differences have been associated with deficiencies emanating from the dominant–subordinate tradition that defines the subordinate as "less than," people shrink away from the unfamiliar.

These differences can come from what Cynthia Garcia Coll (1992) describes as "cultural mistrust or the lack of trust experienced by members of minority groups toward members of a dominant group" (p. 6). Because previous experiences and the sense of trust among participants in a conversation is greatly varied, people enter conversations with highly incongruent expectations around openness and privacy, hopes and apprehensions, comfort and guardedness, and informality and formality, leading to conflicts that need to be anticipated.

Without intentionally creating spaces safe enough for risk taking and where differences are expressed respectfully, self-esteem is valued, and common ground is built, differences usually will not be expressed at all or will be expressed in ways that lead to alienation and rejection (Baker, 2001; Edmondson, 1996, 1999). Amy Edmondson's (1999) work on psychological safety in organizational work teams is informative here. She describes psychological safety within a team as "a shared belief that the team is safe for interpersonal risk taking. . . . A sense of confidence that the team will not embarrass, reject, or punish someone for speaking up . . . stems from mutual respect and trust among team members" (p. 354).

Edmondson (1999) is exploring conditions that promote learning in naturally occurring organizational work groups, suggesting that team psychological safety affects learning behavior and performance. In other words, creating psychological safety where people do not fear being punished involves both the manner of speaking and the capacity for listening. It seems to be a needed precursor for many conversations that might otherwise feel too risky. These ideas are central to work in multicultural teams and are developed more fully in Chapter 8.

Related to these ideas, the most definitive overall finding of this research is the salience of people feeling safe enough to be able to listen to, stay engaged with, and learn from differences in conversations. Second, the interdependence among these five contextual characteristics is unmistakable.

IMPLICATIONS: HOW TO PREPARE, CREATE, AND SUPPORT RECEPTIVE CONVERSATIONAL SPACES

To prepare for, create, and sustain receptive conversational spaces over time is a delicate and multidimensional process. How are these spaces created? Words and ideas like "opening," "encouraging," "allowing," "reflecting," "inviting," and "finding humility" were used frequently by the research participants. Yet they may invoke images that seem too ambiguous and indefinite. Unfortunately, there is not a clear road map or one recipe for creating a receptive conversational space.

Instead, I invite you to open your imagination to conjure up possibilities of new ways to create more receptivity. Try to stretch your vision and the boundaries of the situations that are alive and relevant for you as you are reading. While this section attempts to begin integrating research, literature, and years of experience, the intention is to be provocative, not to be definitive or to provide a map or a destination. Instead, the intention is to offer some highlights rather than to comprehensively explore the complexity of this process. On this journey to creating more receptive conversational spaces, we will explore five general areas:

1. Open the space.
2. Encourage partnership and imagination.
3. Allow for differences.
4. Take time for reflection.
5. A space for humility.

On this brief journey you may want to think of your role as a consultant, manager, facilitator, teacher, or leader in a group, team, or class, whichever of these settings seems most relevant. Or you may envision yourself as a member of a particular group. If you see yourself in a leadership position, this approach calls for a redefinition of traditional leadership behavior. As learning environments become more collaborative, these approaches may be of help to build receptive and trusting relationships that catalyze learning in conversations regardless of the position or status of the participants.

Open the Space

An ethos of openness permeates receptive conversational spaces. Investing time and energy up front or early on is a major part of the effort. Try to prevent negative expectations and try to influence initial interactions to make the later work much easier. Help people come into the group with a focus on inquiry and curiosity to minimize monologues and advocacy that can silence others. Demonstrate respect and curiosity through the choice of words and behavior and by reframing the comments of others, when needed, to help create more open, safer, and more receptive environments.

This process may take longer than anticipated. It may feel like a loss of control. Try to be patient, but not passive. Try to embrace the unknown and celebrate the outcomes that may be surprising. Try to involve people in letting go of expectations for predictable behavior and predictable outcomes. By actively engaging each person in shaping their work together, people can more easily develop shared responsibility to discover unexpected and exciting new directions. Part of opening and supporting the space is the anticipation of new ways of working together in a spirit of inclusion, respect, and collaboration to get people excited about the value of their participation.

The series of conversations with Gloria and Nick and their larger group is an excellent example of a self-organizing process taking on a life of its own. Their conversation began in a space that was safe and receptive enough for people to talk openly over time about controversial issues. Their one-on-one conversation took off and continued to grow beyond the awareness of most of the other members of the group or the faculty. By opening and supporting the initial space and trusting the self-organizing nature of a natural hunger for learning, better understanding became easier. The process of opening the space and letting go can over time even begin to feel more like a relief than fear.

Encourage Partnership and Imagination

Receptivity to differences, safety for risk taking, and creative self-organizing groups typically do not thrive in hierarchical, authority-dominated systems. These elements of conversational learning call for a redefinition of traditional leadership behavior where prople can develop more peerlike, consultative partnerships and more collaborative relationships that can feed positively on each other.

Yet these more collaborative behaviors of partnering call for shifting away from the role of the leader, consultant, teacher, or facilitator as the expert. Embedded within the model of the leader as expert is a deficit of trust in the capacity of each person to make valuable, imaginative contributions. Embedded within the assumption of the model of leader as someone who controls the process is the assumption that people's interactions can be controlled. Embedded in the expectation that learning is a one-way monologue is the lack of awareness that each person has a legitimate and necessary part of the truth and part of the "story." It assumes only one truth, one side to the story, and a fixed unchanging reality, all assumptions that do not have legitimacy in a multicultural, knowledge-intensive world.

To encourage partnerships and imagination, each person can strive to become a trusted partner who does not punish, embarrass, try to control, or try to get even. Trusted partners can, however, make observations and tell his or her own truths to heighten awareness of the group process and group behavior. How the observations are made can tip the delicate balance of the partnership. Not considering how words may feel to others can damage trust while too much attention can make people so self-conscious that their energy and spontaneity are suppressed. To maintain that delicate balance, often in a playful way or in a gentle way, I often use myself as an example of one who has a part of the picture, some of the answers, and needs the assistance of my peers. By my example, I can therefore invite others to become better partners in the process.

Allow for Differences

Conformity without the open expression of differences can breed mediocrity. Closing off the expression of differences can create a picture or story of reality that is incomplete. Yet allowing for differences involves proactive acceptance of differences. It involves honoring and respecting each person and his or her wide range of differences as they emerge, sometimes unexpectedly. It involves using differences as resources for learning. It entails developing and sustaining relationships with people who may seem at times extraordinarily unfamiliar.

Generally, the kinds of differences people think of include race, ethnicity, gender, sexual orientation, nationality, and religion. Differences in values, opinions, ideas, and priorities are also resources. Another form that deserves mention is the recognition of diverse learning styles and preferences for different ways of communicating among group members. Thus, offering only one medium, such as face-to-face meetings, inevitably gives preference and more exposure to people who are especially effective in that kind of setting. Therefore, an essential element of allowing for differences is to offer as many different mediums for expression as possible. For example, providing opportunities for people to work in settings such as large groups, small groups, pairs, alone, synchronous and asynchronous virtual environments, and shared writing in hard copy and in online environments allows for contributions of differing kinds of talent that may otherwise be hidden group resources.

Actively seeking differences also requires being respectful in the face of controversy and differing opinions. It means striving to be curious when the instinctual inclination may be to try to convince others and advocate for a sense of rightness. And it means modeling behavior that is congruent with words.

Take Time for Reflection

Reflection takes time, reflection requires energy, and reflection can look to others like wasting time and energy. Yet without time and space for reflection it is difficult if not impossible to learn from experience. In reflective conversations it can be easier to consider unfamiliar differences and new possibilities than in fast-paced competitive conversations, because it allows for more pondering and consideration. While the more fast-paced approach is appropriate for some purposes, it is often not one that is most conducive to creating receptive conversational space.

The pace of the conversation can be influenced by talking and acting, by not filling up the space with words, and by accepting there may need to be times of silence. Allow time for slow responses when asking for comments or asking questions. Try not to use evaluative comments or questions that make others reluctant to speak for fear of embarrassment or criticism. Encourage reflection by not only inviting it verbally but also by allowing for the space of silence to give people time to be bold enough and wise enough for thoughtful disagreement. Encourage reflective disagreement by responding to differences of opinion by trying not to be defensive, by asking for elaboration, and by not rushing on to another topic or person.

Reflection can be private (within a person) or public (in pairs, small groups, or whole groups). For example, private reflection can take many forms, such as journaling, thoughtful consideration, asynchronous online environments, or writing. Group or small-group conversations can become sources for public reflection. Either one can be encouraged through open-ended questions, experiential activities, brainstorming, and reflection upon past experiences, for example. Reflection can be unstructured and spontaneous by guiding the conversation to explore serendipitous comments, and it can be structured by time and activities planned with the group. In any case, without reflection, potential for learning from previous experiences can be decreased, leading to the repetition of previous unproductive patterns. "Wasting time" on important issues may lead to powerful discoveries.

A Space for Humility

A space for learning in conversation is a space for humility. Going beyond the shift from leader as expert to create receptive spaces means finding the humility to partner with very different people and to often not get recognition. It extends beyond a cognitive knowledge of and intellectual interaction with the person or the group that seems different. Humility fundamentally alters the role of behaving like an expert and calls for listening to learn in collaboration with others. It fundamentally alters how differences are encountered when learning and trustworthy relationships are a priority.

The strength of humility involves examining our own stereotypical, embedded assumptions about other groups, races, sexual orientations, religions, nationalities, and so on. Without a commitment to that work, it is difficult if not impossible to be fully present from a deeply centered place to avoid the dangers that are often associated with unprofessional behavior. This work involves recognizing institutionalized "isms" and our own role in perpetuating those "isms." It calls for competence in surfacing differences to challenge the status quo. For example, those of us who are white need to grapple personally with the white privileges that we usually take for granted to have credibility and viability in creating safe receptive conversations among diverse people (McIntosh, 2001; Shipler, 1997; Takaki, 1993).

The strength of humility and devotion to learning allows us to take in differences with enough self-assuredness to consider and chew on their possible meanings. Helping others create and support receptive conversational spaces also builds professional partnerships to create safe space, to support respectful behavior, and to guide the learning process.

CONCLUSIONS

Underlying the very essence of creating receptive conversational spaces for conversation learning is recognizing its ever-evolving nature and respecting that each person brings to a situation a part of the truth, a legitimate part of the story. This chapter has hopefully offered insight into the nature of this kind of space, with illustrations and examples as well as some practical guidance.

The approach is not easy, because it is often subtle and runs counter to many of the norms in Western cultures. It calls for creativity and imagination to bring both passion and discipline to conversations with respect and curiosity. It calls for careful preparation of receptive conversational space, participants, and the self. It calls for congruent behavior and deliberate initiatives to encourage receptivity to listen to and learn from unfamiliar differences. It calls for thoughtful recognition that everyone brings needed talent, expertise, and experiences to the group for learning. It calls for careful adaptation to the cultural and contextual setting.

Contextual characteristics that can support conversational learning include creating and sustaining a safe, receptive conversational space where listening reflectively to give voice to diverse others is a priority. The proactive recognition of differences and conflict as resources for learning in conjunction with the rhythmic inclusion of both the cognitive and emotional dimensions of learning is fundamental. Without making a concentrated effort to simultaneously attend to all of these characteristics while maintaining a moderate pace in the conversation in ways that are appropriate to each unique context, conversational learning becomes more challenging.

Safe, receptive environments do not just happen; trust is not a given. "People develop trust not by forming affective attitudes or beliefs about persons, but people . . . develop trust through interaction, conversation, in relationships with one another" (Flores & Solomon, 1997, p. 58). One of the challenges is to model trustworthiness and to help others share responsibility for creating trust and psychological safety where people can be vulnerable enough to question, take risks, ask for help, talk about and make mistakes, and listen to learn.

To be receptive to others, both the fears that people perceive from within and judgments that get projected onto others need to be suspended, at least briefly. This chapter has explored the process of creating a space that helps people let go of those fears and judgments.

REFERENCES

Baker, A. C. (2001). *The role of context in connecting individual and organizational learning*. Manuscript submitted for publication.

Coll, C. G. (1992). *Cultural diversity: Implications for theory and practice*. Work in Process series no. 59. Wellesley, MA: Stone Center.

Edmondson, A. (1996). Learning from mistakes is easier said than done: Group and organizational influences on the detection and correction of human error. *Journal of Applied Behavioral Science, 32*, 5–28.

Edmondson, A. (1999). Psychological safety and learning behavior in work teams. *Administrative Science Quarterly, 44*, 350–383.

Flores, F. L., & Solomon, R. C. (1997). Rethinking trust. *Business and Professional Ethics Journal, 16* (1–3), 47–76.

Gadamer, H. G. (1994). *Truth and method* (2d rev. ed.). New York: Crossroad.

Hall, E. T. (1969). *The hidden dimension*. Garden City, NY: Anchor Books.

Kanter, R. M. (1986). *The tale of "O": On being different in an organization*. New York: Harper and Row.

Mathews, D. (1995). Building a strong civil society and a healthy public life. In Marjorie E. Loyacano (Ed.), *Connections* (pp. 27–28). Dayton, OH: Kettering Foundation.

McIntosh, P. (2001). White privilege and male privilege: A personal account of coming to see correspondences through work in women's studies. In M. L. Andersen & P. H. Collins (Eds.), *Race, class, and gender: An anthology* (4th rev. ed.). Belmont, CA: Wadsworth/Thomson Learning.

Miller, J. B. (1986). *Toward a new psychology of women*. Boston: Beacon Press.
Muldoon, B. (1996). *The heart of conflict*. New York: G. P. Putnam's Sons.
Palmer, P. (1990). Good teaching: A matter of living the mystery. *Change, 22* (1), 11–16.
Shipler, D. K. (1997). *A country of strangers: Blacks and whites in America*. New York: Alfred A. Knopf.
Takaki, R. (1993). *A different mirror: A history of multicultural America*. Boston: Little, Brown.

7

Streams of Meaning-Making in Conversation

Patricia J. Jensen and David A. Kolb

> Much—even most—meaning in conversation does not reside in the words spoken at all, but is filled in by the person listening. Each of us decides whether we think others are speaking in the spirit of differing status or symmetrical connection. The likelihood that individuals will tend to interpret someone else's words as one or the other depends more on the hearer's own focus, concerns, and habits than on the spirit in which the words were intended.
>
> Deborah Tannen (1990)

In *The Mechanism of Mind* (1969), Edward de Bono offers a simple metaphor for the way in which the brain becomes mind. He likens the memory surface of the mind to ordinary table jelly made up in a shallow pan. Incoming information is hot water spooned onto the surface in different places. Over time the surface is sculpted and contoured into a unique form depending upon where the hot water has been placed and the ways in which the surface interacts with the water. As patterns develop, depressions and channels are formed, some depressions deeper than others, if more hot water has been placed on or near that particular spot.

One of the implications of the interaction between incoming information and the patterns that exist on the memory surface is that the memory surface may be presented with large amounts of information coming from both inside and outside the individual. In this situation, "when a large pattern is put on the surface, only a small part of the pattern is retained, the rest is simply ignored. . . . A limited attention span means that much is left out, but it also means that something is actually selected. . . . Selection means preference and choice instead of total acceptance of all that is offered" (de Bono, 1969, pp. 88–89). It is this selection process that explains how "the same situation may appear completely different to two different people because the contours of their memory surfaces are such that the selected attention area or sequence of attention areas is quite different" (p. 90).

Viewing the contours of the memory surface as a sculpted record of all that has happened on the surface, these previously developed patterns are the ones used to process incoming information. Thus, the past organizes the present. For de Bono (1969), "Learning is a matter of putting a new pattern on the surface or changing an established one" (p. 274).

We appreciate this graphic image of the process of an individual's "brain becoming mind" in part because it so clearly conveys one vivid image of the complex process of the development of cognitive styles, illustrates individual differences, and simply defines learning. During the past several years we have studied the ways that individuals, with unique memory surfaces, enter into and make sense of their experiences in conversation.

This chapter describes how learning styles get expressed in conversation. We describe ways individuals engage in and make sense of their experience in conversations. We call these patterns of learning streams of meaning-making. These streams of meaning-making were inductively generated from transcripts of in-depth interviews conducted with participants in a Ph.D. seminar based on conversational learning. The development of this seminar is explained in depth in Chapter 5. These interviews asked participants to identify a conversation that stood out for them in the seminar and then analyze it through a structured interview protocol. This study was one part of a larger study on conversation (Baker, 1995; Jensen, 1995). The methodology was based on a naturalistic paradigm (Lincoln & Guba, 1989) to develop a grounded description of ways in which the participants made meaning and learned in and through conversation. Using a dialectic approach, the interview data were compared and contrasted with scholarly literature on learning, meaning-making, and conversation to identify patterns of meaning-making grounded in the experience of the participants. The streams of meaning-making thus identified were then related to participants' scores on the Learning Style Inventory (LSI) (Kolb, 1999).

The five streams are outlined in the following list. In the pages that follow, these five distinctive approaches to conversational learning are outlined, briefly defined, and illustrated with excerpts from transcribed interviews.

Stream I	Stream II	Stream III	Stream IV	Stream V
Resonating and Reflecting	*Expressing and Interacting*	*Attending and Appreciating*	*Interacting and Conceptualizing*	*Listening and Analyzing*
Gaining understanding of the meaning of one's own experience and/or others' experiences through resonating and reflecting in and through conversation.	Gaining understanding about one's own perspectives and feelings through expressing them, and feeling and hearing others resonate and respond during the course of conversation.	Gaining understanding of specific others and self through attending to and appreciating the interaction in the "here and now" of the conversation.	Gaining understanding of one's own and others' perspectives and feelings through interacting in conversation with others who hold and express different perspectives.	Gaining understanding of others' perspectives and feelings about the topic of conversation through listening and interpreting others' interaction in the conversation.
Hearing Others	*Heard by Others*	*Aware of Others*	*Differ with Others*	*Compare with Others*

STREAM I: RESONATING AND REFLECTING

In this stream an individual could be seen as connecting with other(s) in the conversation by hearing them express their experience. Participants described how hearing another and resonating with their experience was the impetus for their own individual reflection, gaining insight and acting on this new meaning.

This led them to reflect on the meaning that such experiences had for themselves and/or the other(s) in their daily lives. Their reflection led them to understand the experience in new ways and to take action for themselves based upon their new understanding. For example,

> I distinctly remember I was criticizing the conversation. . . . I kept saying [to myself] these people are . . . avoiding things that really matter. . . . They are only concerned with concepts and theories. . . . [A colleague] mentioned about sharing experience . . . through the conversation a healing process would take place. And this brought me back to . . . an experience that I had gone through myself, which reflected the same process. . . . And his conversation kind of triggered it all.

Resonating with others' experience served as an impetus for reflection. In the following excerpt a participant recounts how she explored the meaning of differences in her reflection during one particular seminar: "How difficult it is to embrace things. Embrace and not fight. . . . It is not that everybody has to agree with everyone. But how difficult it is to widen our range of acceptance . . . just embrace the difference. . . . The way I embrace the differences, is listening to the different voices."

The ways people acted on their reflection and insight ranged from taking initiative to have more private one-to-one conversation to giving expression in more public contexts. For example, "[This conversation] just convinced me more about the need for conversation. . . . I am [now] taking more effort to converse with people, to be open and honest . . . about my person." One way to characterize Stream I is when one is listening to and resonating with others. One way to characterize Stream II is when one feels listened to and feels others resonating with them.

STREAM II: EXPRESSING AND INTERACTING

In this pattern of meaning-making individuals expressed their views on particular ideas and used the interaction with their colleagues to clarify their own perspectives and feelings about the ideas discussed. Through their participation in the conversation they felt a stronger connection to and acceptance by their colleagues. While initially communicating their feelings and perspectives brought them into the conversation, it was through their interaction with their colleagues that they further clarified their own understanding, of themselves and of others: "I was very much affirmed . . . from the inside . . . and was somewhat reaffirmed by some people who shared."

One participant talked about a subject he was "very passionate" about and described this conversation as assisting both him and his colleagues to clarify their perspectives on the topic. For him, "The dialogue did help bring clarity to my own mind in terms of what I was saying":

> I am having this constant struggle of communicating . . . [and] trying to have an appreciation for other people's points of view. And listening well and incorporate those in my value system or my thoughts. . . . The conversation helped me in that regard. . . . It seemed to me that that conversation helped me in terms of my perception of that group, it made it more cohesive for me. . . . I felt a little bit more a part of the group, having initiated that discussion. . . . I think they did get to know me a little bit better. . . . It was my feeling more comfortable with the group that was meaningful to me.

STREAM III: ATTENDING AND APPRECIATING

Here individuals engaged in the conversation primarily by attending to specific others, by listening to and being aware of these individuals' feelings, perspectives, and interactions. This attention led them to positively value this experience and deepened their appreciation for and understanding of others and of themselves: "For me it meant there was a lot of energy around this subject. . . . I thought we had fun from the . . . beginning. . . . We talked about something real that has meaning to me. . . . I think more than usual we talked to each other, and listened better than we have."

Throughout her interview, one participant gave consistently focused descriptions of many other group members. These descriptions were noteworthy in the ways that she portrayed the feelings and perspectives of each individual. As part of this description process, she said,

> They both were much more vocal today than they had been. . . . I think . . . they felt more aligned . . . with the readings . . . than they had in a while . . . when [one colleague] first started talking about intuition. I immediately drew some understanding of the difference between [that colleague] and I in terms of our thinking by the way that he was talking about intuition.

In the discussion on intuition, this same participant described a number of insights gained through this conversation for herself and about her colleagues. Her clarity about naming her experience combined with her respect for the experience of others, even when the experiences differed, is what stands out.

In Stream III participants experienced others in the conversations in ways that they were aware of both correspondences and contrasts. In Stream IV students listened to and interacted with one another in ways in which their differences were central.

STREAM IV: INTERACTING AND CONCEPTUALIZING

In this stream individuals with strong views on a topic interacted with others who held and expressed different perspectives. Through their interaction and through conceptualizing these varied viewpoints they gained insight into their own and others' perspectives and experience. One described how his clear focus on the conversation assisted him to hear different perspectives: "But then . . . during the conversation, I saw that others were talking in a different way, looking at it from another perspective. All the readings that we had, and I thought for myself, there is another way. That my way is not the only way. . . . These are different ways. . . . They are as valid as my own perception."

In this pattern of meaning-making participants recalled that hearing others who held different perspectives was as important as describing their perspectives to others: "I also became aware of how complicated, or how complex a particular topic is . . . that it can be looked on from several angles. . . . I was listening . . . to what other people were saying . . . [and] asking myself . . . what . . . do [others] say and what is my stance, and can I identify with what they think or what they feel. Try to become more open."

Some participants described new awareness of their own perspectives on the conversation topic as being action oriented. Others described their insights regarding themselves and their own as well as others' perspectives:

> Well, I became more aware of the fact that different people perceive situations differently. . . . I also became more aware of my own personal tendency to feel defensive when I am talking about a viewpoint that affects me personally . . . [and] the fact that different people have different reactions to the same situation. . . . It made me aware of . . . a different point of view. . . . I think it might have made me more accepting of different viewpoints, of the topic that we were discussing. But I do not think that it really changed my basic viewpoint.

In Stream IV participants considered varied perspectives in interaction with one another. One way to characterize Stream IV is as having a listener and a speaker. In Stream V participants described conversations where they listened to their colleagues, privately analyzed the interactions and came to new understandings through their participation. One way to characterize Stream V is as a listener.

STREAM V: LISTENING AND ANALYZING

Here individuals listened to others discuss their perspectives and feelings on a particular topic. This led them to distinguish between perspectives and to clarify the perspectives they heard their colleagues discuss, leading them to compare these perspectives with their own. As they listened throughout the conversation they evaluated the overall conversational flow and drew conclusions regarding their own and others' perspectives on the topic discussed.

Listening to their colleagues engaged in various conversations, they heard and interpreted distinctive perspectives and were aware of what they were thinking and feeling about the overall flow of the conversation. For example,

> It was being taken the wrong way. . . . I would like to help clarify what he is saying, but he is saying it. And I am not understanding his thoughts well enough to jump in and clarify his thoughts for the class, so I did not. . . . As it began to unfold, I was very uncomfortable, because I saw it coming as an open hostility. . . . The way it developed . . . there was no hostility shown, just some very strong opinions. And they were very respectful of each other in offering those opinions.

Another participant described a majority of the participants in this discussion in ways that reflected her understanding of their varied perspectives and learning preferences. She characterized her own stance in relationship to the topic of conversation as follows: "I was probably more receptive . . . trying to follow the conversation. . . . It had to do with the fact that we were . . . talking about something that you could kind of hold on to."

In their interviews the participants named their experiences in these respective conversations in ways that reflected new insights gained or clarifications about their own and other's perspectives: "I like to discuss just from the different perspectives that people bring to the conversation. . . . It did not change my point of view. . . . The conversation with [him] did help me to understand his perspective." Another viewed diverse perspectives as being related to different learning styles and life experiences: "I definitely can sense that we have different learning styles in the class. . . . People are at different points in their lives. . . . The way we see the world is tinged . . . by where we are and who we are, and our experiences. . . . I became more aware of different people's opinions, values, about where they are in terms of their points in their lives."

RELATING MEANING-MAKING IN CONVERSATION TO INDIVIDUAL LEARNING STYLE

Once we established streams of meaning-making in the conversations we overlaid each participant's profile on the Learning Style Inventory (Kolb, 1999) on the meaning-making streams in order to determine if relationships existed between individual learning preferences and patterns of interpreting meaning in and through conversation. In order to clearly present this process, a brief overview of the LSI is provided.

The LSI is a self-descriptive instrument used to assess an individual's preferred learning style. For each of twelve items in the questionnaire respondents are asked to rank four descriptors, from "most like you" to "least like you," that describe the ways they learn. One descriptor in each of the twelve items relates to one of the four learning orientations as explained in Chapter 4: concrete experience, reflective observation, abstract conceptualization, and active experimentation. This self-scoring instrument provides two primary profiles. The first profile represents how much an individual relies on each of the four different learning processes. The second profile represents their preferred dominant learning style: diverging, assimilating, converging, or accommodating.

The participants in this study completed the LSI as part of their preparation for the group session that focused on individuality. LSI scores distributed almost equally across learning-style preferences (N = 16;

accommodating, 4; diverging, 5; assimilating, 4; and converging, 3). We then compared each participant's learning-style preference with the stream of meaning-making they used in conversation to determine if they relied on their preferred modes of grasping and transforming experience in the conversations they selected as the focus for their interviews (see Figure 7.1).

Each of the participants with a preference for concrete experience connected in conversation through one of the three ways outlined in Streams I, II, and III. These ways of connecting are characterized by being attentive to one's own and others' feelings, experiences, and/or perspectives as communicated in the conversation. Each of the participants with a preference for abstract conceptualization connected in the conversation through one of the two ways outlined in Streams IV and V. Both of these ways of connecting are characterized by hearing others talk about their perspectives on the topic of conversation. We then overlaid each participant's preferred learning style on the streams of meaning-making they used.

Learning Styles Emphasizing Concrete Experience

In the divergent learning style participants with moderate to high concrete orientations were described as interpreting their experience in conversation through Stream I (resonating and reflecting). A divergent learning style emphasizes concrete experience and reflective observation. Two of these participants explained that they were having a hard time relating to a conversation that was going on until they heard someone express his or her individual experience. For these listeners, hearing and resonating with something that was meaningful to them brought them into the conversation for a moment. This connection led them to reflect on the meaning of what they resonated with, for them and/or for the other. In a sense, their participation in this conversation reflects a "pure type" divergent learning style. They each acted on their new insights by expressing them to another or to the group and each described ways they took action for themselves as a result of their new understanding.

Reflective of a divergent learning style, these participants connected with the feelings and experience of another and reflected on meaning. The new understanding or insights they described also reflected a concrete feeling orientation. For example, "Figuring out how I could make myself feel better, adjust better, feel connected, feel community, feel at home . . . I was able to take action for myself. It has really changed how I feel about being here."

Another participant with a divergent learning style in Stream I described how she identified with the "anxiety level" and the way that

Figure 7.1
The Relationship between Learning Style and Stream for Each Participant

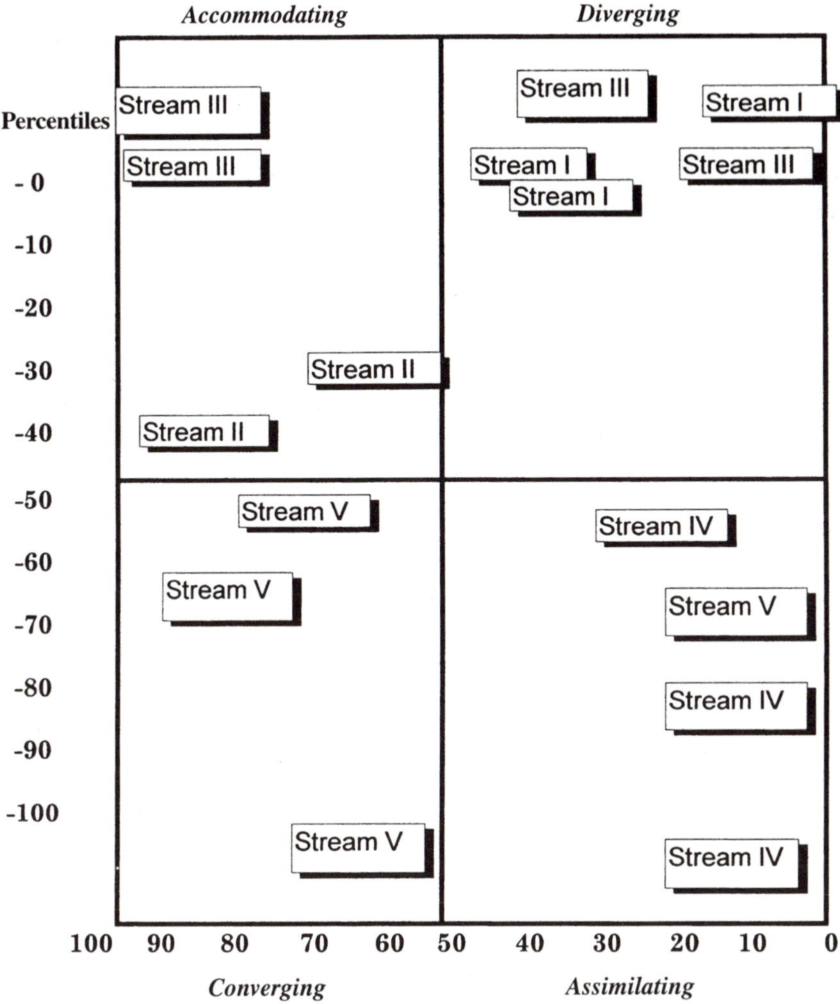

people "struggled with this issue" in the conversation. She further described how a "fruitful discussion does not always have to be based on a cognitive aspect." When asked in the interview if she had a sense of what this conversation might have meant for others, her insight reflected an awareness of the feelings of others.

An accommodative learning style emphasizes concrete experience with an action orientation. Here, participants with concrete orientations closer to the abstract dimension were described as interpreting their experience in conversation through Stream II (expressing and interacting). These participants described how through expressing their perspectives and feelings about the conversation, and feeling others resonate with and interact with them, they came to new understandings about themselves, the topic of conversation, and others. Perhaps reflective of the risk taking that typifies an accommodative learning style, they described how the interactions about feelings and perspectives helped them to become involved in a new way. The insights or understanding they described also reflected both affective and interactive dimensions. For example, "I felt a little bit more a part of the group, having initiated that discussion. . . . I think they did get to know me a little bit better. . . . My being able to share something with other people who were able to appreciate and resonate with what was meaningful to me. . . . I was able to feel . . . a member of the group."

Crossing both accommodative and divergent learning styles, participants with high concrete experience orientations were described as interpreting their experience in conversation through Stream III (attending and appreciating). Participants with an accommodative style described how they connected in the conversation by attending to specific others and appreciating their interaction. Reflective of an accommodative learning style, they described new insights gained in terms that indicated how they could act in the future or reflected a deeper understanding of how their feeling and thinking were connected. For example,

> I think I was thinking what I was feeling. And at times, I was feeling what I was thinking. If I think I am afraid, then I feel afraid. . . . And I took the book to begin reading, thinking I should be nervous, so I was nervous. As I read the book, though, I think my thought process took a back seat and my feeling process . . . there was a conversion that took place. And, as I allowed myself to think out of my emotions. Then I have a different experience. And I think that is the type of transformation that took place.

Learning Styles Emphasizing Abstract Conceptualization

An assimilative learning style emphasizes abstract conceptualization and reflection. In the assimilative learning style participants were described as interpreting their experience through Stream IV (interacting and conceptualizing). Each of the participants described how they connected in the conversation by hearing their colleagues express perspectives on the discussion topic that was different from their own. The differences between what they were hearing and what they thought and felt seemed to be an impetus for them to engage in the conversation by stating their individual perspectives.

Reflective of an assimilative learning style, each of these students described their learning in conceptual terms. For example, "As I said, we have had this discussion over and over again. And I am waiting to hear . . . this is what we should, or can [do]. . . . What I think we need is a national think day. And it will be a day where we think before we do anything. And more or less, saying that thinking will give you control."

Another participant with an assimilative learning style and the participants with convergent learning styles were described as interpreting their experience in conversation through Stream V (listening and analyzing). A convergent learning style emphasizes abstract conceptualization with an active orientation. The participant with the assimilative learning style connected in the conversation by listening to his colleague's perspectives on the topic of conversation. He identified distinctions between his own perspectives and those he heard expressed. Each of the participants with convergent styles connected in the conversation by listening to their colleagues' perspectives and feelings on the topic of conversation, and through reflection made distinctions between their own perspectives and those they heard their group members express.

Demonstrating the often controlled expression of emotion that characterizes this learning style, two participants described how they considered making a verbal contribution to the conversation and for varied reasons did not. For example,

> I was starting to get angry with what I was seeing as sort of the manufactured stupidity of some of those remarks. . . . I was remembering that [in] one of the pieces that we read . . . there were some statistics on [the topic being discussed]. . . . I was about to get on my soap box, and sort of trumpet them. . . . Fortunately, [a colleague] just spoke up very quietly and [quoted statistics on the topic]. . . . I am really glad she did that. Because it was a much nicer way of doing that, instead of me getting up . . . and kind of beating people over the head with facts.

Another participant with a convergent learning style described how at varied points in the conversation she was thinking about other matters that directly involved her, rather than attending to the conversation.

IMPLICATIONS FOR APPLICATION

Most teachers, trainers, group facilitators, and others who work with adults in formal or informal learning settings know from experience that individuals take in, interpret, and act on experience and ideas in different ways. Over 900 studies exploring learning styles in diverse professional and academic areas support the viability of learning styles, as described through the Learning Style Inventory (Kolb, Boyatzis, & Mainemelis, 2000). As suggested through this research, learning styles are a contributing factor to an individual's way of making-meaning in conversation. As such, they are one way to think about pluralism in the learning environment. In light of these differences, diverse approaches to participating in meaning-making in conversation need to be systematically considered.

The participants' experience in this study reflected that verbal interaction in conversation is not the only dependable source of information to gauge if people are involved in learning in ways that are meaningful to them. Listening can be active when it is a form of focused attention to others in the "here and now," or a springboard to personal reflection. Listening can also be a "safe" alternative when speaking is perceived as being disruptive to the conversational focus.

Conversations that highlight ideas and concepts can provide an entry point for learners with an abstract orientation. Conversations in which participants share their experience and feelings provide an entry point for learners with a concrete orientation. A key implication of this finding is that it is important to create multiple entry points into conversation for participants with varied learning preferences. Individuals may be silent because they are not connecting to what is being talked about.

Drawing upon de Bono's (1969) concept of the mind's memory surface, one way to conceptualize learning is to develop new patterns and ways of approaching the learning experience. By developing new patterns of apprehending and transforming experience, learners can increase their repertoire of knowledge acquisition. Thus, for more concrete-oriented learners this could include developing more abstract and cognitive patterns. Learners who are used to hands-on activities might seek out ways to enhance their understanding of specific discipline concepts and the ability to more systematically analyze a situation or problem. For more abstract-oriented learners this could include developing ways to perceive through their senses and attend to their feelings in diverse situations. One critical area where expanding the learning-style repertoire can happen is in conversation. As learners focus on the meaning of learning differences within a group, they find access to other ways of approaching the learning task as peers model other perspectives within the group interaction. This conversation offers learners the challenges and opportunities they need to stretch their learning styles and embrace in a more holistic way the cycle of learning.

Parker Palmer (1990) defines the academy as "a place of true pluralism where many stories can be told and heard in concert" (p. 13), where students not only come to know the ways in which the world works but also come to know their inner selves. Traditionally, education has been equated with mastery of content and has reflected a more abstract, cognitive, and outside-in orientation to learning. If one accepts our experiential perspective of a dual-knowledge theory of learning, then learning styles become a central educational consideration for creating learning environments.

As designers of learning contexts, educators can reconceptualize learning as a process of assisting learners to more fully enter into the ongoing conversation that is a discipline in ways that respect the strengths of distinctive approaches to meaning-making and learning. Ways of knowing by appreciation as well as knowing through criticism can be experienced in the classroom. Conversation can be a way for participants to connect with each other as well as each other's ideas and can serve as the stimulus for solitary or more communal reflection. Reading material can be used in ways that evoke an aesthetic stance and can be integrated with reading that evokes a more efferent stance. Good conversation in learning environments can assist learners to listen to their own inner voices and to each other.

REFERENCES

Baker, A. C. (1995). Bridging differences and learning through conversation. *Dissertation Abstracts International 56* (10A), 00298. (University Microfilms No. 9604634).

de Bono, E. (1969). *The mechanism of mind.* New York: Simon and Schuster.

Jensen, P. J. (1995). Streams of meaning-making in conversation. *Dissertation Abstracts International 56* (10A), 00235. (University Microfilms No. 9604658).

Kolb, D. A. (1999). *Learning styles inventory.* Boston: TRG Hay/McBer.

Kolb, D. A., Boyatzis, R. E., & Mainemelis, C. (2000). Experiential learning theory: Previous research and new directions. In R. J. Sternberg & L. Zhang (Eds.), *Perspectives on thinking, learning and cognitive styles* (pp. 227–247). Mahwah, NJ: Lawrence Erlbaum and Associates.

Lincoln, Y., & Guba, E. (1989). *Fourth generation evaluation.* Newbury Park, CA: Sage.

Palmer, P. (1990). Good teaching: A matter of living the mystery. *Change, 22,* 11–16.

Tannen, D. (1990). *You just don't understand: Women and men in conversation.* New York: William Morrow.

8

Conversational Learning in Multicultural Teams

Esther D. Wyss-Flamm

> Exposure to difference encourages breadth of attention, a way of seeing that underlies ways of continuing to learn as an adult, for every opening to culture [difference] is a rehearsal for dealing constructively with inner or outer change.
>
> M. C. Bateson (1994)

Imagine a team hard at work on a series of projects with a firm deadline. The projects call upon the team to analyze, write up, and present findings, using analytical as well as people-oriented communication skills. The organizational context is competitive, emphasizing efficiency and timeliness; at the same time, team members are urged to attend to their own and each other's skill development and learning. The team is composed of eight members, each contributing a particular expertise. The membership of the team represents five national and subnational cultural identities. English is a second or third language for half of the members; some of them have no prior experience working with people from another culture.

As team members interact, it is apparent that conversational styles vary enormously. Some voices are loud, while others are quiet. Some are outspoken, others keep more to themselves. Some are quick, spontaneous, and witty, others more deliberate and thoughtful. Some appear comfortable with business jargon, others use basic language to communicate. Some seem intent on work, others are chatty and social. Some are big-picture oriented, others more concerned with the details. Some are expressive using gestures, others are more restrained in their body language. Some focus on the logical flow of conversation, others seem to give more voice to their gut feelings. With such a wide array of conversational styles, how does the conversational space develop in this team? How does conversational learning emerge over the course of their time together?

Our organizations are no longer limited by national boundaries: Multicultural teams such as the one described are found in all sectors and occupations. We find ourselves interacting daily with people from differing cultural contexts; more and more we are being asked to perform tasks as members of interdependent teams. Because conversational styles are marked by cultural upbringing—just think about the different ways in which you have observed people speak up and listen—this means an active encounter with a wider array of conversational styles than ever before. Yet our awareness of and knowledge about what happens conversationally in such teams are extremely limited.

From the onset of a multicultural team's first meeting, members are immersed in the flow of conversation, a flow shaped both by the organizational environment and the team members themselves. Inevitably, members "bump up" against each other's styles in conversation, and encounter difference in ways of expressing a point of view, of signaling dissent, of indicating enthusiasm, of taking on a task, or even of communicating humor. Often members are conscious that difference is intriguing and could become a source of powerful insight. However, just as often such difference is considered strange, annoying, and distracting from getting the task done.

This observation highlights a recurring theme in conversational learning: the importance of psychological safety in the conversational space that supports such learning. At the team level, psychological safety is defined as those aspects of the conversational space that promote trust, mutual respect, and well-being among the members, thereby increasing the sense of security in togetherness. In every team, conversational norms develop on issues, including team members' ability to respect each other's differences, unique skills, and talents, to accept mistakes, to bring up the tougher issues confronting the group, to take risks and ask each other for help, and to fully support each other's efforts. Edmonson's (1999) research indicates that these aspects of team psychological safety result in a team environment that can be qualified as high or low in safety, providing an important context for learning taking place among its members.

This chapter seeks to develop the sensitivity of those of us concerned with the learning processes of highly multicultural teams and offers a framework and model for how conversational learning appears in performance-oriented multicultural teams. While honoring the basic premise that conversational learning is organic, contextual, and spontaneous, it is nevertheless helpful to identify elements of such learning to strengthen our awareness about these processes in teams whose functioning and well-being are so relevant to our working lives today.

After a brief mention of the research context, the following pages describe the conversational dynamics of two contrasting multicultural teams working in identical task and organizational environments. The conversational space of one of the teams is characterized as high in psychological safety, while that of the other team is low. Narrative descriptions of the two teams are presented side by side to form a context for subsequently identifying and illustrating a model of conversational learning. Ultimately, this chapter suggests a dynamic interrelationship among psychological safety, conversational space, and the conversational learning that takes place among team members.

MULTICULTURAL-TEAM RESEARCH AND CONVERSATIONAL LEARNING

There is growing concern among those active in multicultural research about the continued difficulties in understanding cultural difference at the team level (Boyacigiller & Adler, 1991; Watson, Kumar, & Michaelson, 1993): Culture is emerging as a far more complex construct than anticipated (Salk & Brannen, 2000). The choice of explicitly situating the research in multicultural teams resides in the desire to better understand an issue of great practical concern as well as to add to recent promising inroads of inquiry into this topic area (Cohen & Bailey, 1997; Kirkman & Shapiro, 1997; Tannen, 1998; Earley & Mosakowski, 2000). Research on such teams that breaks new ground means departing from the mainstream in two significant ways.

First, the approach here explicitly does not use or assume culture-based behavioral generalizations to guide the research. This is not to deny that there is empirical evidence relating to culturally identified behavioral characteristics (e.g., the frequently cited works of Hofstede, 1984; Hampden-Turner & Trompenaars, 1993). However, there is an issue of scale in a team where there are at most two or three members of similar cultural origin. To assume that these particular individuals will embody the behavioral characteristics associated with their culture becomes problematic and may create a false reality around such differences. Anthropologists Kluckhohn and Murray (1949, p. 35), among the first to offer a framework for culture-based differences, warn against seeing individuals exclusively from the viewpoint of such generalizations.

Second, the purpose of this research is not to isolate cultural difference from other differences that abound in a team, but to see it as contributing to the wealth of conversational learning taking place. Locating research in the experience of highly multicultural teams ensures the presence of a wide variety of conversational styles in addition to the many differences (e.g., gender, age, social status, learning style, professional experience) already present in culturally more homogeneous teams. Life at the team level is complex and multifaceted, and both context and interactions among differences need to be fully acknowledged (Luft, 1984; Gillette & McCollom, 1990). Engagement among culturally diverse individuals encompasses different kinds of meaning-making, linguistic, verbal, nonverbal, and sociocultural dimensions in conversation. For team members, this means additional uncertainty in the conversational space that may well contribute to a decreased sense of the psychological safety of the team.

Some additional definitions help distinguish this research from other such efforts discussed in this volume. A primary distinction is the difference between groups and teams. "Group" is the broader, more encompassing term for a community of associated individuals, while a "team" is a group of organizationally affiliated individuals united in performing interdependently on a specific task or series of tasks (Hackman, 1990). A "multicultural team" is defined as a team where more than half of the members identify with different cultural traditions, be this at the national (e.g., Japanese, Russian, Kenyan) or subnational (e.g., African American, Asian American) level (Adler, 1997).

RESEARCH CONTEXT AND DESIGN

Unlike many of the group environments discussed in this volume, the team context in this chapter is highly task and performance oriented. The explicit learning orientation of the two teams discussed in these pages was less apparent than their focus on efficiency and conformity to the ways of corporate business. The two teams described were composed of MBA students on the site of a prominent private U.S. management school located in the Midwest. In an effort to simulate actual workplace conditions, a cornerstone strategy of the two-year MBA curriculum of this business school was to organize entering students into multicultural teams.

All students were assigned to eight-person teams established during their first few hours of contact. Instructors assigned each student to a team with the criterion of maximizing diversity in each group in terms of group-member learning style (based on the Learning Style Inventory, Kolb, 1999), gender, nationality, and ethnicity. Members of these teams worked intensively together throughout the first academic year on a variety of group assignments; contact during the second academic year was more sporadic and voluntary. The team tasks included outdoor activities, group-development activities, financial-analysis cases, an organizational-analysis project, case competitions, and exit-assessment activities.

From a conversational learning perspective the environment of this business school, as that of any other organization, is seen as the discourse within which the teams are embedded. Although the goal of a school is clearly related to learning in the form of managerial skills development, it is in many ways a discourse environment that resembles the private sector in terms of its competitive orientation. Just as the business school environment actively fosters and endorses a certain type of discourse, it plays a powerful role in restricting or submerging others. For example, discourse conducive to networking with the local business community is actively promoted. Discourse that is critical of the motivation of corporate interests or of globalization is less apparent. Clearly, the organizational environment plays an enormous role in influencing the space for conversational learning taking place within the teams.

The two teams discussed in this chapter were chosen for the contrast and similarity in their conversational dynamics. Each team included energetic, ambitious people from diverse backgrounds. Members' concern with getting good grades, being efficiency oriented, and meeting deadlines were also similar. The organizational context and the projects they discussed were identical.

Yet the conversational dynamics evolved differently in the two teams. These differences are evident in their scores on Edmonson's (1999) measure of psychological safety: Team 1 scored high (among the top third of all peer groups) on this measure, while Team 2 scored low (among the bottom third of all peer groups). The team members' own accounts of how they worked together provide a more detailed portrait of contrast and similarity between the two teams. They offer real-life examples of interactions to enrich our understanding of the psychological safety in the conversational space of these multicultural teams. In fact, the stark difference in ratings on psychological safety is often blurred by the quality of their accounts. Taken together, the conversational dynamics of the two teams form a foundation upon which the model for conversational learning is constructed.[1]

A TALE OF TWO TEAMS

Described in the next pages—much of it in their own words in passages excerpted from the validated team narratives—are the two teams as they worked on their projects. Each team was composed of eight members, briefly presented in the following list:

Team 1

Bob: He took on the name Bob to help Americans remember him. Bob has spent his life in China (Beijing) and came to the United States only a few weeks prior to the MBA program. In his mid-thirties, Bob is married; his wife and child stayed behind in China. Bob's conversational style is outspoken, considered a bit rough by his peers.

Brad: He describes himself as a U.S. male Midwesterner: "I have ethnic background, but I'm not strongly tied to it at all—I guess I would call myself white." Single and in his late twenties, Brad is observant, articulate, and quick to respond, to criticize, or to lend a helping hand.

Chandra: "I identify strongly with my country, India. And it's probably become more strong after coming here." Coming from a background of privilege—he refers to his father's prominent role in the publishing industry—Chandra's style is serious, intelligent, hard working, polite, and very insistent when he believes he is right.

Dan: When asked about his cultural background, Dan responds with his vocational identity: "I'm a typical American manager: very focused, driven." Dan is of French and German descent, spent eight years in the U.S. Marine Corps, and talks in a very measured, self-assured manner.

Heetaek: "One hundred percent" Korean, Heetaek is reserved, quiet. He has a passion for numbers and a background in the Korean banking industry prior to coming to the program. He talks about difficulties in expressing himself in English. To an outsider, his English is remarkably clear and expressive.

Team 2

Akira: "I am typical Japanese. Some Japanese are Americanized. I have never been abroad, so I am typical." In fact, Akira says he had never been outside Tokyo in Japan either. Akira's conversational style is marked by attentive listening, frequent clarifying questions and consultations with the dictionary, as well as a good sense of humor.

Anil: Born to Indian parents in Troy, New York, Nil (his nickname) says, "I consider myself half Indian, half American, trying to blend both cultures." Recently married to a young woman from India, Nil says he sees life in the United States in new ways through her eyes. In conversation, Nil comes across as easygoing and articulate.

Gerald: "The English would say I'm Australian; the Australians would say I'm English." He is aware of his penchant for straightforward talk, to "call a spade a spade." A trained accountant, student of Buddhism, and voluminous speaker, Gerald is in his late forties, by far the oldest team member.

Rich: "I am, like, American. That's it." When asked for more detail, he explains he was raised Jewish in the South, something that he says he avoids talking about. His conversational style during the interview was withdrawn, with occasional glimpses of a dry sense of humor.

Sachiko: Having spent the first twenty-seven years of her life in Tokyo, she feels fully Japanese. Three years earlier, Sachiko married an American serviceman and came to the United States, her first exposure to another culture. Her English is clear, slow, articulate; her engagement in conversation is quiet and reflective.

Jane: Like Bob, Jane took on an American name to facilitate communication with Americans. Originally from southern China, Jane worked in the export industry prior to coming to the United States for study. Jane comes across as quick, observant, and a very fast learner. She speaks English very rapidly, adopting numerous slang expressions.

Mike: "I'm basically an American guy. . . . There's no other place I want to live without baseball, football, basketball and golf." Mike adds that "of course I'm African American and have an affinity to our issues, and our culture." In his thirties, married, and a recent father, Mike voices his point of view strongly and convincingly when asked.

Steve: "I'm a mutt!" with a Jewish Russian mother and a Catholic Italian father: "I sort of go with American culture, whatever that is. . . . I'm at the cusp of Generations X and Y, so I'm one of those people that are vague as to where they belong in life." Steve is the youngest team member; he comes across smart, trendy, ambitious, smooth.

Susie G.: With a father from Pakistan and a mother from the Philippines, Susie says, "When people ask, I say I'm an Asian Pacific Islander." At the same time, she was born and raised in central Ohio. Susie speaks rapidly, spontaneously, and uses many colloquialisms. At twenty-three, she is the youngest team member.

Susi S.: "I am completely bi-cultural." Susi has spent half her life in the United States and half in Korea, has worked and grown up in both cultures, has helped teach Koreans about the United States and vice versa. She sometimes finds herself questioning where she fits in. Recently married, Susi comes across as very assertive and articulate about her likes and dislikes.

Thor-Jacob: "Jake," as he asks to be called, has always lived in Norway, where he worked in international business. "Also, I am married to an African who is half Chinese." Jake comes across as intense, intellectual, analytical, and concerned with being precise in his speaking, which, as English is not his native tongue, tends to frustrate him.

Looking at this list, it is evident that the teams were highly multicultural. But they were also diverse in other important ways: Age, gender, expertise, professional background, education, and social status were relevant to their conversational dynamics. It soon becomes apparent that these differences played a considerable role in how team members organized themselves and how they learned.

Both teams chose to focus on the same two events for their individual interviews. The first event was a complex financial-analysis project that included the preparation of spreadsheets and a report. The assignment spanned the time period of the team's first two weeks together. The second event began a few weeks later and was an organizational-analysis project that also included a report and culminated in a group presentation of their findings. This assignment took place over a two-month period.

While both teams completed their assignments, each at first faced difficulty in harnessing the skills of the various group members and in getting the first project done efficiently. Both teams used this experience to help organize for subsequent teamwork. The differences in the conversational space between Team 1 and Team 2 became more pronounced as they worked through the second assignment.

Financial-Analysis Project

The assignment asked the team to analyze and issue recommendations on a new product line for a fast-food company. According to instructions, each team first split into half teams before consolidating their ideas into a large report. At this starting point in both teams, members with more difficulty speaking English played an important role:

Team 1: The work in half teams gave those of us with the lowest level of English speaking ability more of an opportunity to contribute: Heetaek did so by preparing a model spreadsheet, and Bob became very absorbed in applying the textbook guidelines to the case.

Team 2: During our half-team meetings, Akira, who was typically very quiet, prepared a spreadsheet because he really wanted to contribute after feeling like he had not participated much on previous group work.

As the full teams met to consolidate their work, a marked difference emerged between those members who knew about finance and those who were less proficient with numbers. Eventually, these differences led team members to take on more focused roles of either fine-tuning calculations or writing and editing the report. In each team there were some communication difficulties across language barriers and differences in expertise:

Team 1: Our full team meeting went on for six hours, much longer than anticipated. The three of us who had a limited background in finance tended to sit back, sometimes frustrated, sometimes joking about our feeling helpless to contribute. Eventually, Dan and Brad began working on the report that was to accompany the case; Steve tried to look busy on an unrelated task, designing a team logo. . . . Three of us became engaged in a lengthy debate about assumptions underlying the calculations, each using a different tone of voice to affirm our opinion and convince others. Chandra was firm and reserved; Mike soft-spoken but intent; and Bob excited and comparatively loud.

Of the remaining two group members, Jane worked on the computer comparing the two versions of the spreadsheet, pointing out inconsistencies, while Heetaek, who had the most expertise in finance among all of us, remained silent. He did not feel confident presenting his ideas and persuading us in

English. On several occasions Chandra left the room to consult on the project with colleagues from India. Those of us not involved in the debate were increasingly concerned about the time and the group's apparent inefficiency. Jane finally chose the version of the two spreadsheets she was more familiar with to submit with the final report.

Team 2: We met as a full group prepared to push it to its conclusion in a few hours. Many discussions, rewrites and more than 16 hours later, we handed in the report just before the deadline. We used Akira's spreadsheet as a starting point for our discussion. Some of us asked him to clarify certain formulas. Because he had difficulties in speaking in English, Sachiko, also from Japan, sometimes translated for him. Akira found it easier to express his thinking to those of us who were also accustomed to working with numbers and spreadsheets. This dynamic seemed to contribute to our split into working groups, where half of us fine-tuned the spreadsheet while the rest worked on writing the report.

Meanwhile, Jake became increasingly concerned about a particular aspect of the assignment: he felt our group work would be incomplete if we didn't address this concern. Because he too had difficulty explaining higher concepts of finance in English, he stopped us several times, trying to get our attention by waving his arms and even jumping on the table. He excitedly explained his thinking with diagrams on the whiteboard. Some of us recognized the potential added value of what he was saying, but we generally felt that Jake was blocking the group's progress, bringing us back to ground that we had already covered.

By 10:00 p.m., Susie G., who was less drawn to the details of the analysis, ordered pizza and the conversation became more relaxed and social as we ate. Half of us, Stephen, Susie G., Susi S., and Sachiko left shortly thereafter, feeling we had contributed what we could. Of the four of us remaining, Jake seemed to gain energy and continued to ask the other group members to redo certain sections and calculations. As they continued into the night, Gerald became angry at what he saw as Jake's inconsiderate persistence. Jake apologized repeatedly, but maintained that he didn't know how else he could have acted.

Members of both teams remembered debriefing the experience of working together on this project even though this was not an explicit aspect of the assignment. The feedback was spontaneous, informal, and not focused on any particular member in Team 1; it was more formal, calculated, and personalized in Team 2. For both teams this assignment made members more aware of their work patterns and helped them recognize each other's skills and expertise, knowledge that they used to organize themselves for subsequent projects:

Team 1: After handing in our report, some of us wondered about the effect the lengthy debate among three of us had on the group. Those of us who had not been well prepared for this case wondered whether we had let the group down. At a subsequent meeting on another assignment, we discussed the unevenness of contributions, with each of us pledging to come more fully prepared. Personal feelings of dissatisfaction with each other were kept inside, and discussions that explored the evolving relationships among us were avoided in favor of maintaining momentum. Most of us agreed not to "screw up our progress by getting personal."

Team 2: The following day, Gerald called for a team debrief of this experience, which took place in the afternoon. Most of us agreed it was a useful reflection on our process. However, Jake felt the debrief was intended to single him out to be sanctioned for his intrusive working style. Indeed, Gerald had hoped this debrief would be a mechanism to ensure Jake got the message not to overwhelm the group with his presence again.

Organization Analysis Project

Here each team was asked to act as a management consulting group to assess the functioning of an organization in the local area over a period of two months. Differences between the two teams became more apparent in the way they organized and maintained the goal of efficient, rapid, deadline-driven performance required by the business school environment. Team 1 spent significant time together, organizing two group visits to their client organization, pairing up, verbally debriefing and discussing their findings, and spending some social time together. Team 2, having endured continuous power and interpersonal struggles among four of its members, kept full group meetings and contact with their local client organization to a minimum and organized this project so that group members could contribute with individualized tasks requiring no direct interaction with each other.

Team 1: One of the highlights was when we met at the site of the organization that we were studying, occupying one of their conference rooms which had been set aside for us through Brad's prior connections to the firm. Being on site brought a sense of excitement and a commitment to professional behavior in us all: for Bob, Heetaek, Jane, and Chandra, it was our first real contact with an American business organization. We spent the first hour coordinating a plan to gather information through the firm's intranet and through interviews, for which we broke into pairs, usually combining a native English-speaker with a less fluent speaker. After several hours of collecting information, each pair in turn debriefed the group as a whole, with other group members incorporating comments into the report. Four of us, Brad, Bob, Chandra, and Heetaek, topped off the day with a lunch together, which we recalled as particularly enjoyable.

Team 2: The project was particularly memorable for some of us, and not so for others. This difference seemed to depend on our level of involvement in the project. Susi S., who had contacts with businesses in the local area, was instrumental in identifying and gaining access to the organization we analyzed. During one meeting to organize the project, she had taken the initiative to assign interviews to the non-Americans among us, including Jake, who expressed anger at not having been consulted previously about whom he would interview.

We had all agreed that those of us who preferred to work on a parallel finance case (e.g., Akira, Stephen, and Jake) could limit our involvement in this project to conducting one telephone interview, writing up the interview notes, and e-mailing them in to Susie G. Both Sachiko and Akira conducted their interviews by e-mail. Susie G. then cut and pasted the interviews, added an introduction, and, together with Susi S. consolidated the report.

Contrast in the conversational dynamics of the two teams was also apparent in their description of the presentation of their findings for this project. Again, there was more of a social yet at the same time nonconfrontational component in Team 1, while interpersonal animosity and "just getting the job done" seemed the norm in Team 2:

Team 1: We were concerned with coming up with a concept for the final presentation that was novel and imaginative. We all met at Steve's place to work on this, watched some comedies on video, drank some beer, and ate pizza. Then, armed with computers, we engaged in an extensive brainstorming session, as we pushed each other for better, more interesting, more humorous ideas to incorporate into the presentation. As the presentation concept became clearer, ideas just fell into place, and a number of us were aware of the synergy in the room, of ideas appearing spontaneously as we built on each other's contributions. Although the Americans took the lead on being playful with ideas, in the end we were all able to incorporate our unique styles and some of our cultural characteristics into our roles. As we were planning, humor often needed some explanation for Bob, Jane, and Heetaek.

We made sure to rehearse several times before the actual presentation. Again, the Americans among us were more comfortable with the presentation format, and coached the rest of us who felt more nervous and were concerned with memorizing our lines. Even right before the presentation, we continued to add on humorous ideas and props to enhance our roles. According to everyone, the presentation went beautifully, and we always considered it a real high point for the team.

Team 2: At the end of the semester, we had to present our project findings. Nil who always enjoyed working with computers, helped locate clipart to prepare the slides. The two Susis called for a full group meeting, where they handed one or two slides to each of us to present, and we briefly brainstormed to come up with a concept that would guide the overall presentation. We developed an outline of what would be included in the presentation, practiced once, and found ways to shorten it by removing some content from group members' slides who appeared slowest in presenting in English. A few of us practiced individually before the presentation. Because he'd been sick, Jake didn't see the slides until minutes before, and Gerald arrived late which forced us to postpone the presentation for half an hour. This caused frustration especially for the two Susis, adding fuel to an already raging fire among us concerning punctuality and apparent lackadaisical attitudes.

Tracing the conversational dynamics of two multicultural teams during two memorable events underlines how no two teams will strike out on the same path, even if context and task are identical. Team 1 developed a conversational space that was psychologically safe. This does not mean that the members of this team did not encounter initial communication difficulties, but they were able to transcend these to develop a strong performance mode, where individual skills were respected and utilized, risks could be taken, and they were able to ask each other for help. Members commented on valuing the cultural differences within the team. The psychological safety of the conversational space in Team 2 was low: Members seemed unable to move beyond intense interpersonal conflict that manifested itself from the beginning. Ultimately, despite open communication about their differences, team members were annoyed at each other's work styles, unwilling to lend a helping hand, and found ways to organize themselves to minimize contact with one another.

EMERGING MODEL OF CONVERSATIONAL LEARNING

Our exploration of these two teams continues with an overview of three recurring assumptions about conversational learning. A first assumption is the assertion that human beings are fundamentally a learning species guided by curiosity (Freire, 1994), by our very human ability to wonder. Our orientation toward learning is enacted through conversation that exposes both our individuality and our ability to construct joint understanding with others.

This assumption is closely tied to a second one. The encounter of difference in conversation is essential for learning: It is bumping up against difference that can stimulate our curiosity, our drive to learn, and our ability to actively try to enter each other's experiences and perspectives. Indeed, from this perspective learning without the experience of difference is an impossibility: Difference exposes us to an awareness of what we know and don't know, without which we cannot imagine alternatives. From this perspective we also recognize that internal personal and external social aspects of the experience of difference interact with one another to further learning in the conversational flow.

A third assumption concerns psychological safety and relates to how we experience and explore difference. A team with conversational space where we feel safe, trusted, respected, and able to make mistakes is one where we are more able to connect and enter each other's experiences. Conversely, a team with conversational space where we are uncomfortable asking for help, don't feel valued, or are unable to express our differences is one where we are more prone to becoming self-protective, disengaged, or unwilling to reach across to understand another member's experience. Thus, we would expect the level of psychological safety in the conversational space to set a strong tone for the potential for conversational learning in a team.

These assumptions helped guide the development of a model of conversational learning grounded in the data on the two teams. The analysis continued with the identification of statements by team members that communicated awareness of difference, be it between team members, between the team and other teams or groups, or between concepts that emerged in the content of group work. These passages were loosely grouped, then categorized according to clarity of expression, intensity of tension, and integration of differences as conveyed in the statements.

As the research progressed through the examples across the teams, comparing and contrasting statements, it became possible to refine the statements into phases positioned on the framework depicted in Figure 8.1. An outward-directed spiral depicts both the recursive and discursive flow of conversation within a team. The dotted line indicates how the flow of conversation cycles between internal personal and external social dimensions. The model is rooted in the initial experience of difference and moves through four identifiable phases of how team members learn from difference. At each phase there are certain experiences of difference that become dropouts as there is no further mention of them in the data.

Phase 1: Perceiving Difference

The onset of conversational learning is the individual team member's experience of difference: This is where he or she perceives that there is another point of view present in the team's conversational dynamics that is in some way unlike his or her own. This phase is about noticing or discernment, where the team member mentally separates some aspect of an experience from other aspects surrounding it. As the team member is in conversation with the other team members, there are many such experiences where a seed is planted that is the source of an emergent distinction.

Figure 8.1
Model of Conversational Learning

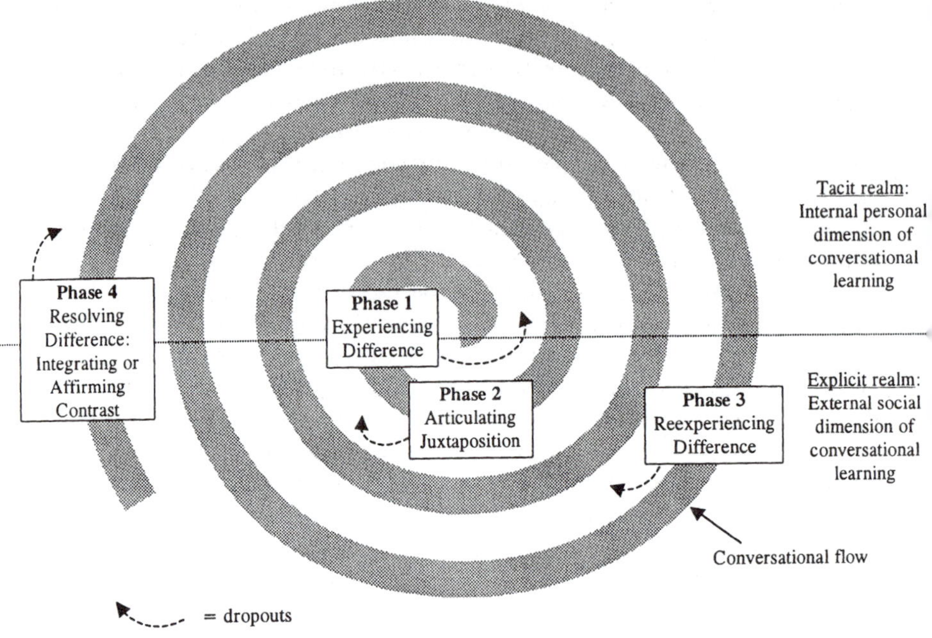

This phase resembles Kolb's (1984) description of what he calls concrete experience: The individual is grappling with the tangible qualities of the immediate experience of the conversation. The grasping of an experience becomes possible through a jolt in the flow that comes with the sensation of difference, where the familiar meets the strange. This awakening touches our deeply personal, mostly unconscious tacit knowledge (Polyani, 1966): Only the individual team member can know when this is happening in conversation. The onset of conversational learning is feeling-based, suggestive, allusive, and often elusive to the outsider.

One gets the sense that at this point the team member becomes more aware of his or her desire to clearly express and put words to a sensation, to relate an idea in conversational terms that make it accessible to others. This desire helps push him or her toward the next phase of conversational learning. At the same time, one also senses a self-monitoring taking place in how voice is given to experience: Even at this early stage of conversational learning, some perceived differences are filtered out for appearing too fleeting or too unimportant, or perhaps for being socially unacceptable for conversation in that team.

The first phase of conversational learning is thus rather difficult to discern in interview data: While it may be quite common, it usually resides in the mind of the individual team member and is not directly articulated. Despite this difficulty, it is possible to identify its occurrence, and the following examples demonstrate the onset of conversational learning in the two teams. Team members talk about feeling "vibes," a sense that they cannot readily put into words that will engage others, especially in teams that place a premium on efficiency and rationality in their process.

One example of this initial phase surfaces feelings about using ethnic humor in the team. Brad ostensibly pokes fun at Bob by using the term "Asian Tiger" to describe his assertive style of interacting in the group. Bob senses an undercurrent, and here we see Bob talk about his reactions to Brad's humor: "It's not a friendly way to say that 'Asian Tiger,' and also I can sense that, you know, sometimes he [Brad] just didn't, he didn't say any derogative words, but you can from his, you know, expressions, or his way to laugh at you, to talk with somebody about you seemed, 'look at that guy,' you know? Those kind of things, you can feel that. Right. You can feel that."

Bob powerfully grounds his statement in language related to his feelings. At the same time, there is a tentative tone to Bob's statement. It is difficult to know whether this is anything more than a temporary feeling of one group member toward another. It is only by Bob coming back to this issue that we can know more about how Bob continued to derive learning from his observation about Brad.

In another example, we see Gerald allude to a distinction that is meaningful to him: "We didn't do an all-nighter to prepare for it [the presentation]. It was much more pleasant, and people were guarded by that point." To the outsider, Gerald's use of the words "more pleasant" and "guarded" seem somewhat incongruous. His words are based on feelings that are not clearly articulated, reflecting a possible nuance in perception, an undercurrent or gut feeling that was triggered by the concrete experience of working in this team.

Phase 2: Articulating Juxtaposition

At the next phase, conversational learning is more clearly articulated and thus more readily identified in the data. The team member has devised a mechanism to more explicitly verbalize his or her experience of difference. The conversational experience that has created an awareness of difference (Phase 1) has gone on to stimulate his or her ability to articulate the different perspectives or points of view in the form of juxtaposition.[2] When alternative ideas or perspectives appear in conversation with the intent to make a point or to emphasize an aspect of an experience, the team member steps out of the descriptive talk and into a more explanatory, clarifying, and connective mode of conversation. This phase is characterized by the act of placing words and concepts onto the felt difference, resulting in the introduction of new ideas into the conversation.

In conversational learning the formulation of juxtaposition can be seen as a deepening of individual meaning-making of larger conversation. It moves the learner across a dialectic from concrete experience to abstract conceptualization (Kolb, 1984), from awareness of difference at a more tacit to a more explicit level (Nonaka, 1994). It takes an individual team member's internal feeling and brings it into circulation through "a social process *between* individuals and not confined *within* an individual" (Nonaka & Takeuchi, 1995, p. 61). At the same time as it connects, juxtaposition remains the unique individual expression of experience.

Examples of juxtapositions in the interview data are rich and abundant for both teams. There is a playful, creative element in these statements that seem to represent a release, a rejoicing at having found concepts to more fully capture the difference evoked by a feeling at Phase 1. These juxtapositions are engaging and evocative for both the speaker and the listener. The act of articulating juxtaposition offers team members a foothold upon which they can temporarily position themselves in a team environment with unfamiliar and sometimes unnerving differences. Team members use juxtapositions to verbalize many types of difference: in task orientation, social interaction, background, analytical approaches, communication styles, humor, time, work ethic, education level, perspectives on leadership, and participation.

In one example, Chandra juxtaposes his engagement with this team with his former group experiences in India:

> We [Indians] become very friendly, and very involved with each other. And, we can be very strong in making sure our point goes across. Keeping in the back of mind that the person whom I'm enforcing my view on is my friend, and he's my countryman. And, so he knows my behavior. . . . [In our team] I could not behave in the same way I would have behaved with an Indian, because I was at that stage not sure if they understand my behavior or not.

Chandra clearly articulates his learning about working in a culturally diverse team by comparing it with experiences working in more homogeneous groups. He identifies his style of forcefully pushing his point of view as entirely typical in the Indian setting, whereas he notes that it may not be understood in the same way when working in this multicultural team. In another example, Rich juxtaposes Jake's energy level with his own: "From what I can recall, Jake seemed to get more energy as the evening wore on and everyone else got more tired. I usually get really tired late and so I have trouble inputting; I have trouble doing much after ten o'clock." In this juxtaposition Rich clearly articulates an important difference in work style he has noticed between himself and his fellow group member. To the extent to which this juxtaposition recurs in the group, this difference can go on to become the source of deeper conversational learning.

Phase 3: Reexperiencing Difference

This third phase is intimately connected with the recursive aspect of conversational learning. Team members, having experienced difference (Phase 1) and articulated it in the form of juxtaposition (Phase 2), sometimes found themselves reexperiencing that difference as significant, trying—with more urgency this time—to articulate it in the team's conversational flow. It is possible to recognize this phase of conversational learning when a particular juxtaposition occurs repeatedly and its verbalization does not seem to alleviate the team member's experience of tension relative to the perceived difference. The team member recognizes that there is something more to this particular juxtaposition than to others residing in the conversational dynamics of the team: It seems to resonate with particular intensity, appear particularly annoying, or continually challenge his or her sense of the way things should be. As the juxtaposition recurs, the perspectives within the juxtaposition are reinforced and become amplified, more powerfully polarized, and dichotomous. While in many ways an extension of Phases 1 and 2, Phase 3 distinguishes itself as a separate phase by the strong element of tension that comes with the reexperience of difference.

In the interview data this phase of conversational learning appears when a juxtaposition makes repeated appearances within and across interviews. Phase 3 also includes the occasional direct statement of need to do something to alleviate the tension felt by a particular team member. This tension reflects team members' desire to push understanding toward some kind of resolution, which propels the team member toward the fourth phase of conversational learning.

Examples of Phase 3 conversational learning typically reflect a preoccupation with aspects of group work that affect group performance. Mark refers to Heetaek's lack of verbal input by juxtaposing Heetaek's English-speaking ability with his quiet personality: "With Heetaek, there was really not anything in the language or anything that we had to overcome, it was just having him open up."

Throughout the data, Mark as well as other members of his team make statements reinforcing the importance of having Heetaek "open up" to the group, speculating about how Heetaek's language ability and personality were affecting this dynamic. Another example of repeated juxtaposition is Anil's laid-back grade orientation and other team members' need for As. Susie G. frames the juxtaposition this way: "Nil, you get a 'C' and he is happy. So there are just different priorities in this team. . . . That's one thing about our group except for Nil is that we all want to be at that 'A'-level before we let people just run with it whichever way they want." Other team members, including Nil, talk about this difference in grade orientation as important to understanding the conversational dynamics of the team. The recurrence of such juxtaposition in Phase 3 builds tension that pushes for some kind of resolution.

Phase 4: Resolving Difference

The fourth phase is about coming to some sort of temporary personal resolution on a particular set of perspectives that first appeared as juxtaposition. This means inventing verbal expression to help release the tension apparent in Phase 3. There are two alternative scenarios, which can be likened to the two sides of a coin, through which this sense of completion is achieved. Phase 4 can be distinguished from the other phases by its attempt to put to rest a certain recurring tension or dilemma that team members have identified in the group. Overall, examples of resolving difference are less frequent in the data than examples of the preceding phases.

Scenario 1: Integrating Difference

There are different traditions of conceptualizing integration of difference. In Western dialectical thinking it represents the synthesis between thesis and antithesis. In the Christian tradition integration is framed as reconciliation after strife. In Eastern terms it is the insight hitherto unseen that springs forth from the interplay of two positions. Integration implies a letting go of one's own firmly held perspective, cultivating one's ability to see a situation through new eyes, and, through a committed, respectful listening stance, opening up and entering other ways of seeing a situation. A team member learns to see the value of joining one perspective with that of the other in an innovative way: "either–or" becomes "both–and." There is no doubt that in today's interconnected world this form of resolving difference plays an increasingly important and vital role.

The examples that occur reflect a sense of connection, a recognition or shift made possible by the experience of difference in the group. In the interview data the team member articulates a new insight or way of looking at the tension derived from the perspectives in the juxtaposition. Dan describes how he is becoming more open to differences by integrating his Marine Corps experience with civilian experience:

> Although now that I'm out, you know, and more in the civilian world, I'm prepared.... I still am driven like, you know, a Marine Corps type manager in that I do expect everyone that's getting a paycheck that works with me to be working just as hard as me. But, I'm much more open to, you know, situations where I might have to, you know, change my philosophy a little bit. And, say, "Okay, now this is a person who I might need to adjust a little bit for."

Dan describes and affirms aspects of his Marine Corps experience that he continues to value, while at the same time he articulates a broadening and acceptance of the different ways in which people work. In a second example, Anil is able to connect with Jake's thinking on a particular task, which he then shares with the other team members:

> So he [Jake] realized, "Okay, let me try [to explain my point] again," and I can't read his mind, but I think he realized, "let me try with Nil." So he said, "Nil, you are trying to understand this?" And I said, "Yeah." I think he could see I was trying to understand. So he explained it one more time, and then what I do is I explained it back to him. And he said, "Yeah, that's right!" And I explained it simpler and easier. So then I knew I got it right, and then I turned to the others and said, "Okay, what he is saying is very important."

This example profoundly underlines how respectful listening, speaking, and repeating are essential aspects to arrive at this scenario of conversational learning: Anil joins Jake's painstaking explanation with his own ideas and is able to bring other group members to a new way of understanding the task. Both examples imply the need for open, expansive, broadly inclusive conversational space to support team members' ability to identify ways to integrate difference.

Scenario 2: Affirming Contrast

While this second scenario is also about arriving at a sense of resolution on a particular tension that first appeared as a juxtaposition, it is a situation where one side of the tension is declared correct while the other is dismissed as flawed or wrong. The "either–or" thinking is maintained and leads to an affirmation of one perspective over another; the conclusion itself reinforces the contrast and the dichotomy in the larger team conversation. The team member decides that one position in the juxtaposition is correct, and maintains that the other is false or flawed in some way. In so doing, he or she often falls back on a prior-held point of view. A team member's stance in this scenario is less exploratory and more closed, restrained, and absolutist than in the first scenario.

Examples from the two teams have a finality in their tone, a sense of separating out one or more persons from the rest of the team or of holding one idea above another. They are based on a difference that has recurred and persisted over time in the team. This first example follows numerous references to differences between Americans and non-Americans made by many of the group members. Bob articulates how team members who are American hold the advantage in terms of language and knowledge of the territory: "They [Americans] are better than us. They should take that leadership. They have experience there. They know the people there. And, you know, it's their task so there's nothing wrong there."

As opposed to articulating ways in which American and non-American team members contributed to the team, which would be a form of integrating difference, Bob's statement separates and affirms the contrast between the group members based on nationality. A second example follows many comments by team members about how Susi S. and Gerald often disagreed. Susi S. talks about the ongoing animosity between herself and Gerald: "I didn't really go out of my way to ease the tension between me and Gerald because I just didn't like the guy and I wasn't sure if being personal with him would ease the situation. My way of dealing with it was to be more professional." Susi deliberately turns her back on the potential for integrating difference by affirming contrast with her stance of not liking Gerald. One gains the sense from these examples that the conversational space underlying this scenario tends to be rather tight, narrow, and restricted.

THE CONVERSATIONAL LEARNING SPIRAL AND PSYCHOLOGICAL SAFETY

This overview of the four phases of conversational learning identifies steps within a process that is flowing, spontaneous, and highly context dependent. In the team setting, such learning cycles back and forth between insights that are highly personal and individualized and ones that are derived socially through conversation with each other. Relative to certain differences, team members come back to some juxtapositions again and again, reinforcing their importance in the conversational flow of the team. This cycling back and forth revolves around the principle of recursiveness, which in the model is depicted in the form of a spiral.

As a representation of the conversational flow, the shape and density of the spiral can vary: In teams where the tension in juxtapositions tends to be resolved by integration (Phase 4), the coils of the spiral appear looser, more expansive, and able to cover more space. In teams where such tension is more likely resolved by affirming contrast and one point of view over another, the coils are more tightly wound upon each other. The shape of the spiral can thus also be seen as a reflection of a team's conversational space.

As they journey through the phases of conversational learning—consciously or not—team members drop ideas. There are issues that are not carried further from one phase to the next for further meaning-making. Not all feelings of difference (Phase 1) are translated into juxtapositions (Phase 2). Not all articulated juxtapositions (Phase 2) recur (Phase 3). And not all of those that recur (Phase 3) are brought to a sense of resolution (Phase 4). The ideas that are dropped in and of themselves tell a story and become another reflection of the dimensions of a team's conversational space. This story would be interesting to pursue in future research.

The model is based on the experience of two teams with contrasting levels of psychological safety. While there are examples of all phases of conversational learning in each team, an important distinction between the two teams resides at Phase 4. In Team 1, the team with a high level of psychological safety, the examples integrating difference are more numerous and encompass a wider range of topics than the examples affirming contrast. Meanwhile, there are more examples affirming contrast than integrating difference in Team 2, which reported a low level of psychological safety. This suggests a dynamic interrelationship among three key concepts: psychological safety, conversational space, and conversational learning at the level of resolving difference. An image of this interrelationship emerges by revisiting the two teams.

In Team 1 an early conversational norm focused members on the team's ability to efficiently produce outstanding work. Team members knew they could count on each other, helped each other overcome communication and language barriers to draw out the best in each other's skills, found ways to take risks, and fully stood behind each other's contributions. At the same time, they were very cautious about addressing interpersonal differences and held back from giving each other feedback, aspects of teamwork normally associated with high psychological safety. This might have been a function of the nature of the dominant discourse, which upheld the importance of keeping a fast pace and meeting deadlines. It could also have been related to the multicultural character of the team: Interpersonal feedback is more commonplace in some cultural contexts than in others, where it is perceived as threatening to relationships. Overall, the conversational space in this team was expansive and open to different ways of seeing the world. The examples of conversational learning in the team indicated many ways in which team members reached into each other's lives, professionally and interpersonally, enriching their own perspectives by exposure to each other.

In Team 2 an early conversational norm formed around upholding open communication at all costs, reinforced by Gerald, the team's oldest and most outspoken member, who, during the first meeting, proclaimed himself as devil's advocate out to challenge the others in the group. Half of the team became locked into open, loud, and personalized conflict, which manifested itself in almost every meeting, while the other half shied away from participating in conversation beyond a bare minimum. While one would expect open communication to be an important aspect of psychological safety, how such a norm comes into being becomes key. The team's approach to openness could also have been a function of the multicultural nature of the team: Open communication comes more easily to members of some cultures than others. Ultimately, in this team, conversational space was constrained, and examples of conversational learning, especially among the four feuding team members, were mostly limited to a narrow range of categorical statements about their experiences of each other.

The example of these two multicultural teams opens up some interesting questions about the interrelationship among psychological safety, conversational space, and conversational learning. What aspects of psychological safety appear most important in the experience of such teams? How does conversational space reflect a particular level of psychological safety? What differences are developed through all four phases of conversational learning? What differences typically drop out?

CLOSING THOUGHTS

This exploration of the conversational dynamics of two multicultural teams results in an emergent model that begins with individual team members' experiences of difference and spirals outward through four phases that encompass conversational learning. Team members each experience difference differently; at the same time, team members' conversational engagement influences that of the other members. Some differences become salient to conversational learning of team members and are developed through all four phases of conversational learning, while other potential threads are lost along the way.

The context of the multicultural team presents more opportunities for examining difference and higher levels of uncertainty than culturally homogeneous teams. In many ways this characteristic allowed us to distinguish a framework for conversational learning and for understanding psychological safety that may be more difficult to pinpoint in groups that are not as diverse. It will be interesting to apply this model to map out juxtapositions, integration, and contrast affirmation in other teams.

This chapter raises numerous questions for further research on psychological safety, conversational space, and conversational learning. At the same time, it outlines a vital learning process that explicitly links the individual and group experience and that is wider in scope than predominant outcome- and performance-based models of team learning. Conversational learning emerges as a group process based on team members' own meaning-making of their conversational interactions that can encompass the full range of cognitive, perceptual, and feeling-oriented expressions underlying the experience of difference. Ultimately, the research suggests that the level of psychological safety in the conversational space helps frame whether the difference is experienced as an opportunity to integrate difference or as a way of affirming one point of view. For researcher and practitioner alike, such inquiry develops our awareness of the conversational dimensions influencing our profoundly human ability to connect with one another across difference.

NOTES

1. Research design note: Teams were invited to participate in the present study at the end of their second academic year. Each team was asked to identify two memorable events. Sixty- to ninety-minute individual face-to-face interviews were conducted with each team member on these two events. Based on the interviews, the researcher wrote a narrative for each team that was circulated, reviewed, and edited during a group validation session. The validated narratives give voice to each team and provide a portrait of the way in which teams perceived their conversational dynamics.

2. The term "juxtaposition" deserves some explanation here. Defined in the *Oxford English Dictionary* as "the action of placing two or more things close together or side by side, or one thing with or beside another," the term has its roots in the Latin *juxta* (near), the Old English *joust* (engage in combat), and the Indo-European *yug* (closely connected) and *yeug* (connected by yoke). In French, it is a grammatical term referring to propositions where connection is implied without one being subordinated to the other. The *American Heritage Dictionary* adds intention to the definition: The verb "to juxtapose" is the act of "placing side by side especially for comparison and contrast." Past usage of the term is suggestive but not restrictive of the relationship among the ideas being juxtaposed. The concept that ideas set side by side influence each other comes from the visual arts: When colors are juxtaposed, they become influenced as to their hue. Juxtaposition thus also implies creativity. Particularly relevant to the present

research is how philosopher John Locke used the term in 1690 to explain how we draw relationships between ideas in his theory of knowledge: "When the Mind cannot so bring its Ideas together, as by their . . . Juxta-position or Application one to another, to perceive their Agreement or Disagreement."

REFERENCES

Adler, N. J. (1997). *International dimensions of organizational behavior.* Cincinnati: South-Western College Publishing.

Bateson, M. C. (1994). *Peripheral visions.* New York: HarperCollins.

Boyacigiller, N. A., & Adler, N. J. (1991). The parochial dinosaur: Organizational science in a global context. *Academy of Management Review, 16,* 262–290.

Cohen, S. G., & Bailey, D. E. (1997). What makes teams work: Group effectiveness research from the shop floor to the executive suite. *Journal of Management, 23,* 239–290.

Earley, P. C., & Mosakowski, E. (2000). Creating hybrid team cultures: An empirical test of transnational team functioning. *Academy of Management Journal, 43,* 26–49.

Edmonson, A. (1999). Psychological safety and learning behavior in work teams. *Administrative Science Quarterly, 44,* 350–383.

Freire, P. (1994). *Learning and hope toward personal and social transformation.* Transcription of speech delivered at the International Experiential Learning Conference, Washington, DC.

Gillette, J., & McCollom, M. (Eds.). (1990). *Groups in context: A new perspective on group dynamics.* Reading, MA: Addison-Wesley.

Hackman, J. R. (Ed.). (1990). *Groups that work (and those that don't): Creating conditions for effective teamwork.* San Francisco: Jossey-Bass.

Hampden-Turner, C., & Trompenaars, A. (1993). *The seven cultures of capitalism.* New York: Currency Doubleday.

Hofstede, G. (1984). *Culture's consequences: International differences in work-related values.* London: Sage.

Kirkman, B. L., & Shapiro, D. L. (1997). The impact of cultural values on employee resistance to teams: Toward a model of globalized self-managing work team effectiveness. *Academy of Management Review, 22,* 730–757.

Kluckhohn, C., & Murray, H. (Eds.). (1949). *Personality in nature, society and culture.* New York: Knopf.

Kolb, D. A. (1984). *Experiential learning: Experience as the source of learning and development.* Englewood Cliffs, NJ: Prentice-Hall.

Kolb, D. A. (1999). *Learning styles inventory.* Boston: TRG Hay/McBer.

Locke, J. (1990). An essay concerning human understanding. *Great books of the Western world.* Chicago: Encyclopaedia Britannica.

Luft, J. (1984). *Group processes: An introduction to group dynamics* (3d ed.). Mountain View, CA: Mayfield.

Nonaka, I. (1994). A dynamic theory of organizational knowledge creation. *Organization Science, 5* (1), 14–37.

Nonaka, I., & Takeuchi, H. (1995). *The knowledge-creating company: How Japanese companies create the dynamics of innovation.* Oxford: Oxford University Press.

Polyani, M. (1966). *The tacit dimension.* Garden City, NY: Doubleday.

Salk, J. E., & Brannen, M. Y. (2000). National culture, networks, and individual influence in a multinational management team. *Academy of Management Journal, 43,* 191–202.

Tannen, D. (1998). *The argument culture: Moving from debate to dialogue.* New York: Random House.

Watson, W. E., Kumar, K., & Michaelsen, L. K. (1993). Cultural diversity's impact on interaction process and performance: Comparing homogeneous and diverse task groups. *Academy of Management Journal, 36,* 590–602.

9

Extending the Conversation into Cyberspace

Ann C. Baker

> Whether social uses of the Internet have positive or negative effects may depend on how the Internet shapes the balance of strong and weak network ties that people maintain. Strong ties are relationships associated with frequent contact, deep feelings of affection and obligation, and application to a broad content domain, whereas weak ties are relationships with superficial and easily broken bonds, infrequent contact, and narrow focus.
>
> Kraut et al. (1998, p. 1019)

At times a conversation ends with the feeling that there was not enough time to finish talking. Other times a conversation ends with a sense that there was a misunderstanding. Given the pace and complexity of contemporary life, it is not uncommon to wish there was more time to talk with work colleagues, in learning environments, among family members, and with friends. Depending entirely on face-to-face (f2f) conversation is limiting, given the geographic dispersion among people who work and play together, congested traffic in cities, frequent travel needs, different time zones, and differing internal body clocks among those who are "morning" people and those who are "night owls." Yet depending entirely on f2f conversation is no longer necessary.

Cyberspace not only offers an alternative medium for extended conversations; it has become an integral part of life for many people in the workforce, in education, and among friends and families. A seemingly infinite capacity for extending the conversation across physical space and time becomes available, not as an alternative to other forms of conversation but as a complement. Cyberspace offers an entirely different kind of venue for interpersonal interaction from the traditional same time–same place medium. The medium of cyberspace is more comfortable for some people and for some kinds of conversations. It expands the venue alternatives to accommodate, for example, communication-style differences, language-of-origin differences, learning-style differences, and cultural differences.

This chapter offers an extension of ideas explored throughout this book in the form of a case study in which f2f conversations are being complemented and extended in cyberspace. As an illustration of ways that conversational learning is evolving and coming to life in cyberspace environments, the case study hopefully will ground what otherwise may seem like abstract or idealized ideas in a real-world example. This example is intended as a jumping-off point for imagining applications in a variety of similar arenas that have relevance for the reader. Thus, the illustrations offered in this chapter are not intended as prescriptive to provide a method or "how-to" recipe. Instead, the intention here again is to be provocative, to stimulate your imagination, and to engage you in conversation about learning in virtual environments.

At the heart of conversational learning is social, relational learning among people who each have experiences and ideas that become vital resources for new possibilities yet to be discovered. Herein lies a fundamental assumption to guide the reading of this case study. Another assumption is a clear distinction that is being drawn here between the linear transmission of existing information and the creation of new knowledge and new ways of knowing that can be discovered and created among people in their conversations.

A social, relational perspective is necessary to recognize that "knowledge is not just embedded in the invisible cognitive worlds of individuals, but exists within the multiple relationships and evolving memberships of individuals and groups in society" (Richter, 1998, p. 312). This case study is about relationships among people and groups within an ongoing learning community that recognizes that learning is not limited to the individual cognitive process. It is about a learning community of people who are not satisfied with the linear transmission or sharing of existing information or knowledge. Instead, the emphasis is on seeking alternative ways of creating new ways of knowing to enable systemic change in the status quo of organizations.

To move beyond a linear and individualized perspective, the emphasis shifts toward more collaborative interactions in social, relational learning. This collaborative creation of new ways of knowing is found in the organizational-learning literature that draws attention to double and triple loop learning (Argyris, 1994, 1985; Isaacs, 1993; Romme & van Witteloostuijn, 1999) and the unearthing and examination of mental models and assumptions (Senge, 1990).

Without getting sidetracked by a treatise on these ideas, triple loop learning "entails . . . developing new processes or methodologies . . . [to facilitate people in] learning to see things in totally new ways" (Romme & van Witteloostuijn, 1999, p. 439). Thus, in this case study the f2f and virtual learning spaces are designed to assist people in learning how to perceive themselves, their organizations, and the larger world in "out of the box" ways. While transmission and sharing of existing information is a valuable by-product in this example, the primary intention is more transformative. The focus is on helping the participants remove the blinders of unexamined assumptions by listening to and learning from people who see the world differently. Creating receptive spaces for interactions among people in virtual space is as essential as it is in same time–same place space.

To allay reservations up front of readers with limited computer experience, this case study about creating a virtual conversational space is being written by someone with a totally nontechnical background. As a professional whose disciplinary education and research is in organizational behavior and whose work as a professor, manager, and consultant has emphasized the importance of f2f interactions and multiculturalism, I came to this work in the cyberspace environment as a skeptic. Yet my perspective has changed considerably by using, observing, and participating for five years in multiple online conversational environments. My primary experiences in virtual space are as a consultant and as a faculty member in the learning community of the Masters in Organizational Learning Program at a research university in the Mid-Atlantic region. This university learning community provides the setting for the case study.

In setting the context of this case study, I will describe at least one way of extending social learning among people in conversation into cyberspace. Drawing upon this experience, some of the benefits and limitations of this approach will lead to recommendations for people who may consider a similar venture. Along the way I will share parts of one specific conversation that spontaneously emerged in the community as an example.

SETTING THE CONTEXT

Virtual conversational spaces are commonly referred to as online conversational environments. These two terms are used interchangeably in this chapter. These online environments are being used among people in the global workplace, in traditional and nontraditional educational and training settings, and in informal, avocational communications among people with shared interests. This case study involves creating an online context in conjunction with classrooms, seminars, group meetings, and other forms of professional development to increase and complement learning opportunities for both students and faculty.

Online conversational environments offer opportunities for interaction that are distinctly different from e-mail conversations. E-mail is often a highly efficient medium for the linear transmission of information. It is often an essential part of sharing existing information and thus not "reinventing the wheel," and can be effective for coordinating activities.

However, this chapter is about providing opportunities for interaction in a "shared virtual space" that is conducive to discovering new ways of thinking and seeing unexpected possibilities. This process is similar in some ways to striving to provide a conversational learning space in a classroom, seminar room, or other f2f meetings. Access to the classroom and to this kind of virtual space is limited to a mutually agreed upon predetermined group of participants. Unlike the f2f space though, where time and space are limited, in the virtual space each person can contribute to as many of the threaded (topical) conversations as they want, can initiate new threads (topics), can join the conversation at whatever time of the day or night is convenient for them, and can join from almost anywhere in the world. This anywhere–anytime capability is referred to as asynchronous interaction.

The case study is set in a program that complements the more traditional medium of f2f interaction for organizational-learning and knowledge-management studies with shared virtual conversational spaces. For some content areas, courses can be effectively delivered in an exclusively distance-learning (online) environment. However, for the content and nature of my teaching and consulting expertise related to organizational behavior and organizational learning, my experience thus far strongly suggests a combined approach is most effective.

An underlying assumption of this chapter relates to my understanding of learning as a process whereby individuals create knowledge by transforming their experiences. Conversation in its multiple iterations (f2f, in written texts, in cyberspace, teleconferencing, etc.) is one of the most readily available and yet too often taken for granted and thus underutilized resources to stimulate learning. Virtual conversations can extend opportunities for learning into yet another venue.

Cultural norms, learning styles (Kolb, 1999), and interaction preferences (such as introversion and extroversion) vary widely among people. Varying teaching and learning approaches to respond to these diversities takes time. The experience of most faculty is that they never have enough contact time with students to sufficiently cover the content, allow for cross-cultural learning, and offer enough experiential learning opportunities for iterative learning within the confines of the typical semester or quarter course. Expanding the number and nature of learning venues can extend learning opportunities while also more effectively meeting the needs of diverse students. In addition, it is increasingly crucial to expose students to collaborative groupware technologies that are becoming commonplace in the workplace, where employees are often dispersed geographically across multiple time zones. Therefore, there are many advantages to incorporating online conversational environments that depend on groupware technologies into the curriculum.

As mentioned, the context for this case study is a professional master's degree program in organizational learning. Generally, the students are required to have at least five years work experience prior to admission into the program. Courses are taught in an evening–weekend format to working adults, who range in age from the twenties to the sixties. These adults typically include people from many professions, countries, races, and ethnicities. Students enter the program each fall as a cohort and typically complete the degree in approximately two years, taking most of their courses together until their last two semesters.

I have used online conversational environments thus far in two ways in the program. The first format, which I began using in the spring semester, 1998, is in a core course that I teach to the first-year students in their second semester and is referred to here as the Organizational Learning Course (OLC) format. The course is a foundational theory course on organizational learning. One of the course requirements is for students to initiate and participate in online conversations reflecting and building on their readings for the course, other relevant literature and concepts, classroom interactions, and possible connections and applications to the workplace. Approximately 20 to 25 percent of their grade is based on this online work.

Access to the online conversations is limited to the students in the course, sometimes one other faculty person well known to the students, and myself. Their participation is not anonymous, because the person's name appears with each of their postings (comments, entries) in the online conversation. This lack of anonymity seems to contribute to people feeling more responsible for the nature of their participation and the kinds of comments they make in the threaded conversations. Students also know each other and the faculty prior to taking this course, and these relationships are relevant and emphasized throughout the program as important to the social processes involved in learning collaboratively.

The second format for online conversations that informs this chapter is a communitywide, online conversation for everyone in the degree program. It is intended to help build a collaborative learning community among the faculty and all current student cohorts who are in the program at any given time. This communitywide online work was initiated in the fall of 1999 to support a three-hour required course, Creating a Learning Community (the Learncom). Students are enrolled in the Learncom throughout their participation in the degree program (usually for twenty-one to twenty-four months). The purposes of the Learncom are to facilitate learning and networking across the community, to provide varied forms of interaction among the students and faculty, and to offer a real-life experience of creating and participating in a collaborative learning community. The online conversational environment used to support the Learncom is referred to here as the Virtual Learning Community (VLC). Typically, the f2f contact time for the Learncom includes three Saturdays each semester over the approximately five semesters most students are in the program.

The VLC is intended to offer another complementary venue for interaction, relationship building, exploration of concepts and ideas, and experiential learning. Access to the entire VLC is typically limited to all current students and faculty. However, there are some parts of the VLC that also are open to graduates of the program. This limited access is important, because it allows students to get to know the people who are in the conversation and the people who are reading their postings (comments), and because issues of confidentiality are sometimes critical for personal and organizational topics. Other than required periodic postings of reflective papers, all student participation in the VLC is voluntary and not a consideration of their grade for the Learncom course. In each environment (OLC and VLC) the importance of good facilitation is increasingly obvious, and I will elaborate more later.

To participate in both formats, each student must have access to a computer with at least a minimum capacity, use of a Web browser, basic capability to use the software, and Web authoring tools for the Web–technical facilitator (as distinct from the conversation facilitator). Minimum computer requirements are given to students as an enclosure with their acceptance letter to the master's program, and they are expected to have them in place when they begin classes. While in the past different software and authoring tools have been used for these two environments, they all allow for threaded (topical) conversations grouped according to themes. The students typically initiate these themes, and faculty members read and occasionally participate as the conversations develop over time.

For the OLC, the software we have used is a Lotus Notes database delivered through the Internet using a Lotus Domino server in the R5 version. It allows participants access through the Web. Therefore, participants do not need to have Lotus Notes software loaded on their computers. The only training to learn how to use the software is a several-hour session offered during the orientation for the program prior to the beginning of classes. This ease of use is necessary, since many of the students' previous computer experience is limited to e-mail and word processing. My facility now with using the necessary tools is indicative of the relative ease of use, since I was one of those with similarly minimal computer skills in 1996. Generally, most students are able to use the software relatively easily.

Although we use these tools frequently in most courses, some students do not initially find them easy to use and are frustrated at first. To facilitate the transition, we encourage students to help each other, and we offer them other resources, such as access to doctoral students who are knowledgeable about the software, for assistance. Having adequate computing power and being able to use the software easily is directly related to the levels of participation.

For the first year (1999–2000) of the VLC, the software used was the Web-based application WebCT (Web Course Tools). However, because the design tools and participation patterns within WebCT are somewhat difficult to use and because students wanted to be able to use only one software program throughout the whole master's program, as of fall 2000 Lotus Quickplace replaced WebCT. Lotus Quickplace is currently being used in courses throughout the program, again to facilitate ease of use and minimal preparation.

BENEFITS FROM THE EXPERIENCE

While an extensive research project is underway and not yet complete, there are already many lessons learned from the experience since it began in 1998. Overall, the benefits far outweigh the limitations, given the purposes for the inclusion of online conversational environments in this learning community. Some of the unmistakable benefits of complementing f2f, hard-copy written texts, and e-mail interactions with cyberspace conversations to build and support the learning community are the following:

- Increased opportunities for reflection, reflexive listening, and learning.
- Alternative venue or medium to better accommodate participants' diverse communication styles, cultural differences, language capabilities, learning styles, individual preferences, and so on.
- Alternative venue or medium for building relationships, trust, and psychological safety.
- Increased time and space available for ongoing communication and exposure to the thoughts, feelings, ideas, and experiences of others beyond the more commonly used and time-limited f2f, written texts, e-mail, telephone, and conference-call formats.
- Asynchronous opportunities for participation on a twenty-four-hour, seven-day-a-week basis almost anywhere in the world.
- Increased opportunities for discovering other people with similar interests, experiences, expertise, curiosities, and so on.
- Opportunities for developing experience and competence in the use of groupware technologies.

The virtual environment offers an alternative format for people who may be quieter or more reticent in groups, for people whose language of origin is not English, for people whose cultural norms are not to be assertive, and so on. I have found that it is an easier medium for many people to express themselves and to speak more readily. In addition, because the virtual space does not prompt people as strongly for as immediate a response as a f2f conversation does, it makes possible and can encourage more reflective listening and consideration. Especially around controversial topics, when someone says something in f2f conversation that stimulates a reaction or disagreement, the listener may feel compelled to respond immediately. In the virtual space, when the person reads the same comment they can choose not to respond at that time or at all.

An Example

One of the conversational topics that stimulated the most participation in the VLC was diversity. An important reminder here is that all participation in the VLC was voluntary and was not tied to grades. In a long series of conversations on race that extended over many months, people who felt passionately about the issue expressed many direct and candid statements and feelings. Many more people read the entries and seldom or never posted their own entries. Thus, they were relatively quiet or silent participants. The software being used at the time did not offer the capability for participants to monitor who was reading or not reading the various conversational threads. In other words, there was no way for the participants to know who was reading the conversational thread unless a person made an entry. However, the Web–technical facilitator was able to monitor participation.

Both in the online conversation and in my interviews later with participants as part of my research, many people brought up spontaneously that they had strong reactions when they read some of the diversity entries. Several people said that if some of these comments had been made to them in a f2f conversation, they would have felt compelled to respond immediately, and that their responses would have been far more reactive or defensive than they were in the online space.

To illustrate this phenomenon and some of the highlighted benefits, one specific extended conversation in the VLC about race will be described using some of the actual words posted in the virtual space. In this specific conversation there were three people who were the primary participants. Of these people, one was a white male (wm), one was an African-American female (AAf), and one was a white female (wf). At the beginning of the fall semester, the first semester of the VLC in 1999, this AAf was asked to facilitate the diversity thread.

The following entry was made a few days after the orientation at the beginning of school where the second-year class had just met the new people in the first-year class. Each class is referred to as a cohort, since new students enter together only once a year. About a week after the orientation, in the diversity thread of the VLC, the AAf said, "I was struck by the fact that there was only one person of color in [the new] cohort—did anyone else notice?" A wm in the new cohort responded by saying, "I didn't notice. I do believe diversity in personal schemas is what's important. . . . Color is a factor as well as many other environmental influences. I'm sure we are lacking in diversity in many areas but have enough to go around in others." The AAf then responded with

> Welcome to the fray! As you will learn, I can be like a dog with a bone when it comes to issues of race. Having said that, I hope that you will continue to interact even though things may get a little "heated" from time to time.
>
> My first reaction to your posting was "how white of you." It is always amazing to me how white people will say that "I don't notice race, I just look at the person." That in and of itself is a "privilege" of being white.

Over the next week and a half this conversation continued among the AAf and several other people. Then the wm who had made the comment about "not noticing" and who became one of the three primary people in this part of the diversity thread said

> I may be beginning to understand. Or at least realize that I really haven't noticed as I said earlier. It's hard to understand something that I haven't expe-

rienced (can't in most environments) as a Middle Aged, White Male in Corporate America. As you said "How White of Me."

Having grown up in the south in the 50's and 60's, I've come a long way—but not as far as I may sometimes give lip service. You are getting my attention.

A few days later, the wm said, "So far I have enjoyed being a member of a privileged class and haven't taken the time to think much about discrimination. This discussion offers a small, but somewhat impersonal, way to learn from each other. Isn't that what the VLC is all about?"

The next day the wf that became one of the three primary people in this conversation responded to the wm's comment. The wf responded by asking him some very direct questions inquiring into how he might not see or think about some of the inequities and discrimination that she saw very clearly. At the end of her long entry, she said that she meant "these questions sincerely. If I've gone too far, I apologize." He responded, "You haven't gone too far. And I am going to answer your question. However, it is late [it was 11:25 P.M.], and I want to give some time to my answer and not just fire off a quick response. So I'm going to mull this over tomorrow and try to paint a picture of who I am and how my beliefs about racial issues were formed. And they go way back to 1947."

His response the next day involved a series of stories from his childhood that he was realizing had contributed to forming his previously unconscious assumptions about race. And his candor and stories prompted this response from the wf:

First, I must tell you how much I appreciate your response to my questions. As I said earlier, I knew when I asked them that I was, without invitation, potentially entering into the no fly zone. I can't tell you how much I admire and appreciate your willingness to be in this zone with me. Some face time in this dialogue would be valuable some time too.

I learned something HUGE from this exchange.

She then similarly told some stories from her childhood about how her perceptions around race had developed. This part of the conversation between the wf and wm took place over a weekend. At about 1 A.M. on that Monday morning, the AAf added this entry to the online conversation in the diversity thread:

I'm back! (really, I've been out of town). In reading through your postings, I feel like I've been ease dropping on a very private and personal conversation between two friends. I really enjoyed the conversation and appreciated your openness. Although I may have a point or two that, upon reflection, I may come back to.

Given the fact that we are all from the South [she means specifically these three people] and grew up in the same era, we have a common environment to draw from in the development of our experiences. It would be interesting to take a look at how the environment and our experiences in the environment have shaped our present reality and what kind of opportunities do they provide for our social and organizational learning as well as that of others.

She then began to tell her own stories from childhood, followed by some similar storytelling from several other people who had been "silent" readers for the previous week or longer in this diversity thread.

Soon the wm made this entry:

I decided to reread all of the postings in the Diversity discussion. Today, when I looked at my note and your response to my "I didn't notice" comment, I felt a different tone and noticed other points. Why?

The first time I read it, I took it personally and became defensive. This caused me to put up my own blinders to what you were saying about the lack of AA's [in my] Cohort. . . . [The VLC] does offer a unique space for discussing emotional topics like race. I have found that the opportunity provided by this e-world to take some time to think before responding is very helpful. It gives me a chance to disengage some emotion and use the little gray cells more effectively. While the emotional parts are authentic, they can sometimes impede learning.

Again, after many entries as this conversation continued, about a week later the AAf said, "I am so excited! I am finally getting to the place where I had hoped that this program would lead. I would love to get together." The three of them were now planning to meet f2f for coffee.

In addition to the wm's learning and new insights here, there were many other people who reported they had learned a lot from this experience. Gradually many people participated in this virtual conversation about race by making similar entries and telling their stories, asking questions, or making statements.

In my research interviews about a year later some people talked about how much they had learned from this conversational thread. I also learned that many people were uncomfortable with the directness of this particular conversation and with what they perceived as confrontational and too much conflict for them. Some of these people said they stopped reading the diversity thread because of the confrontational tone of the interactions. A few people said they stopped participating at all in the VLC at least partially because of their discomfort with this conversation.

In my interview with the wf she brought up this conversation in the diversity thread. Specifically she talked about her inquiry to the wm after he said that previously he "hadn't taken the time to think about discrimination." When she responded to him, she was intentionally different in her comments in that entry than she had ever been before. She said that the difference in her behavior was at least partially because she saw these two other people as so "honest and intimate." She said,

> I made myself do something different than I usually . . . had been doing on-line, because I recognized that a lot of times I would push out . . . very crisp . . . cutting comment. . . . That was when I was . . . start[ing] to work on how I can be a better instrument [an instrument for change as an organizational development consultant]. And so I made myself, I remember, like, sitting there—I probably waited 12 hours . . . before I responded . . . intentionally, which was different, because I . . . thought a lot about, who do I want to be? How do I want to respond to, create an opening and not anger, not bring up someone's anger . . . and push him against a wall. . . . My response to him was very different. I asked him a question. . . . It created a completely different conversation than most of the kinds of conversations I had. . . . I was proud of myself for taking the time to think about what . . . [and] who I wanted to be in that conversation.

The AAf talked in our interview about how much she had learned from this experience in the diversity thread. Specifically, she said,

> And so that was . . . probably, for me, one of the most rewarding moments in the program, and it said to me that—and it has opened up a whole place for me that I want to pursue—it says to me that online conversations can be very rewarding for dealing with difficult conversations. It can be a good place to begin to deal with difficult conversations, because he [the wm] also told me that he doesn't think that he would have gotten there in face-to-face, because he would have disengaged. . . . One of the things that he said to me afterwards was that he felt after having that [online conversation] . . . he was ready to have face-to-face conversations and engage around the issue of diversity and race finally in face-to-face. He could do it without feeling like he was shut down or feeling that he was being attacked.

This AAf also said that in her online experience while in the master's program,

> One piece of learning that I take away is about the need to . . . to be reflective even in an on-line environment before you act, before you speak. I mean it's the same thing. Your speaking is being done in a different manner, but you still have to be reflective before you open up your mouth . . . because you have the dynamic of interfering with relationships again . . . if you're interacting with another person.

She talked about how much the online work gave her more opportunity to reflect, saying,

It's not like being in . . . a face-to-face conversation with them. I can go back and think about it and, you know, ponder it, and turn it over, and whatever, and then respond later whenever, and so it has been good for my own personal growth and development, because I've noticed there are times when I'm not ready to take in information that I see on-line, and then at some point later something happens in my life that will trigger that, and I can go back and reread it, and it makes sense. The aha comes, or I can . . . accept the feedback, you know, and say, "Well, yeah, that may have been right." . . . I'm engaged enough to note that I want to go back and look at that. . . . I will just download it to a file and keep it and then have it to go back [to].

She talked about how her experience of being a facilitator of the diversity thread really helped her learn about her own style of facilitation. Her increased self-awareness was having a substantial impact on her efforts toward new directions at work and on her efforts to become a more effective facilitator. She had developed her own process of being able to watch herself while facilitating, and said, "So afterwards when I reflect on it, I can remember not just that engagement that's going on, but also what I was feeling at the time and how that was seen to the other person. . . . A lot of times it's more work than I want to do, but I have been able to do it a lot better as a result."

She also describes that she learned, from reading other people's thoughts and ideas online, how they came to think as they do: "One of the big learnings, at least for me . . . that I could really see, probably for the first time in my life, how people arrived at conclusions . . . or took positions that they took without . . . judging it [the conclusions, positions of others]. I mean . . . that was their experience and [I could] value it."

The value of expanding the space and time available for learning from others and for reflection was a common theme throughout the interviews and can be seen in this woman's words:

I think that a lot of the ahas that I have gotten through the course of the program have been a result of participating . . . on-line. . . . Because we don't have enough time in class necessarily to have conversations around issues . . . to really get a full grasp of what it means—the whole interaction piece or feedback. . . . But you really don't get a good understanding for it until you start to have to deal with . . . the giving and the getting [of feedback]. . . . I think that concepts started to make sense to me. . . . You start to see. . . . The dots started to be connected between theory and practice.

For many of the students the combination of the f2f and the virtual conversations offered potent stimuli for learning. The online conversations allowed them to reflect and build on their readings, have regular f2f interactions, and make connections and applications to the workplace. Overall, they were able to move their conversations to a more reflective and deeper level.

LESSONS LEARNED, RECOMMENDATIONS, AND IMPLICATIONS

While there are many benefits to using virtual space, it is critical to emphasize that its effectiveness and appropriateness is inextricably connected to the purpose of the group's interactions and to the culture and context where it is being used. Probably regardless of the purpose or the context, there are limitations that need to be anticipated and addressed. These recommendations and suggested implications for use in other contexts are related to concerns raised earlier in this chapter.

An Inclusive and Evolving Sense of Purpose and Expectations

It is crucial to work collaboratively with participants to develop and implement online conversation environments. In the case study this kind of joint effort increased participation among the students and stimulated faculty members to be more open to making changes. Being able to collaboratively develop clarity of purpose is directly related to the expectations that participants bring into the experience and the kinds of norms that get established. Thus, there is a benefit in offering both a required and a voluntary arena for online participation. In the required virtual space (OLC), students learn how to use the groupware. Then they are offered another arena where they can choose to extend their participation and influence in shaping the conversation and gain experience in facilitation. In both arenas students create their own threads (topics) for conversation and shape the conversation. Another form of influence comes through a committee made up primarily of students, with some faculty input, that makes decisions about what software changes are needed each year. Also, the Web managers for the VLC are always students, again giving them experience and considerable opportunity for input and influence.

When participants are encouraged to offer their input to shape the virtual space, they are more likely to be open to change and strive to create a more inclusive learning environment. In my syllabus for the organizational-learning core course I include an introduction to my philosophy about learning experientially through conversation in multiple venues, and I outline what is expected of the students in the online conversational environment in terms of frequency, nature, and scope of contributions. I revise my syllabus each year based on my experience and students' input. For example, one year the syllabus stated that each person needed to initiate at least three new threads and participate in other ongoing threads of conversation. However, students felt that this expectation was overly restrictive in terms of ways they could make substantial contributions to the conversations. Given the appropriateness of the concern about the need for more flexibility and the generally high quality of the responses added to already existing threads, I agreed with this concern and in the next year the syllabus asked students to

> both initiate new topics and contribute to ongoing threads of conversation and . . . focus more on making substantial, thoughtful comments that reflect that you are reading the course material and giving thought to both the concepts and possible applications of relevant ideas. Consistent with the essence of learning, your contributions need to attend less to agreement or disagreement with the texts or other people and attend more to respectful inquiry into each other's ideas and exploration of . . . previous assumptions.

This selection from the syllabus also reflects another realization I learned from the students: that I needed to give more explicit guidance regarding ways to deepen the conversational level in the online environment.

In the VLC, while the community talked about its purpose, my impression is that the faculty and second-year students need to expand this effort considerably. We need to explore more explicitly with the new cohort and returning cohorts ways that the VLC can better complement the creation and support of our learning community.

For use of online conversations in the workplace, this recommendation for full inclusion and participation would also be relevant. For example, in this chapter references to "students" could be replaced with the terms "group members" or "workers," and references to "faculty" adapted to refer to "managers" or other people in positions of leadership. This adaptation for managers would be especially relevant when the content or results of the online conversations are a component of performance review, promotions, and the like. The need to offer multiple options for participation where the group members have more choice about participation has relevance in many different contexts. For example, in the VLC many of the students talked about their disagreement with faculty decisions about changes in grading criteria and other wide-ranging criticisms of the degree program, offering them a much-needed venue for expression. While not always pleasant for the faculty to read, it offered the faculty insight into concerns that people in positions of leadership (e.g., managers) often do not hear. The use of the "syllabus" could be thought of in the workplace as guidelines, memos, procedures, and so on that offer ways for the people with positional leadership to communicate necessary considerations.

Another aspect of creating an environment of ongoing, inclusive participation is to encourage the group to intentionally and collaboratively consider at least some flexible, fluid norms for their online etiquette. For example, encourage group members to consider, before their work together or soon after it begins, their preferences for conversational norms such as level and nature of directness, respect, feedback, humor, setting boundaries, confidentiality, and so on. The deliberate creation of group norms is a learning process itself. It also gives everyone a touchstone to go back to as the conversation evolves; not to be rigidly adhered to, but to be used as a starting point for future consideration as changes are discovered and become important.

Context-Appropriate Choices

Recognizing and responding to cultural and contextual differences is endemic to learning and important to create receptive learning environments. When the online environment is used for conversations about sensitive, proprietary, and other similarly controversial topics (such as race or gender discrimination), these considerations are especially necessary. These topics and experiences are embedded within institutional and societal systems of power inequities and can be used for recrimination. Building trusting relationships and assuring protection from use of the conversations beyond the boundaries of a protected environment is essential for learning. While some people find it easier to speak out and be heard in the online environment, many others are more reluctant to write down their ideas, opinions, and so on out of a fear that the retrievability of this text could be used in ways they would not choose. Providing enough psychological safety (Edmondson, 1999) for people to have less fear of recrimination and punishment and to be able to trust the intentions of their colleagues is fundamental to learning.

Thus, although context appropriateness is critical, I suggest that when the purposes of online conversation extends beyond the linear transmission of information, consideration be given to limiting participation to people who have ample opportunity to know each other initially in f2f work projects, classes, meetings, conferences, and the like prior to the use of online work and to have at least periodic f2f contact over time.

Facilitation of Online Conversations

Generally, my approach is to see online conversations as venues that are primarily the students' environs or in other contexts the group members' environs rather than as belonging to the people in positions of leadership. Thus, limited faculty or leader participation has distinct advantages, especially in a context like the VLC, where participation is voluntary. The more the students or group members help create the context, facilitate it, and feel safe and comfortable participating openly in it, the more the online environment is a safe place for all participants to learn. Avoiding anonymity increases the personal responsibility for each person's contributions and diminishes flaming, disparaging outbursts, and recriminations that impede learning.

To guide these complex dynamics, skilled facilitation of the conversational threads is vital and is a good opportunity for students and group members to gain training and experience. Unlike f2f conversation, in the online environment visual cues such as readiness for next steps, who is taking the lead, and whether people are being heard, understood, or misunderstood are not available.

The facilitator can help participants better anticipate how their behavior might be misunderstood and can model ways to converse constructively, respectfully, and honestly about issues that could or are becoming serious problems. Sometimes a facilitator needs to have an offline, one-on-one f2f conversation with a group member to offer feedback. Also, the facilitator can give the online conversation enough structure to keep it from meandering off topic into side conversations that can often lead to a loss of interest by the larger community. At the same time, it is critical that the facilitator does not control the conversation so much that the potential for creativity, catalytic possibilities, and enjoyment are impeded.

In the OLC, where the grade for the course is linked to online participation, I think that the faculty member has more responsibility to participate. I suggest that faculty read and participate at least every seven to ten days. A response to at least each person's initial entry, if possible, offers needed reassurance to students that their comments are not "lost in cyberspace." It reaffirms that what they are writing is being read, gives them some feedback, and encourages continued participation. Also, this venue provides increased opportunities for faculty to ask questions and bring in ideas and resources that there was not time for in the f2f context. These dynamics are similar again to other contexts such as the workplace, where the online work is tied to performance evaluation, promotions, and so on.

Technical and Training Support

Prior to beginning conversations in the virtual space, if possible, it is critical to assure that all participants have adequate computing capacity and training to assure their easy and fast participation in the online conversation. Especially for people with limited confidence and experience in cyberspace, without this ease and speed their level of participation is likely to be limited and frustrating. These initial experiences and impressions are typically difficult to change later. Also, having technical support systems in place to answer participants' questions on a twenty-four-hour, seven-day basis, to address hardware and software problems that inevitably accompany this kind of effort, to update Web sites, and so on is directly related to the level of participation and to minimally equalize the technical facility of the participants in online conversations.

CONCLUSIONS

Extending the conversational learning approach into virtual environments offers another medium for interaction through time, across physical space, and into alternative venues. Growing out of five years experience, this chapter describes the use of multiple online conversational environments as a part of the master's in organizational learning program in a university. Written from the perspective of someone with a nontechnical background, my viewpoint has changed considerably by using, observing, and participating in online conversations that extend venues available for learning.

The primary benefits include the almost infinite expansion of time, space, and access by participants for interaction and conversation. In addition, when implemented with cultural and contextual awareness, it is possible to offer another medium for expression and for learning beyond more traditional technologies (meetings, lecture, classroom or seminar conversations, writing, e-mail, group projects, etc.). It also offers participants valuable training and expertise in groupware technologies that are widely used in businesses, governments, and nongovernmental organizations in the current knowledge-intensive world.

The virtual environment offers alternatives to people who may be quieter or more reticent in groups, for people whose language of origin is not English, for people whose cultural norms are not to be assertive, and so on. It is an easier medium for many of these people to express themselves and to speak more readily. In addition, it allows for and can encourage more reflective listening, because in the virtual space people perceive themselves as having more choice about whether and when to respond than in face-to-face conversations. This combination can offer potent stimuli and support for conversational learning.

REFERENCES

Argyris, C. (1985). *Strategy, change and defensive routines*. Boston: Pitman.

Argyris, C. (1994, July–August). Good communication that blocks learning. *Harvard Business Review*, 77–85.

Edmondson, A. (1999). Psychological safety and learning behavior in work teams. *Administrative Science Quarterly, 44*, 350–383.
Isaacs, W. N. (1993). Taking flight: Dialogue, collective thinking, and organizational learning. *Organizational Dynamics, 22*, 24–39.
Kolb, D. A. (1999). *Learning style inventory*. Boston: TRG Hay/McBer.
Kraut, R., Patterson, M., Lundmark, V., Kiesler, S., Mukopadhyay, T., & Scherlis, W. (1998). Internet paradox. *American Psychologist, 53*, 1017–1031.
Richter, I. (1998). Individual and organizational learning at the executive level: Towards a research agenda. *Management Learning, 29*, 299–316.
Romme, A.G.L., & van Witteloostuijn, A. (1999). Circular organizing and triple loop learning. *Journal of Organizational Change, 12*, 439–453.
Senge, P. M. (1990). *The fifth discipline*. New York: Doubleday.

10

Extending the Conversation into Professional Conferences

Ann C. Baker, Patricia J. Jensen, and David A. Kolb

> Do you know the conversation is one of the greatest pleasures in life? But it wants leisure.
>
> William Somerset Maugham (1980, p. 751)

All too often conversation is not a part of the formal meetings or sessions during professional conferences. Instead, professional conferences operate from a premise that one or a few people have the knowledge and are thus the experts and that they must convey that knowledge to the learners in a one-way exchange. Often lost in this approach is respect for the experience and expertise that each person brings into the arena and appreciation for the infinite learning that can occur synergistically among people through their conversations with each other. This chapter illustrates how a conversational learning approach can be applied during professional conferences and meetings by describing a successful example. The chapter offers an example of an innovative way to design a conference explicitly to promote learning through conversation.

CONFERENCE LEARNING

The traditional conference format is all too familiar. Conferences open in large plenary sessions with a few experts speaking to the crowd, the participants seated in rows of chairs too close together, and then there are break-out sessions where experts speak to smaller groups of people, seated once again in rows with little opportunity for interaction or conversation except for brief questions and answers. Ironically, the most substantial conversations at conferences occur informally during the coffee breaks, meals, and cocktail hours rather than during the formal meeting times. The challenge that faces conference planners is how to bring new life and energy into the formal sessions.

Conference participants usually attend meetings and conferences to meet new people, to get together with old friends and colleagues, to make connections with individuals they have heard about, to learn about what is new in their field, to learn about things they need to know, to network, and to learn about new ideas and ways of getting things done. Yet when conference participants sit in rows and get talked at hour after hour in dark rooms where slides and overheads are all they can see, people get bored, feel disconnected, and may feel they are not getting what they want and need. Moreover, when new participants enter this kind of conference arena they may often find it difficult to make the initial connections that would help them feel comfortable enough to want to return to subsequent meetings.

In the fall of 1994 there was a very different kind of conference that actually did promote conversation in innovative ways that brought new life and energy into the traditional format and can serve as an example for conference planners of professional organizations. The postconference survey indicated that, overall, participants left the meeting with a sense of great fulfillment. As a result of being in conversation with different people, they felt they learned new things and began to think in ways they never had before.

The first International Experiential Learning Conference in the United States was held in November 1994 in Washington, D.C., with over 1,500 participants attending from approximately thirty-three countries. After three previous conferences in the United Kingdom, Australia, and India, planning began in 1992 for the U. S. conference, which was cosponsored by the Council for Adult and Experiential Learning (CAEL), the National Society for Experiential Education (NSEE), and the International Consortium for Experiential Learning (ICEL). The theme for the conference, "A Global Conversation About Learning: Exploration, Reflection, Action," raised the critical question of how opportunities for good conversations among the participants might be created. The intent was to bring new life and energy into the entire conference, operating out of the assumption that each participant brings valuable expertise and experience. Thus, it became critical to create a context where participants could share their knowledge and experience through conversations with each other.

According to experiential learning theory (Kolb, 1984), people need to reflect upon their experiences before they can begin to make meaning and learn from them and then progress to take some new kind of action or adopt new behavior based on what they learned. Thus, the question facing the meeting planners for this international conference was how to create the time and space for conversation and reflection among conference participants. Although over 1,000 people were expected to attend, it was decided that conversations needed to take place in small groups no larger than ten to twelve people. If the groups were larger, each person would not have a chance to talk and be heard. It was also decided that participants would gain the most benefit from their conversations if they stayed in the same group throughout the conference. In this way, people could get comfortable with each other, begin to really get to know each other, and talk more openly. With such considerations in mind, the exploration and reflection (E&R) group was created as a hospitable space for conversation. In addition, the conference was designed in such a way that there were no alternative events or sessions planned when the E&R groups were in session.

There are at least three considerations worth exploring to learn from this example: why conversation groups at all, how to facilitate the groups, and how to plan for them within the body of a conference. What is the reason to have conversation groups at all? If people come to meetings and conferences to meet, talk with, and learn from others, the idea of bringing their conversations into the formal content and body of the meetings seems critical. If people who share interests, expertise, knowledge bases, and a common language and vocabulary are all attending the same meetings, then tapping into those extraordinary resources can be an invaluable source of learning as they share their experiences, best practices, approaches that did not work, ideas, and so on. A conversational approach recognizes that much learning takes place through conversations among people as they explore both their similar and divergent experiences and perceptions.

A second consideration is how to facilitate conversation groups, especially within the format of a large conference. In this international conference, substantial attention and preparation was given to facilitation. The guiding principle was that less intervention, rather than more, was most appropriate. The assumption was that knowledge and expertise rested among the attendees. Space and time needed to be created and held to allow for the conversation to happen, not to try to make it happen. Partially because there were people coming from all over the world and because three organizations had combined to cosponsor the meeting, the idea of the facilitators hosting as well as facilitating was also prominent. Thus, in this example the role was referred to as the Host/Facilitator.

To prepare the Host/Facilitators, a two-and-a-half-day retreat was held for the people from the United States a month prior to the conference, and a one-day retreat was held at the conference site for the international people the day before the conference began in Washington. Participants in the longer retreat conducted a month earlier expressed a profound sense of confidence and camaraderie gained through the experience of being a part of those sessions. Yet a careful analysis of the postconference evaluations suggests that, for most conferences, a one-and-a-half-day on-site retreat prior to a conference would be adequate.

The third consideration is the logistical and substantive planning that obviously must precede such an effort. The decision was made to set up the opening session of the conference with circles of twelve chairs and no tables because hearing across tables would have been more difficult. Host/Facilitators greeted attendees and helped them fill in chairs away from the door first. Participants were encouraged to form diverse groups to increase their chances of meeting new and different people. Ultimately, people chose where they wanted to sit and could sit with a friend(s), but in most cases they did form quite diverse groups.

After a brief opening program on the stage that included a conversation among five leaders in the field and several very brief opening remarks, participants engaged in their own conversations in their E&R groups. All the several years of planning and addressing endless concerns truly paid off when over 100 circles of people engaged in conversation for over an hour with enormous enthusiasm and concentration. The real sign of success came when the only real complaint was that one hour was not nearly long enough and when most of the conference participants returned the next day for their next E&R group meetings.

E&R group meetings were scheduled each day at a different time, with no competing events. Several meetings were planned immediately after plenary sessions to facilitate reflection and discussion about those sessions. One was held just before lunch. Groups were encouraged to then have lunch together, and many did. Another was planned at the end of the day to give more flexibility for time and some social time together. In all cases, the groups created their own agendas and were thus responsive to the interests and needs of the multiplicity of groups.

On the afternoon following the conference closing, both oral debriefings and written evaluations with the E&R group facilitators were completed, with follow-up written evaluations mailed out to all E&R group facilitators who could not attend the debriefing. The anecdotal responses during the conference and the generalized feeling that something quite valuable and unusual had happened were strongly supported in the debriefing and evaluation. When asked to rate the overall value of the E&R groups in terms of providing the conference participants an opportunity to engage in conversations of exploration and reflection, on a 5-point scale (with 5 as the most valuable) the facilitators gave a 4.5 rating. Of the sixty-four facilitators who responded to the written evaluation, approximately fifty said the groups provided structured opportunities for conversation, global conversation, exploration of ideas, reflection and integration of learning experiences, and, finally, being able to give voice to participants. Almost as many (about forty-two) referred in some way to the increased opportunities for connection, personal contact, and more genuine human interactions. Over one-third pointed out the opportunities they had to get to know people from diverse backgrounds.

There were six overall themes to the responses from sixty-four of the facilitators, and the essence of their responses can best be understood by sharing their actual words. These comments are grouped by theme: overall success, the creation of a space and time for conversation, the learning process, the diversity of the people, additional activities that grew out of the E&R group contacts, and the value of making connections with others.

Overall Success

Frequent comments from over one-third of the facilitators were that the E&R groups were

- one of the "best parts" of the conference.
- "great."
- "wonderful."
- "highly valuable."

In addition, the E&R groups provided

- the opportunity to take "the content and [make] meaning together."
- "expanded perceptions by exchanging them."
- a chance to "slow the pace and talk with new perspectives."
- opportunities "to engage deeply in conversation that ranged from reflection on content, to discussing nuances of particular practical experiences, and to sharing reflections on the personal experience of the conference."
- "Uniform agreement in my group of the value of this time to share stories, ask questions, and share our thoughts with real people over sustained period of time."

Diversity

Comments included the following:

- The E&R groups gave them the "opportunity to explore and reflect with people I normally would not gravitate towards, developing a cohort group to think with and learn from."
- They had met "many people that I wouldn't have otherwise—not the usual contacts."
- E&R groups were "providing a focus for sharing experiences with a diverse, yet consistent group."
- The groups were valuable because of "connecting and sharing with a diverse range of individuals."
- There was the personal value of having the "opportunity to hear what others were doing [and the] reassurance that all over the world people are grappling with similar concerns."

Activities

Facilitators said that in addition to the scheduled group time, groups took "group photos," "took off together for a museum sojourn," and "saw [them]selves as extra sets of eyes and ears for one another [in their E&R groups] and worked hard to bring back information or contacts that would help others in their quests." One said, "Hosting the E&R group pushed me to be more adventurous in my choice of sessions and truly to take advantage of the international aspects of the conference."

Making Connections

Here are some comments that seemed to primarily focus on the connections made in the E&R groups:

- "Often in conferences, people new to the organization find it difficult to link into already formed friendship groups. . . . Participants in my group really linked together and quickly found thinking and discussing together a stimulating and enriching experience."
- "It provided a space where a few of us could get to know each other in a more substantial way."
- It "offered a chance to be personally connected on an individual level."
- It was an "opportunity to connect personally with about half a dozen individuals I didn't know before."
- "People really *valued* the chance to connect."
- It was a "way to make the meeting more personal."

- "The honor and respect each member gave to each other . . . the warmth and openness and ability to share quite deeply—the continuity."

Overall, the specifics of the way that these groups were planned, formed, and conducted can be adapted to the context and nature of most conferences. Yet some overarching themes may be critical for conversation groups to be successful regardless of the professional group or the setting:

- The space and time for conversation should be explicitly created.
- The leadership or facilitation should be provided, but minimal.
- Attention should be given to hosting the participants.
- Group size should be kept small.
- The same group should meet over several days.
- The agenda and content of the conversations should be fluid and responsive to the membership of the groups.

The challenge in bringing new life and energy to conferences and in promoting learning in these formal settings is to become more responsive to how much people want to be in conversation with their old friends and colleagues, want to have conversations with new and different people, and want to have conversations that are sources of both learning and fun.

REFERENCES

Kolb, D. A. (1984). *Experiential learning: Experience as the source of learning and development*. Englewood Cliffs, NJ: Prentice-Hall.

Maugham, W. S. (1980). *Family quotations John Bartlett* (Emily Morrison Beck, Ed.). Boston: Little Brown.

11

Conversational Learning in Organization and Human Resource Development

D. Christopher Kayes

> A highway has no meaning in itself; its meaning derives entirely from the two points that it connects. A road is a tribute to space. Every stretch of road has meaning in itself and invites us to stop. A highway is the triumphant devaluation of space, which thanks to it has been reduced to a mere obstacle to human movement and a waste of time.
>
> Milan Kundera (1991, p. 223)

FROM METHOD TO CONVERSATION

Kundera's distinction between a road and a highway provides a good place to start a conversation on learning and contemporary organization and human resource development (OD/HRD) practices. Organization and human resource development practices often resemble speeding down a highway. Learning is viewed as an end and methodology is the vehicle for reaching that end. Like a highway, conventional methods often act as obstacles to organizational learning by minimizing the role played by experience in the learning process. In contrast, a conversational approach to OD/HRD is akin to walking down an underdeveloped road, revealing and deliberate, toward meaningful learning encounters in an inviting space. This chapter poses conversational learning as an alternative to conventional OD/HRD methods. Conversational learning is grounded in five dialectics: apprehension versus comprehension, action versus reflection, discourse versus recourse, individuality versus relatedness, and status versus solidarity. Conversational learning promises an innovative approach to current OD/HRD practices, including organizational knowledge creation, change, developmental learning, time, and instructional delivery. Conversational learning creates a more holistic approach by providing an alternative set of practices to compliment extant OD/HRD. By creating a safe space that values conversation, individual experience can become transformed into group knowledge.

From the outset, this chapter sets out to create a distinction between conventional and conversational approaches to OD/HRD by exploring the dialectics of conversation. The distinction between conversation and convention is often drawn sharply to illustrate how conversation represents a significant renewal of practice. Drawing such a sharp distinction highlights the challenges that professionals may face when seeking to employ conversation in their methodological routines. Extending such a clear distinction between two interrelated practices, however, seems overdrawn. Unlike Kundera's highway, which is "a waste of time," conventional methods add value to learning by keeping a practical focus and an end in sight. Conversation invites us to stop along the way. Thus, Kundera's road–highway distinction helps frame this conversation, but it only takes us so far, as conversation and convention may best be viewed as two interconnected OD/HRD practices. Understanding the relationship between conversation and convention begins with a look at the status of method in OD/HRD.

Method in Organization and Human Resource Development

Human resource development and training professionals widely believe that the principle role of learning is to improve organizational performance and productivity (Rowden, 1996). This belief has led to a proliferation of new training methods designed to improve performance and productivity. Willis (1996), for example, has compiled a "filing cabinet" of OD/HRD methods that include training, delivery, advising, coaching, designing, managing, leading, and peer consulting (p. 38). The underlying objective of most of these methodologies is congruent with the values of the contemporary economic organization (Kayes, 2002; Ritzer, 2000). Ritzer suggests that contemporary economic organization embraces three dominant values: calculability (measuring bottom-line results), predictability (setting clear and achievable goals), and efficiency (taking the least expensive and most direct means to reach an outcome). The values of calculability, predictability, and efficiency continue to have an important impact on OD/HRD practices around the globe, as evidenced in increased calls for professional credentials, standardization of training methods, renewed interest in outcome-based training, and improved measures of evaluation (Kayes, 2002). These conventional practices, however, seem incomplete in light of the new, more complex, fast-changing, and technology-intensive organization. Conventional practices cover only half the distance.

The introduction of conversational learning into the OD/HRD lexicon challenges a commonly held assumption about OD/HRD methods: that learning results from good design and delivery of training. In other words, good learning results from good method. Conventional wisdom goes something like this: Identify the training need, develop the proper design, and deliver it effectively, and then learning can be properly achieved and evaluated. While at first there is an appealing certainty and conventionality to this logic, the introduction of conversation in OD/HRD reveals another side to practice. Conversational learning presents a different logic, one that is driven by different ideology, by meaning rather than method, deliberation rather than delivery. In simple terms, conversation eludes convention.

The philosopher Hans Georg Gadamer (1989) pointed out the limitations of method. Gadamer argued that modern society, overrun by the philosophy of science and commerce, has mistaken method for truth. Methodology prestructures thinking so as to predetermine the outcome. Method mediates experience to make it conform to certain expectations. Richard E. Palmer (1969), in his analysis of Gadamer's philosophy, explains that methods "prestructure the individual's way of seeing. Strictly speaking, method is incapable of revealing new truth; it only renders explicit the kind of truth already implicit in the method" (p. 165).

A similar logic applies to conventional OD/HRD training and development methods. Conventional OD/HRD methods predetermine outcomes by reducing the range of interpretation. By prestructuring the learning space, method narrows the range of meaningful experiences that emerge in conversation. Under the compliance of method, experience does little more than conform to the predetermined expectations of the method. What becomes measured is not the learning but the effectiveness of the method in predetermining the outcome. When method is the dominant vehicle of learning, meaning becomes reduced to an obstacle on the way toward a measurable achievement. This methodological prestructuring reduces the scope of learning to ensure that interpretation arises at the expected destination. The process of conversation provides an alternative strategy for learning, one that avoids the obstacles posed by conventional OD/HRD methods.

Conversational Learning in Organization and Human Resource Development

If contemporary human resource development and training methods strive for efficiency, calculability, and predictability, then conversational learning, by engendering deliberation, immeasurability, and uniqueness, represents a fundamentally different approach to conventional OD/HRD. These three values—deliberation, immeasurability, and uniqueness of experience—provide an invitation to rethink OD/HRD practices in light of conversational learning.

Conversation engages the uniqueness of experience as the foundation of learning. As an extension of experiential learning theory (Kolb, 1984), conversational learning moves from the particulars of experience to the generalized concepts of society. Learning begins with an individual experience that becomes transformed through conversation. Unique experience becomes the raw data for learning in the conversational space. Richard E. Palmer's (1969) definition of hermeneutics, the study of interpretation, is instructive in understanding how experience moves beyond the individual into the conversation. Palmer suggests three interpretive processes that can be adapted to explain how experience is transformed in conversation:

- saying, "expressing [experience] out loud in words."
- explaining, as in giving details of an experience.
- translating, as in using different words to describe experiences such as "translation of a foreign tongue" (p. 13).

Saying, explaining, and translating individual experience in conversational space transforms individual knowledge into a form that is accessible to others in the group. This process of interpreting experience describes how conversation invites unique meaning into the learning process.

Because experience is unique to the individual and given meaning through expression in conversation, the learning often eludes quantification and thus remains immeasurable by conventional standards. Because experience, even experience that is made explicit in a social context of conversation, often remains unavailable to traditional methods of educational validation (e.g., standardized tests, outcome evaluations, and proficiency examinations), learning remains largely a factor of individual and group subjectivity.

For Gadamer (1989), conversation was closely tied to the concept of deliberation. Deliberation was not tied to methodological purity, but rather was more about developing a kind of proficiency in knowledge creation. Deliberation leads to understanding experience in context, and proficiency emerges as one begins to recognize that deliberation is a continuous, dialectical process of inquiry. Deliberation moves to "clarify the conditions under which understanding takes place" (Palmer, 1969, p. 184). Deliberation points to a careful consideration of multiple explanations and connotes a slow but focused movement toward understanding (Thompson, 1996). Deliberate conversation enhances learning by increasing one's capacity to consider multiple sides of an issue, debate, or problem. Unencumbered by traditional methodological constraints, deliberate conversation engenders meaningful learning encounters in the course of conversation. Through these learning encounters, meaning emerges in various conversational contexts.

Eleanor Duckworth (1996), a student of Piaget, observes that learning space should value "not knowing" as much as it does knowing. Deliberate conversation embodies the value of "not knowing" as it intends to "provide occasions, such as those [that encourage] accepting surprise, puzzlement, excitement, patience, caution, honest attempts, and wrong outcomes as legitimate" parts of learning (p. 69). From this value of "not knowing," embodied in deliberation, emerges the distinction between efficiency and deliberation in OD/HRD practice. Efficiency leads to learning one best way of doing or understanding; deliberation leads to multiple meaningful possibilities. Efficiency leads one down a highway, quickly glossing over variations and uniqueness in the conversation. Deliberate conversation leads down a road, engaging the moment in order to create and interpret new encounters along the way.

Valuing uniqueness, immeasurability, and deliberation presents a challenge to conventional OD/HRD methodology. The challenge is not intended to completely undo conventional OD/HRD practices; rather, it is an attempt to engage in conversation about important issues that may be overlooked in the rushed response prevalent in the fast-paced, technology-intensive, and change-oriented organization.

FUNDAMENTAL DIALECTICS OF CONVERSATION IN OD/HRD

The addition of unique, immeasurable, and deliberate conversation to conventional OD/HRD practices can be considered within the broader dialectics of conversational learning. Kolb, Baker, and Jensen (see Chapter 4) outline five dialectics of conversational learning: (1) apprehension versus comprehension, (2) action versus reflection, (3) discourse versus recourse, (4) individuality versus relatedness, and (5) status versus solidarity. Each of these five dialectical tensions plays a role in a conversational approach to OD/HRD.

Conversation and Organizational Knowledge Creation

A shift from conventional methods to conversational learning can be considered a qualitative difference in the type of knowledge creation that emerges from the learning process. Nonaka (1994) makes a distinction between internalization (knowledge created when an individual receives the values and routines of a culture or social system) and externalization (knowledge created when an individual makes implicit assumptions, experiences, and abilities available to others). In the rush to increase efficiency of delivery and design of training, the importance of externalization processes in OD/HRD has been largely overlooked. Conventional OD/HRD focuses primarily on internalization, making the practices and values of the organization available to individuals within the organization. Conversational learning is more likely to engage both externalizing and internalizing as means to create organizational knowledge.

Because it is grounded in the data of personal experience and not simply the normative values of the organization, conversational learning represents a bottom-up approach to knowledge creation in organizations, beginning with individual experience and moving to more general knowledge. This movement from experience to concept represents the apprehension and comprehension dialectic of conversational learning.

Nonaka's distance between personal and social knowledge creation, however, seems overextended from the vantage point of experiential learning theory. Kolb (1984) reminds us that social and personal knowledge stand in constant conversation. "Social knowledge . . . cannot exist independently of the knower but must be continuously recreated in the knower's personal experience, whether that experience be through concrete interaction with the physical or social world or through the media of symbols and language" (p. 105). Thus, the movement between social and personal knowledge cannot be captured in any formal way through conventional evaluation measures.

Modification of traditional methods to include deliberate conversation as a legitimate part of training and development may lighten the load in creating the meaningful learning encounters that engender externalized knowledge creation (Baker, Jensen, & Kolb, 1997). A bottom-up approach can be contrasted to most OD/HRD methods because traditional methods attempt to identify generalized rules and procedures and then replicate them across individuals within an organization.

Bridging the distance from personal to social knowledge appears to present an overwhelming challenge to the OD/HRD professional. After all, most OD/HRD professionals receive training that helps them to indoctrinate individuals by teaching the institutionalized values and practices of the organization. Little time is devoted to navigating the bumpy road of individual experience.

Conversation and Change

Another division between conventional and conversational learning mirrors a distinction found in classic epistemology (Miller, 1996). Aristotle (1953) drew a clear distinction between practical knowledge (*phronesis*) and the poetic knowledge (*poiesis*). Practical knowledge concerns itself with achieving specific ends, while poetic knowledge concerns itself with "coming into being, i.e. with contriving and considering how something may come into being . . . and whose origin is in the maker and not in the thing made" (p. 141). Knowledge of how to manipulate various parts to achieve a specific measurable goal drives outcome. Knowledge of how things originate drives understanding, especially as this understanding enlightens how individuals create and then relate to their world. Practical knowledge implies objectivity, a clean slate, where the individual manipulates a series of variables unencumbered by personal interest. Poetic knowledge implies a subjectivity, an act of creativity, where perception and experience contribute to understanding. To emphasize the difference, Aristotle noted, "Neither is acting making nor is making acting" (p. 141).

The relationship between practical and poetic knowledge reveals itself in the action–reflection dialectic, where action implies an active engagement with the world and reflection implies a making of oneself through reflection. In more contemporary terms, Aristotle's practical knowledge is represented in the methods abundant in OD/HRD, which focus on achieving specific organizational or institutional outcomes such as productivity and performance. Poetic knowledge increases the capacity, interest, and sustainability of learning in the individual by engendering meaning and purpose through organizational membership. Practical knowledge leads to manipulation of the outside world to reach external goals, while poetic knowledge leads to becoming a more holistic individual.

In light of experiential learning theory, Aristotle's distinction between practical and poetic knowledge seems overdrawn. Practical and poetic knowledge remain in constant conversation in the dialect of action and reflection. For poetic knowledge to be of value, it requires actions that change the way one relates to the world. Similarly, for practical knowledge to be useful, it requires constant scrutiny of reflection. Coming into being, the process of poetic knowledge creation, results in greater understanding of oneself and one's abilities and shortcomings. Understanding oneself, however, is never accomplished in a vacuum. Self-understanding happens when one comes into contact with practical problems, such as falling short of goals or achieving victories, and the various challenges encountered on the way. Richard Miller (1996), an ethicist who draws heavily on Aristotlian thinking, comments on the fuzziness of Aristotle's categories. He states, "Making may not be acting, strictly speaking, but we would be ill-equipped to act rightly without first making sense of our contexts or cases" (p. 224). If practical knowledge goes hand in hand with personal knowledge, than conventional OD/HRD practices only cover half the needed distance. Conversational learning provides a vehicle to cover more of the knowledge-creation territory.

The active–reflective dialect of conversational learning exposes another missed opportunity in OD/HRD. Team building enjoys popular use as a strategy for organization and human resource development. Yet little evidence has been found to support the connection between team building and organizational change (Woodman & Sherwood, 1980). One reason for the failure lies in the strategic focus of most team-building programs. Traditionally, the goal of team building has focused on building camaraderie among team members, creating synergy, and building capacity to perform in the face of a limited number of predictable tasks. Such approaches often ignore the demands of the contemporary organization: dealing with differences, creating new knowledge, understanding the inner motivations of self and others, sharing knowledge in the face of complex problems, and so on. Conversational learning provides a direct means to cultivate these important team processes that remain virtually ignored in most current team-building programs.

Conversation and Developmental Learning

As if learning in organizations itself were not difficult enough, the move to conversation in OD/HRD practices carries a more complex agenda than just day-to-day learning. Conversational learning also proposes an agenda for development, the progressive change over time that increases one's capacity to deal with complexity, difference, and change. The individuality–relatedness dialectic captures this developmental agenda. Robert Kegan (1994), a developmental psychologist, provides an appropriately complex first step in the developmental agenda that is captured by the individuality and relatedness dimension of conversational learning. Kegan writes,

> The ability to construct one's own point of view and to recognize that others are constructing their own as well, coupled with the *inability* to coordinate these points of view, to construct the self or the other not only in terms of one's own point of view but in terms of the relation of one point of view to another—this simultaneous achievement and constraint allows one to take others into account to the extent of providing them with the sense that they are understood, although one's intent has mainly to do with the pursuit of one's own goals and purposes. (p. 39)

It is important to note that understanding that one's own individual viewpoint exists in the context of others' viewpoints begins the process of development, eventually leading to a deeper appreciation of others' positions.

Few existing human resource programs address developmental learning because development has been considered a function of various biological, educational, life and career stage, and even gender factors. Such issues are far removed from the ongoing slate of OD/HRD programs in most organizations. Helping individuals appreciate differences in point of view is behind most one-shot diversity, sexual harassment, and cultural awareness programs sponsored by organizations.

Unfortunately, most of these programs are too limited in scope and time to foster sustainable developmental learning, such as the ability to think critically and appreciate difference. This is one conclusion that resulted from Jaye Goosby's (2002) study of diversity learning. Goosby studied how learning occurred through several mediums: in- or out-of-class conversations, in- or out-of-class readings, or videos. Participants reported in-class conversation as being the primary source of learning nearly twice as much as any other method. Because much of the diversity training conducted in organizational settings encompass only one or two information-intensive sessions and little opportunity to interact in conversation with others who hold different viewpoints, the deeper complexities involved in understanding individual differences is never achieved. Without deeper attention to understanding the relationship between individuality and relatedness, existing human resource practices amount to little more than social etiquette, teaching others how to interact in difficult social situations without getting to the deeper beliefs that underlie social interaction (Neilsen & Rao, 1990).

Conversational learning, however, provides a promising developmental tool. By creating space that is both supportive and challenging in the correct balance, conversation enables developmental learning (Kegan, 1994). Kegan provides a simple formula for developmental learning that can be easily adopted as part of a conversational learning engagement. He suggests an agenda where "the trainees work in groups," pay attention to "their need to learn each other's skills and limitations as well as their own," and "to hold the other in mind even as they pursue their own ends" (p. 47).

Conversation and Time

A further complication for integrating the developmental learning agenda into OD/HRD lies in the fact that it requires complex, sustained, expensive, and intense commitment over long stretches of time, often putting developmental learning practices beyond the reaches of most human resource efforts. The time dimension represented in the dialectic of discourse and recourse presents one of the most elusive and abstract concepts in conversational learning. As Anthony Aveni (1998), noted astronomer and anthropologist observes, "One's comprehension of time . . . is conditioned by the world one experiences, together with the ways in which one articulates that which is experienced" (p. 331). The recursive dimension seems a particularly difficult concept to grasp. Most OD/HRD professionals are indoctrinated to experience time discursively as a linear, narrow, and finite commodity. In this way, time usually presents itself as an obstacle to achieving a goal. Time is seen as a constraint under which one must work. Such a limited view of time can threaten developmental learning processes because it invites too few challenges to moral reasoning, extensions to critical thinking, integrations of complex ideas, and other processes that may be tied to more recursive learning.

Developmental learning requires revising ideas time and time again, where each time a new insight is gained in the conversation. Ongoing conversations that foster returning to prior ideas make connections that risk being overlooked in the rush to get through material. That means that conversational techniques such as keeping up the pace, covering large amounts of information, glossing over objections and criticisms, stamping out silence, moving along, and failing to return to difficult material may create roadblocks to development. Instructors often evoke these delivery "tactics" in the name of time, and sacrifice learning for method.

Learning is not a clean orderly process, but rather one that is characterized by "slippage" as knowledge moves between the social and personal realms, "deception" as individuals attempt to interpret their experience through language, and "twisting" as one works through the various phases of learning (Kayes, 2001). Linear time characterized by discourse, while providing a comforting coherence to the learning process, lulls the learner into the deception that learning is more straightforward. Conversation reveals the cyclical nature of recursive time by exposing experience to the complex world of social intercourse.

Conversation and Instructional Delivery

A conversation on OD/HRD remains incomplete without attention to the role of the OD/HRD professional in instructional delivery. Conversation challenges convention once again by rethinking the role of facilitator, trainer, or teacher as the primary source of knowledge and expertise in OD/HRD practice. In conversation, knowledge is no longer limited to the OD/HRD professional but reciprocates between group members as the conversation unfolds. Conversation provides an important addition to OD/HRD practice because it migrates knowledge creation from inside the minds of individuals to the external interactions of the group itself. Scholars and practitioners alike call this process "organizational learning" (Argyris & Schön, 1996; Senge, 1990), but another phrase better captures what occurs in conversational learning. "Proximal learning" (Vygotsky, 1978) describes the process that transforms individual experience into group knowledge through conversation. The influential child psychologist L. S. Vygotsky coined the phrase "the zone of proximal development" to describe how children solve complex problems in the company of more advanced peers. Vygotsky describes proximal development as "the distance between the actual developmental level as determined by the independent problem solving and the level of potential development as determined through problem solving under adult guidance or in collaboration with more capable peers" (p. 86).

Proximal learning is not limited to children. Adults too must learn from others and share what they know when they face situations that are beyond their current capacities to know as individuals. Adults have access to the benefit of conversation to expand learning capacity, however, and children do not. This expanded learning capacity is expressed in the dialectic of status and solidarity. Proximal learning describes the process where expertise, defined in the accumulated experiences and capacities of the individual, move from status to solidarity in the face of increasingly complex conversations. First as a ranking process, expertise becomes distributed among groups members as individuals express their strengths and weaknesses in relation to the current conversation. In this process, individual knowledge becomes explicit and becomes distributed in the conversation among various members. Finally, knowledge is linked together in deliberate conversation to create meaningful learning encounters. Conversation maintains the status differentials in the group but also links the differences through a common space.

The OD/HRD professional is stripped of totalitarian status and authority becomes distributed across the conversation. Authority now rests in the conversation, not just the OD/HRD professional. Nor does it rest in the method or delivery. The proximity of group members links experience through both status and solidarity based on the course of conversation. This occurs regardless of whether the conversation occurs between individuals in face-to-face interaction or through technology. The role of the OD/HRD professional in conversational learning focuses on creating space for conversation, inviting different voices into the conversation, and cultivating a safe space for deliberation about difficult but meaningful issues.

The characterization of conversational learning provided in this chapter runs the risk of oversystematizing the informal nature of the process. Conversation marks a less formal process, one that seems to defy conventional method but that promises to enhance the learning experiences of organizational members. Conversational learning suggests a fundamental rethinking of conventional OD/HRD practices because it shifts thinking from individual learning to group learning. With conversation as the vehicle for learning, learning no longer remains trapped in "images of organizations held in its members' minds" (Argyris & Schön, 1996, p. 16), but begins to emerge in the conversation of members.

At the end of the route, learning rests in the meaningfulness of the conversation and not the conventionality of the method. If we return to Kundera's words that began this conversation, we might be bold enough to say that conversation invites meaningful pathways to learning. Considered alongside conventional method, conversational learning promises an exciting way to transform highways into roads, where learning derives from triumphant valuation of space in conversation.

REFERENCES

Argyris, C., & Schön, D. A. (1996). *Organizational learning II: Theory, method, and practice*. Reading, MA: Addison-Wesley.

Aristotle. (1953). *The Nicomachean ethics* (David Ross, Trans.). Oxford: Oxford University Press.

Aveni, A. F. (1998). Time. In M. C. Taylor (Ed.), *Critical terms for religious studies* (pp. 314–333). Chicago: University of Chicago Press.

Baker, A. C., Jensen, P. J., & Kolb, D. A. (1997). In conversation: Transforming experience into learning. *Simulation & Gaming, 28* (1), 6–12.

Duckworth, E. (1996). *"The having of wonderful ideas" and other essays on teaching and learning* (2d ed.). New York: Teachers College Press.

Gadamer, H. G. (1989). *Truth and method*. New York: Crossroad.

Goosby, J. E. (2002). *Black, white and shades of gray: Exploring differences in diversity learning and development between black and white graduate students*. Unpublished Ph.D. diss., Case Western Reserve University, Cleveland, OH.

Kayes, D. C. (2001). *Experiential learning and its critics: Preserving the role of experience in management learning and education*. Working paper, Department of Human Resource Development, George Washington University.

Kayes, D. C. (2002). Sociological issues in human resource development. In M. Marquardt (Ed.), *Encyclopedia of life support systems: Human resources and their development*. London: UNESCO.

Kegan, R. (1994). *In over our heads: The mental demands of modern life*. Cambridge: Harvard University Press.

Kolb, D. A. (1984). *Experiential learning: Experience as the source of learning and development*. Englewood Cliffs, NJ: Prentice-Hall.

Kundera, M. (1991). *Immortality* (Peter Kussi, Trans.). New York: Perennial Classics.

Miller, R. B. (1996). *Casuistry and modern ethics: A poetics of practical reasoning*. Chicago: University of Chicago Press.

Neilsen, E. H., & Rao, H. (1990). Strangers and the social order: The institutional genesis of organizational development. In W. Pasmore & R. Sherwood (Eds.), *Research in organizational change and development* (pp. 67–99). Stamford, CT: JAI Press.

Nonaka, I. (1994). A dynamic theory of organizational knowledge creation. *Organization Science, 5* (1), 14–37.

Palmer, R. E. (1969). *Hermeneutics*. Evanston, IL: Northwestern University Press.

Ritzer, G. (2000). *The McDonaldization of society*. Thousand Oaks, CA: Pine Forge Press.

Rowden, R. W. (Ed.). (1996). *Workplace learning: Debating five critical questions of theory and practice*. San Francisco: Jossey-Bass.

Senge, P. M. (1990). *The fifth discipline*. New York: Doubleday.

Thompson, D. (Ed.). (1996). *The pocket Oxford dictionary of current English*. Oxford: Oxford University Press.

Vygotsky, L. S. (1978). *Mind and society: The development of higher psychological processes*. Cambridge: Harvard University Press.

Willis, V. J. (1996). Human resource development as evolutionary system: From pyramid building to space walking and beyond. In R. W. Rowden (Ed.), *Workplace learning: Debating five critical questions of theory and practice* (pp. 31–39). San Francisco: Jossey-Bass.

Woodman, R. W., & Sherwood, J. J. (1980). The role of team development in organizational effectiveness: A critical review. *Psychological Bulletin, 88*, 166–186.

12

The Practice of Conversational Learning in Higher Education

Alice Y. Kolb, Ann C. Baker,
Patricia J. Jensen, and D. Christopher Kayes

> Though technique-talk promises the "practical" solutions that we think we want and need, the conversation is stunted when technique is the only topic: the human issues in teaching get ignored, so the human beings who teach feel ignored as well. When teaching is reduced to technique, we shrink teachers as well as their craft—and people do not willingly return to a conversation that diminishes them.
>
> Parker Palmer (1998)

Participants in these conversations are scholars and teaching professionals who were members of the doctoral seminar on learning and development at Case Western Reserve University, where conversation was practiced as a medium for teaching and learning for twelve years, from 1988 to 1999. As developed in this book and grounded in the theory and practice of experiential learning, conversational learning is a learning process whereby learners construct meaning and transform experiences into knowledge through conversations. Ann Baker was a member of the seminar in 1990, Patricia Jensen in 1989, and Christopher Kayes in 1996. Upon earning their doctorates in organizational behavior at Case Western Reserve University, they took upon themselves the challenge of creating conversational learning spaces in the institutions they joined as faculty members. Ann Baker is currently an assistant professor at the School of Public Policy in the Program on Social Organizational Learning and Women's Studies at George Mason University. Conversational learning has become an integral part of her teaching and research since she first joined George Mason University as a faculty member in 1995. Patricia Jensen is an associate professor of business and management at Alverno College. She has been practicing conversational learning with a primary focus on creating a hospitable learning space where learners feel welcomed and supported in their learning process. Christopher Kayes is an assistant professor of human and organization studies at George Washington University and a strong advocate and practitioner of conversational learning. His graduate course curriculum is designed around principles and practices of conversational learning.

Through the conversations, three major themes emerged as unifying threads: the concept of learning space as the central tenet of conversation learning, the egalitarian role of the instructor in relationship to learners and its challenge and implication to learning, and what is seen as the important contribution of conversational learning to higher education and what the future challenges or good things to come are. As readers will be able to observe, these themes intermingle and echo each other consistently throughout the conversations. Each conversation has nevertheless its own unique voice, expressed by the distinct personality and style of the speaker. Readers will also note at many points in the conversations that the struggles, uncertainty, and excitements speakers face in the classrooms through the practice of conversational learning ultimately converge in a shared commitment to the value and experience of learning through conversations.

AK: Why conversation learning? When and how were you attracted to conversational learning?

AB: When I entered the doctoral program in 1990 at Case Western Reserve University, I attended David's learning and development seminar. In comparison with other classes, David's seminar was markedly different. David did not conduct himself as an authority figure who needed to remind us of his position and expertise, and we had much freedom and influence in the classroom and in our conversations together in the seminars. Also, I was profoundly influenced by my continued and expanded readings for the seminar on experiential learning. They were just wonderful, provocative, and really relevant to what I was looking for at that time. The experience of being in the seminar was so good that we did not want it to end. This desire among many of the doctoral students to continue our conversations together led us to start the advanced learning and development seminar in 1992. Throughout the seminar, David's style was to let the energy of the group be. His style was much more conversational and nondirective than other faculty or leaders in most contexts. Both in the learning and development and the advanced learning and development seminars we had much more influence on how the conversation developed. In advanced learning in particular, there was such a diversity of voices that amazingly rich conversations evolved. The excitement generated in the seminar was not because we agreed on the issues. There was lots of disagreement, likes, and dislikes among us. But the freedom and flexibility to be ourselves and discover new possibilities together was there.

AK: How was your experience, Patricia?

PJ: For me it started in 1977, when I was first introduced to experiential learning during one of my MBA courses. In the organizational behavior course, the teacher used David's *Organizational Behavior Reader*, grounded in experiential learning theory. Experiential learning just made sense to me. Since then, experiential learning theory has become the major framework that informs the ways I design courses and assignments and interact with students. When I went to Alverno in the fall of 1979, I had never taught before. As I was oriented to teaching in Alverno's ability-based curriculum, I learned that faculty at Alverno were also knowledgeable of experiential learning theory and incorporated it into their teaching. As I developed as a faculty member, moving between my experience in the classroom with students, to reflection, to considering varied theoretical and practical perspectives, experimenting with approaches in the classroom has become a important part of my ongoing professional development. Later, when I went to Case to get my doctorate, I realized that I was a good teacher not only because Alverno's curriculum was well designed to support students' learning, but also because I came to teaching as learner, not solely in the role of a teacher. Another factor that influenced me was David's style. I was impacted by David's example of absolute strength of theoretical understanding integrated in the whole process of human development. He sat in the class as learner himself. He created a hospitable space for learning, in part, because he did not call attention to himself as the expert in the room, and at the same time was willing to share what he knows and has experienced, in responsible ways. Just take the syllabus he created as an example. To see somebody who is as smart and accomplished as he is and able to keep the attention off himself is something that I respect. He kept his attention in the classroom in the conversation.

AK: What about you Chris? What was your experience?

CK: Similar to Patricia and Ann, I started by attending David's learning and development seminar in 1996, then I continued on with the advanced seminar. I was first exposed to experiential learning by David Luechauer at Butler University where I got my MBA. David L. encouraged me to apply to Case Western's doctoral program in organizational behavior because he felt they were doing the most cutting-edge stuff in learning and groups. I was completely hooked on the conversational approach the first time I attended David Kolb's class. Like Patricia just said, David was such a model of learning. The "conversational space" was so exciting that I looked forward to coming for every session because I was a participant and I could enter the learning on my own terms. Something that I hadn't felt in most of the other classes I had attended before.

AK: Tell me about the challenges as well as excitements you have encountered as you developed concepts and practices of teaching that distinguishes your approach from traditional methods of classroom teaching.

CK: First of all, I felt a dramatic change from being a participant of a conversational space to being responsible to create the space. When I first started teaching at George Washington using conversational learning format, my first challenge was how to communicate the concept of what I was about to do. That was the hardest part. To convey the idea of conversational learning, on the first day of class I would hand out an interview with David on the concept of conversation and proceeded to design the course readings using several articles that featured conversations with seminal thinkers such as Erik Erikson, Abraham Maslow, and Howard Gardner. In one of the master's courses on design of learning, participants were mostly trainers who were used to a cookie-cutter training format. Very traditional approaches to learning. Needless to say, the conversational format totally contradicted their mode of learning. They felt I was not teaching. They expected me to stand and teach them when the whole point was not to teach them in a traditional sense. Students expressed frustration at first but two-thirds into the semester they really started to get it. Many times, when I deliberately tried to redirect the conversation, they would immediately redirect me. Another aspect of the class that students reacted to was the physical arrangement of the classroom. I had students create a circle in the middle of the room and did not allow desks. They resisted the idea of sitting in the circle because they felt very exposed. In the beginning the circle looked more like a square, students resisting sitting close to each other. However, as the semester progressed, the circle started to look more like a circle. The circle became rounder and rounder and they sat in the circle close to each other.

As a way to start the conversation I tried to introduce the conversation starter, a one-page summary of thoughts, ideas related to readings, or experiences students had had in class interactions but it did not work. Instead, I had people pair up on a formal topic and asked the pair to come up with questions that would generate conversation. At first, the groups wanted to do a formal point-by-point presentation because when they asked questions, nobody would respond. This created a very uncomfortable environment at first, as you can imagine. Over time, however, the class itself took responsibility for the conversation. I've used this format in several classes now and the class nearly always owns the conversation in the end. But it takes a while. There seems to be a dialectical tension between content and process often expressed in terms of wanting "concrete application" and "theory" rather than conversation. This desire for theory and application in the class often manifests itself in frustration and it is not uncommon for the frustration to be directed to the instructor. I realized that the dialectical tension created by the conversation often creates a cycle of frustration between the students and me. Students seem to want to hold onto the theories and application more and more. Since my approach to conversational learning has been more about asking, "What do you think?" versus "Here's what I know" this only confounds the frustration because I am not directly answering their call for more theory or application. I often ask a participant to draw on their own experience through reflection or to try to figure out how they might apply a theory from the reading to a problem they face. Because they are frequently hesitant to do that, often times they see me as the person who should be doing such work, it just confounds the frustration they feel with the process. I wrote in my journal about one such experience as feeling "hurt, incompetent, pain, failure, concern, frustration, although not completely surprised." I realized that I might be going through the same process they do, I'm having the same feelings. In retrospect, I figured, these are the kinds of emotions the students experience in the conversation, there is no reason I shouldn't feel that way too.

This experience almost made me resort to using lectures again. But I'm glad I stuck with the process. One evening we held class out of the classroom and all of a sudden the whole conversation really took off. Everyone really got into the conversation, they were asking questions of one another, telling stories, laughing, people got up to go to take short breaks but the conversation kept going for two hours. At the end of the class I realized that it takes some time to get the conversation going.

AK: What about you, Ann?

AB: I very much agree with Chris in the sense that it is very challenging to start something new in a setting where students expect the instructor to have all the answers and to be responsible for their learning. I am fortunate, however, to be teaching primarily graduate level students in their thirties, forties, and fifties, and they have a rich array of work and life experience. They typically recognize that they bring valuable knowledge, experience, and wisdom into the university and are not as likely to expect the instructor to have all the answers. The learners that I get to work with want to have lots of opportunities to talk and share ideas with each other. I don't think that adult learners want to be lectured at—in fact, I question whether any learning is optimal in such a one-directional way.

Even so, especially in the beginning it was challenging for me when I had not yet established my credibility as a new faculty member. I did not feel like I could walk in with flowers and a wagon full of books like David used to do in the learning and development seminar at Case. I did not, as a new member of the faculty, want to be misinterpreted as a lightweight. However, David's influence as well as the other literature I was reading and some of my colleagues were very helpful to me. I also was older when I began teaching in the university and brought with me years of experience as a working adult. That helped me feel less intimidated by the typical academic expectations for faculty than I would have felt when I was much younger.

From the very beginning of my university teaching, I rarely lectured. I try to create lots of open space for conversation among the seminar and class participants and frequently use experiential exercises. I do frequently bring into the conversation references to literature or readings and share ideas, concepts, and theories in what could be called brief, mini lectures when I think it is relevant and appropriate. I typically prepare overhead transparencies that I may use, but often do not, depending on how the class evolves.

I always arrange the classroom in a circle. At the beginning of each semester, some of the students typically resist, but I take the initiative and in a matter of fact, upbeat way, I ask them to help me arrange the room in circle. I do not use a desk to sit behind. I do often have a table behind me with an overhead projector and my course materials so that I can reach them as I need them.

At the beginning of each new seminar, class, or semester, I spend time helping all of us in the group to get to know each other. Through my own behavior, through the syllabus, and through the kind of space I strive to create, I try to open and support a collaborative learning environment of colleagues who will be learning together. Typically, participants say that the classes are not business as usual in the university. We can talk about anything as long as it is done respectfully. I encourage differences of opinion by welcoming people who disagree. Sometimes, if nobody talks, I sit in silence and don't fill up the silence with my own talking. Also, to reinforce the idea of us as fellow learners, I refer to myself as Ann, not as Dr. Baker or Professor Baker and sign my e-mails as Ann. Some students express discomfort with calling me Ann, which usually surprises me.

Especially because I am striving to create an environment where difficult, controversial topics can be talked about, I feel a special responsibility to be accessible to participants who may be uncomfortable with this approach. I try to make sure that I am available and really present and attentive before and after class if somebody wants to talk. I am careful to check my phone and e-mail messages and respond as promptly as possible. Along with the increased flexibility and openness in a conversational learning approach, I think comes an increased responsibility to be accessible and to create a safe, respectful learning space.

PJ: My situation is different from Ann's and Chris's. Students at Alverno College learn in a variety of ways so they become familiar and for the most part comfortable with a more conversational approach. In our undergraduate program we have eight broad abilities that students need to demonstrate in increasing levels of complexity as they progress in their studies. One of these abilities is social interaction. In our master's program we have five abilities that students need to demonstrate in order to successfully complete the program. One of these abilities is called Integrative Interaction, and it requires of these learners that they collaborate with other colleagues, mentors, faculty, readings, etc. in the learning process. For example, I teach the first required course that all of our beginning master's students take in their first semester.

One of the first assignments that the students read in orienting to the program is taken from the *Tao of Conversation*. They consistently work in small and large groups in unfolding whatever learning content is present to them. For some of the students, this focus on conversational learning is, at least initially, a real challenge. They often come from settings where they have been "directors" of learning, using traditional "stand and deliver" teaching methods. Because of the consistent insistence on collaborative and conversational learning across our program, they soon come to learn the benefits of the process.

AK: How did your students react to the idea and approach of conversational learning you have developed?

CK: There was one particular student who became adamantly against this method. She vehemently challenged my approach. She asked me about the concept and theory behind my method and I told her there was no clear way to do it. The irony is, I realized that the more she challenged me the more I became committed to something I am still not clear about myself. What the student was struggling with, it seemed to me, was the ambiguity around the method. The question I asked myself was, how do I help the students deal with the ambiguity around the method? In my doctoral class I had somewhat contradicting reactions from students. They feel I don't say much. I just let it happen. On the other hand, they feel less manipulated. They feel this class is more egalitarian and there is not only one way to think about an issue or topic. However, I also don't bail them out when they run into something challenging or conflicting or when they run into silence. Over the course of the semester it became normal that in the middle of the conversation a student would imitate my words. For example, one student would say, "as Chris would say, say more about that." And, they would take charge of the conversation. Sometimes conversation just takes off and all I do is to put some clarification points on the board but they too become irrelevant. Students glance at them, ignore them, and continue with their course of conversation. In one class where I began with a conversational approach, a student commented that all of the objectives stated in the syllabus were process oriented and not outcome oriented. After two class sessions, the student came up to me after class and commented that he and a few other students did not think the class was moving fast enough, that we hadn't covered enough content. This is a pretty typical with the conversational approach.

PJ: From the beginning I draw upon Parker Palmer's idea of knowing in community, in contrast to some traditional views of teaching where there is a clear separation between "the objects of knowledge, the expert teacher and the amateur learners." The students and I read the chapter in Palmer's book *The Courage to Teach,* in which he describes how in this knowing-in-community there is a subject at the center of the communal circle. In addition to this and other readings, the students are assigned to write a brief paper on their understanding of "the human development of their learners." Students in this program are K through twelve teachers and instructional designers in business, so we have a rich diversity of work contexts, years of experience, and perspectives. In the first class I arrange the chairs in a circle around a small table in the center of the classroom on which I've placed flowers and have music playing in the background as students enter the class. I provide a brief orientation to our four-hour class together, suggest that what we do is to begin our knowing together in community, and ask people to share their perspectives on the development of the learner that they prepared for class. We sit in a circle and listen to each person. Each learner puts their paper on the table in the center. In this way, we each begin to create our relationships with each other and with our subject so that the Palmer reading comes alive for students in very experiential ways. In the second day of the class, I sometimes sense that some students begin expressing suspicion: "This is not for real. There is no way this class will go on like this." I think it is understandable from the vantage point that they are not used to equality in the classroom. They feel any time I will go back to being the authority figure and run the class as business as usual. What I try to do is to bridge the theory and practice through conversation. In one particular class, the theme of the day was Bronfenbrenner's ecology of human development. In particular, I hoped that we would come to a clear understanding of "proximal processes" enduring patterns of relationships. It happened that in that particular class, a mother and daughter, both teachers, had started the program together. I asked them if they would be willing to be interviewed by their colleagues on the nature of their relationship based on this particular theoretical framework. I brought in a stool so that the daughter who was shorter among the two could be seen and heard by the twenty people in the class. What I recall from that class is the powerful conversation that was generated. The interesting thing that happened was, at first, both of them were interviewed by students representing varied perspectives on Bronfenbrenner's systems, however, at some point in time, the mother and daughter started to talk to each other about the patterns of their relationship over time. We just sat there and listened to their conversation. It was a very powerful and enlightening experience in several ways. I think this is an example of what I learned in my research on conversation described in Chapter 7. People do make meaning in conversation. If some people are being quiet, I don't assume that they are sitting there not participating but rather experience them as being attentive or reflecting. In those situations, I don't say, "So and so, we haven't heard from you for awhile, what's your perspective?" I believe that as adults, we are each ultimately responsible for our own learning and I don't have to force students to do anything.

AB: Most of the students love the course format. Some of them take longer. At first some people struggle and feel weird sitting in the circle. By the end of the semester students typically ask why all classes can't be conducted this way. However, sometimes it gets very challenging to hold the space. I had a situation one time in an undergraduate class with about forty students. Near the end of the semester one of the class teams was giving their final team presentation on "gossip in the workplace." To demonstrate potential distortions in gossip, the team opened their presentation by playing a round of telephone tag starting a message to be whispered around the class and reported out by the last person to hear the message. The message that was started was about two members of the class, Sue and Joe. Sue and Joe at that time were each in a steady heterosexual relationship with someone else not in the class, information that was well known among class members. The initial message described seeing Sue and Joe going to get a drink together after class, speculating that they might be romantically interested in each other. Prior to class, the team members had asked and gotten the ok from Sue and Joe to use their names in this made-up story for the exercise. After the message had been whispered around the room, the last person to hear the message was asked to announce to the class the message that they heard. However, the final message had been dramatically, and apparently intentionally, changed to introduce an entirely new topic. The message was that Joe was a homosexual.

Given the immediate and consistent response of the team presenting and many of the class journals (an assignment for the class was to keep a personal journal about their learning) that I read over the next two weeks, I felt confident that the final message was not even similar to the original message. The incident disturbed me a great deal and when I read the students' journals, many of them expressed distress and confusion over what happened. I decided to bring the subject up in the next class. I felt that the topic was important and yet often charged with tension, stereotypical assumptions, misunderstandings, and pushed under the rug and not talked about in classes. Once I had opened the door to talk about the incident, the first people to speak were members of the team who designed the exercise followed by almost everyone in the class. The incident became a teachable moment and generated an energetic conversation filled with opportunities for learning about discrimination, stereotyping, implications for the workplace and for people's lives, group responsibility, etc.

I struggle internally many times to decide when it is appropriate to address those moments and which of these opportunities are likely to lead to the most learning. Being able to discriminate between when and how to speak up and follow these teachable moments is part of the challenge. And holding the space to allow the conversation to develop is also often a challenge.

Many times I have to restrain myself to be sure that I do not talk too much. And many times, questions are directed to me. It is easy to fall into a pattern of being asked questions, answering them, followed by more questions being directed to me as the instructor who is expected to have answers. And to me that is not conversational learning. To create a more conversational learning space means that at times I say something like "please don't direct your comments or questions to me. Talk with each other." Often they try to talk more among all of us as peers, but quickly fall back into the same old pattern. I find that especially at the beginning of the semester I have to be persistent or silent to be more of a guide. And when difficult conversations like the one I just mentioned arise, it is important to set some clear boundaries and intervene quickly if disrespectful and inappropriate things are said.

AK: It seems to me that the key factor in conversational learning is the idea of a space. It is invisible and yet, it is there, holding the conversation. What is this space and how do you create it?

PJ: I am interested in creating an environment as if I were inviting students to my living room where we could sit comfortably and be ourselves. A place that people experience as a hospitable space. What I try to teach is how important it is to engage in good teaching and learning. What I am trying to do is to create a space where both careful reflection and interaction are encouraged. In this way, all are invited into the conversation and each can benefit from it. Another advantage to this process for our students has been that learning through conversation has allowed us all to experience the interweaving of intellectual and emotional content in the learning process. All the students in the MA program are professional working adults. They attend classes every other Saturday in four-hour time blocks. I remember sitting with a group of a dozen or so students who were in the process of completing their MA action research projects. One of the texts for this course was *The Courage to Teach*. For that particular class we had read a chapter on paradox in teaching and learning. Palmer describes six paradoxical tensions that he builds into teaching and learning space. It was the middle of the semester and tensions were mounting among students. We were having a conversation on the dimensions of hospitable space and the paradoxes involved, when they engaged each other in a conversation about the struggles of their learners in urban classrooms and the challenges of getting timely information from corporate training programs, their own emotional reactions to the project completion, and the musings of how to communicate the impact of this project to their colleagues. The conversation was rich and full, and not only accessed the concepts of hospitable space as theorized by others, but brought out their own grappling with how to create such space across several settings. Indeed, they were creatively engaged in the paradoxes in ways that their process clearly reflected the content. Because they were so able to speak their frustrations, they could then help each other to work through assumed barriers to their projects and find creative resolutions to problems.

AB: Early in the semester I emphasize the importance of all of us mutually creating a safe place where we can talk about all kinds of issues. I encourage conversations about controversial topics such as race, gender, social class, etc. when it is relevant, and I think they can promote more learning opportunities. And my experience tells me that by going below the surface, easy-to-talk-about topics, group members can become enthusiastically involved and make memorable connections with their workplaces and their own lives. Helping participants learn how to share responsibility for creating an environment that is safe enough to have these conversations is especially gratifying. Yet ultimately I think that it is my responsibility to hold the space and make sure that interactions are respectful. It is all such a delicate balance though. Sometimes during the conversation a student may say something that feels like I am being verbally attacked. And sometimes I think the most learning emerges when I don't respond, although it can be very hard not to be defensive. But if a student attacks another student, I intervene immediately. The longer I teach, the more I become aware of the delicate balance in creating receptive spaces for conversational learning between allowing the conversation to evolve and taking the initiative. Conversational learning is not a passive approach at all. I try to be attentive and fully present in the learning space. I watch for warning signs from students who show signs of confusion or distress. I feel like it is my responsibility to be accessible to students when that happens. I initiate contact with them either during or after the class to continue the conversation.

CK: The so-called goals of conversational learning are embedded in the conversational space, in the process itself. Patricia's comment about the space being like her living room is a good one. I recently had a student say that he felt the class was his only "safe space" away from the office. In Patricia's terms, something that is "comfortable and hospitable" where questions are put on the table for future consideration, reflected upon, and brought back into the conversation. The novelist Milan Kundera, who wrote *The Unbearable Lightness of Being* and other books, said the novel should ask the right question and refrain from giving an answer. I think that might be a good description of the conversational space: It asks the right question but refrains from answering.

AK: What I sense from this conversation is that what you are proposing as conversational learning requires a dramatic shift from the traditional format of student evaluation. How do you know students are learning? How do you evaluate students when your teaching is based on conversational learning?

CK: This is a dilemma I face all the time. How do I know if students are learning? The experiential basis of conversational learning allows each person to define his or her individual outcomes, share that with the group, and take personal responsibility for achieving it within the conversational space. So that learning is defined individually, even within the context of the conversational space. My sense is that even class preparation does not work in a traditional way. Yes, you have the syllabus and the readings that give the overall structure of the class. However, what happens in a particular class is totally unpredictable. You never know which way the conversation will go. In that sense, for me, the preparation comes after the class. Perhaps it is also due to my learning style; I reflect on the experience of that particular class in order to get ready for the next class. I go to class to see what emerges in the context of the last class. Another factor that makes the evaluation difficult is that the conversation keeps going outside the classroom. Conversation keeps going electronically, they anticipate about the readings, and I can see that a broader conversation is going on in people's minds. This is a very exciting and interesting aspect of the class. I require students to present a paper in both my master's and doctorate classes at the end of the semester. Doctoral students produced very creative papers. Master's students, however, were disappointing. In spite of having this great conversation on using innovative learning methods and conversation all semester, every group ended up doing a stand-up Powerpoint presentation like they had never heard of the conversational format at all. I think it may be related to their career stage. Most of the master's students were used to very traditional training methods and stand-up presentations. In that sense, I think the conversational format was too intimidating for them. Doctoral students came with lots more managerial experience. I think they felt more comfortable with the conversational approach and even found it refreshing, as Ann has mentioned.

My experience is that the standard evaluation does not capture what goes on in conversation. The stressful part of it is that this approach is extremely exciting and frustrating at the same time because you do not have control over it. All you can do is to hope that people will get something out of it. Many times I feel like I am walking a fine line between being innovative and incompetent.

AB: One of the things that I do not do in my classes is grade students based on participation. Participation has a connotation of assigning good grades for those who talk. Instead, in the syllabus, one part of the course evaluation is a category that I call effort and approach. The syllabus explains that each person is mutually responsible for creating a learning space where everybody can feel safe and learn together. I suggest that people who think they may be inclined to talk a lot make an effort to be silent or to ask questions of their peers so that others can speak. Those who tend to be silent in groups may need to speak up more and share their thoughts with others. Effort and approach accounts for 10 to 15 percent of the total grade. I let students know that I make notes after each class that I use at the end of the semester to evaluate effort and approach. I think this approach has an impact on students. For example, I remember a white male in a recent class, who had been very vocal during the beginning of the semester began to be much more reflective and thoughtful toward the middle of the semester. He began to ask his peers more questions in class. In the same class, a black man who had been silent throughout most of the semester began to speak up a lot. In one class he repeatedly shared many powerful and insightful thoughts. The class seemed surprised, and somebody said, "John, where have you been all year?"

There also is a level of readiness that gradually develops that is pretty unpredictable so that I never know when it will happen. I remember about halfway through one semester we were having a conversation about Schön's work on the "Reflective Practitioner." The conversation just took off and got energized. I was quiet and would stand up from time to time and write on the whiteboard some of the polarities I noticed that they were talking about in their conversation, such as, intrinsic–extrinsic, lazy–self-motivated. I said very little, a few people just glanced at the board, and continued with the conversation. Then near the end of the class I commented on what was on the board and said that I thought I had been hearing these polarities come up in the conversation. And that led to yet another conversation. Sometimes I start doubting the whole process and I get nervous. Then I remember conversations like that one and try to remember to just trust the process.

PJ: Alverno has had an ability-based curriculum since 1973. One of the implications of our outcome-based curriculum is that we have a pass–fail grading policy. Students progress through the curriculum as they successfully demonstrate outcomes that relate to the abilities set forth by their discipline. So for each class that a student takes she or he often is responsible for demonstrating several abilities at a time. For example, the student may be demonstrating her ability to accurately analyze a business plan. This is one of the abilities directly related to the business and management curriculum. At the same time and in the same class, she may be required to demonstrate an ability to effectively interact with other students and/or professionals.

She may additionally need to demonstrate that she can integrate the needs of a social group or citizen concern into her plan. From the beginning of a student's study at Alverno, we emphasize the role that self-assessment plays. One of the implications of this approach is that students are given the criteria that are used to evaluate their ability development and asked to self-assess. Students experience receiving constructive feedback on their performance from faculty members and peers, in addition to reflecting on their own development. Through these processes they can clearly name and come to a deeper sense of appreciation of their unique capabilities. I'll describe a way this works. In the master of teaching, learning, and assessment program, students are assessed on their demonstration of five abilities at increasingly complex levels of mastery. Therefore, in any class that I teach, I am noting learner progress in a variety of ability areas. Rather than assign percentages to an ability, I look for ways in which each learner comes to the ability as a whole person and I gauge what they are learning related to each ability. This feedback is given to the students in writing as well as in discussions with individuals. For instance, if a learner has a clear comprehension of the content of the class and the theoretical concepts in it and clearly presents this in his or her written assignments, then I know that the learner is meeting the conceptualization ability. However, he or she may be less confident about their capability to present their understanding in more oral modes and so may set that as a specific learning goal.

AK: I would like to raise an issue regarding faculty evaluation. Is traditional faculty evaluation suited to conversational learning? If not, what should the evaluation look like?

PJ: Our master's program is fairly new. The faculty evaluation instrument that our undergraduates use to evaluate our teaching did not seem appropriate. So a few years ago, I developed my own faculty evaluation questionnaire. One of the goals of our program is to assist our learners to become more reflective practitioners who actively engage in inquiry regarding their professional development. This goal also challenges me to engage in this process. Drawing on course content, I used Parker Palmer's six paradoxes of teaching and learning and asked the students to use these as the basis for giving me feedback on my strengths–course strengths as well as on areas to be developed. I found that students were particularly insightful in the ways that they used these concepts to write a narrative about their experience of being a learner in my class. They then carefully included suggestions for future classes that could help with issues of hospitable space. I found that the tone and content of student comments addressed me as a colleague in learning, one with whom they had been in conversation over the course of the semester.

AB: The University requires that I use the traditional evaluation forms in my classes. However, I also have created various other ways for me to get feedback both verbally and in writing through cards and forms that participants can fill out anonymously. Overall, though, I have had high course evaluations and my classes have good enrollment so I don't think the traditional evaluations have been a problem.

CK: I have difficulty with the whole evaluation issue. It's challenging. I have developed my own evaluation form that I use to supplement what the institution requires. This allows me to gauge my own effectiveness in creating the environment, or as we call it, the conversational space. The measure is based on what I call proximal process, based in part on Lev Vygotsky's concept of proximal zone of development which David introduced to me. The measure tries to get at issues of shared expertise, awareness of other class members' opinions, helping others to understand class concepts, knowledge sharing, and a form of psychological safety. I think these processes are in line with the values of conversational learning because they focus on how individuals learn from each other and how they interact rather than just their level of satisfaction with the class or the instructor.

AK: What are your colleagues' reactions toward your approach? In a broader sense, do you think conversational learning can have an impact at the departmental, institutional level?

AB: My colleagues who know my work the most closely have expressed a positive reaction to my approach and they want for me to be actively involved in teaching the students in our degree program. And the more students get to participate through a conversational learning approach, the more they expect and ask for more opportunities in their other classes.

CK: One colleague asked me why I had flowers in the middle of the classroom. He though it was some experiential exercise or something. I had a hard time explaining it and simply said, "No, it just adds to the conversation." He was so interested he ended up trying a conversational approach in his organizational behavior class the next semester. Another colleague thought it would be a great method to teach economics.

PJ: I feel fortunate to work in a setting where my approach to teaching is shared by my colleagues. Many who teach at Alverno use a similar approach to the teaching–learning process. We can participate in faculty workshops where experiential learning is encouraged and creative approaches to collaborative method are modeled and explored.

AK: What are your future perspectives on conversational learning in higher education? What are the challenges and excitements you anticipate?

CK: I used a conversational approach for a class I taught in Singapore and this raised several questions about the cultural aspects of a conversation and introducing it as a method for learning when the expectations of teachers and learning are different. This experience in Singapore made me think of using conversational learning as one of a variety of methods. I was asked by some students in my doctoral class to get involved with some undergraduate living programs. Student affairs kinds of things. They were specifically interested in the use of conversational learning to teach about student life issues. I think this points to conversational learning as an opportunity for learning in some nonacademic experiences that are so key, yet often overlooked in much of higher education. For example, conversational learning may be a less threatening way to introduce and facilitate learning with more controversial or sensitive issues such as sex education, substance use, and diversity. I think most conversations still happen outside the classroom. Think of the potential learning if people were learning from all these conversations they were having all over campus!

PJ: To borrow on a common saying, "So many good books and so little time to read." One of the challenges I feel as an educator teaching adults who are professionals working full time while also enrolled in a master's program is making judgments about what to include as reading materials in the course syllabus. I respect the limited time these learners have to read in a given semester and the relevance good theory can have for practice. With all the information available from myriad sources, I view the choice of material as a primary challenge. I trust the conversational learning process as an essential way for learners to bring together theory and experience, reflection on practice, and talking about experimenting with change. Understanding and appreciating the world and life we have will keep me meaningfully engaged for years to come.

AB: One of my primary interests is in the increasingly multicultural dimensions of the university, the business world, and the global economy. Using a conversational learning approach fundamentally recognizes and values multiple interpretations and ways of understanding and seems to me to be absolutely critical for higher education to encompass more fully in the future. When learning spaces are created that give voice to people who traditionally have been silenced and disenfranchised, groups and organizations gain access to new resources for learning that are essential to them in a rapidly changing world.

REFERENCES

Bronfenbrenner, U. (1979). *The ecology of human development: Experiments by nature and design*. Cambridge, MA: Harvard University Press.

Kahn, M. D. (1995). *The tao of conversation*. Oakland, CA: New Harbinger Publications.

Kundera, M. (1984). *The unbearable lightness of being*. New York: Harper and Row.

Osland, J. S., Kolb, D. A., & Rubin, I. M. (2001). *Organizational behavior reader* (7th ed.). Upper Saddle River, NJ: Prentice-Hall.

Palmer, P. (1998). *The courage to teach*. San Francisco: Jossey-Bass.

Schön, D. A. (1987). *Educating the reflective practitioner: Toward a new design for teaching and learning in the professions*. San Francisco: Jossey-Bass.

Index

About the Authors and Contributors

Ann C. Baker is an assistant professor at George Mason University in the Program on Social and Organizational Learning and Women's Studies in the School of Public Policy. Her research focuses on organizational learning, differences in conversation as catalysts for learning, multiculturalism, organizational change, group dynamics, and conversational learning in virtual space.

Patricia J. Jensen is an associate professor of business and management at Alverno College in Milwaukee, Wisconsin. She teaches undergraduate students in organizational behavior and master's students in adult learning, action research, and organizational learning. Her research focuses on ways individuals make sense of their experience and learn through conversation.

D. Christopher Kayes is an assistant professor in human and organization studies and the director of the master's degree program in human resource development at George Washington University. His research focuses on how individual experience is transformed into group knowledge.

Alice Y. Kolb is an independent scholar and researcher and the vice president of research and development for Experience Based Learning Systems, Inc. Her research focuses on artistic learning and the role of play in learning and development. She is currently involved in projects that promote learning in higher education through institutional building.

David A. Kolb is a professor of organizational behavior at the Weatherhead School of Management, Case Western Reserve University. His research focuses on learning and the role of conversation in learning. He is best known for his research on experiential learning and learning styles. He is the author of *Experiential Learning: Experience as the Source of Learning and Development* and coauthor of *Organization Behavior: An Experiential Approach* (with I. Rubin and J. Osland), *Changing Human Behavior: Principles of Planned Intervention* (with R. Schwitzgebel), and *Innovation in Professional Education* (with Richard E. Boyatzis and Scott S. Cowen).

Esther D. Wyss-Flamm is a Ph.D. student in organizational behavior at Case Western Reserve University. She is completing her dissertation on conversational learning and psychological safety in multicultural teams, and has been active in promoting multicultural teamwork through her teaching and consulting work with domestic and international organizations.